FOR THE LOVE OF THE GAME

FOR THE LOVE
OF THE GAME

*An Oral History
of First-Class Cricket*

DAVID LEMMON

Foreword by Peter May

MICHAEL JOSEPH

LONDON

MICHAEL JOSEPH LTD

Published by the Penguin Group
Penguin Books Ltd, 27 Wrights Lane, London w8 5tz
Viking Penguin Inc., 375 Hudson Street, New York, New York 10014, USA
Penguin Books Australia Ltd, Ringwood, Victoria, Australia
Penguin Books Canada Ltd, 10 Alcorn Avenue, Toronto, Ontario, Canada m4v 3b2
Penguin Books (NZ) Ltd, 182–190 Wairau Road, Auckland 10, New Zealand

Penguin Books Ltd, Registered Offices: Harmondsworth, Middlesex, England

First published in Great Britain 1993
Copyright © David Lemmon, 1993

Typeset by Datix International Limited, Bungay, Suffolk
Set in 12/14 pt Van Dijck
Printed in England by Clays Ltd, St Ives plc

A CIP catalogue record for this book is available from the British Library
ISBN 0 7207 2000 1

The moral right of the author has been asserted

CONTENTS

Acknowledgements ix

Foreword xi

1 A Little Lower Than Angels 1

2 Far Too Much of the Business Element 39

3 A Lovely Life 73

4 They Were All Good Cricketers in Them Days 101

5 They Were Good Days 133

6 A Most Enjoyable Experience 173

7 I Count Myself Lucky 199

8 To Delight in the Performance of Others 229

9 It's Got to be Your Life 269

10 For the Love of the Game 289

Dramatis Personae 303

Index 313

The disadvantage of men not knowing the past is that they do not know the present. History is a hill or high point of vantage from which alone men see the town in which they live or the age in which they are living.

G. K. Chesterton

ACKNOWLEDGEMENTS

This book has evolved over a period of years from my meetings and conversations with first-class cricketers of several generations. It is an attempt to piece together a history of cricket from the words of those who played it. In the period before 1920, I have obviously had to refer to written memoirs and interviews. For more recent times, the story is told in words that have actually been spoken to me or which have been sent to me as tape or video recordings. At no time have I altered words that have been spoken although, on occasions, I have rearranged the sequence of statements in the interests of chronology or fluency.

I am deeply indebted to John Bridges for providing me with the fascinating interview with Sir Jack Hobbs, and my thanks go to Ashley Mallett for interviewing Sir Donald Bradman, and to Chris Harte for supplying the interviews with H. G. Owen-Smith, Peter van der Merwe, Trevor Goddard and Peter Kirsten.

This book has been a long and hard process with many hours of travel and some excellent lunches. It has been a wonderful experience to meet so many of the people who feature in this book. My thanks are due to them for their time, their patience and, in very many cases, their warm hospitality. It is to them that this book is most sincerely dedicated.

DAVID LEMMON
Leigh-on-Sea, 1993

FOREWORD

When I was at Charterhouse 'Hopper' Read, the old Essex and England fast-bowler, came down to play against us. He was at the veteran stage for a cricketer, but, for schoolboys, he was very quick. It was one of my early links with the history and traditions of the game, but I remained ever aware of these traditions during my years at the Oval. Jack Hobbs and Maurice Allom were among those on the Surrey committee at that time, and one was conscious of their achievements, although, as dear old Stuart Surridge was always ready to point out, the last time Surrey had won anything before those great years in the nineteen-fifties was 1914.

The former players never imposed themselves upon us, but they were ready to advise and to reminisce if we wanted. Andy Sandham was the coach at the Oval, and it was to him that I turned for help. If I was having a problem, he would suggest a couple of things, usually to do with grip or stance, and invariably he would correct a fault.

I was always an avid watcher of the game. There are some players who rarely watch, but I enjoyed watching, and I believe that it is only by watching great players that you learn. My particular models, or heroes, were Len Hutton and Denis Compton, and I learned much from watching them.

My first Test match was against South Africa at Headingley in 1951, and I sat and watched Len Hutton and Frank Lowson, another Yorkshireman who was also playing his first Test, put on 99 for the first wicket. Frank was out, and I joined Len. I got a rather lucky four down the leg-side first ball, and at the end of the over Len came up to me and said, 'Are you all right?' I said yes, and he never said another word. He didn't have to. He scored a century and I watched and studied and learned, and I was lucky enough to get 100, too.

David Lemmon now has an acknowledged reputation among cricket authors and avid cricket readers. His attention to detail and his obvious affection for our great game are both very apparent in his latest work, appropriately named *For the Love of the Game*.

I commend it to all cricket lovers who involve themselves in memorabilia and recollection of things past – a certainty for their bookcases.

Peter May

1

A LITTLE LOWER
THAN ANGELS

John Nyren

Revd John Mitford

William Beldham to Revd James Pycroft

Richard Daft

William Caffyn

Herbert Jenner to A. W. Pullin

Revd James Pycroft

John Jackson to A. W. Pullin

Fred Lillywhite

Emerson believed that 'there is properly no history; only biography', and more than a century later Henry Miller asserted 'the history of the world is the history of a privileged few'. This book claims to be neither a history of the world nor, indeed, a history of cricket, for hard facts and precise statistics will rarely be found here. It is a memory book, the story of a game told through the recollections of 'a privileged few' who enjoyed their moments of triumph and encountered their share of disappointment.

Our sources tell us that it is likely that a form of cricket existed by the end of the thirteenth century and that it was certainly played in the sixteenth century. John Derrick, a witness concerning a disputed piece of land in Guildford, testified at proceedings on 16 January 1598 that, 'being of the age of fyfty and nyne yeeres or thereaboutes', he had, when a scholar at the 'free schoole of Guldeford, runne and play there at Creckett and other Plaies'.

In the next century, Henry Teonge, chaplain on HMS *Assistance* and HMS *Royal Oak*, told of cricket in Syria. Writing in his diary for 6 May 1676, Teonge tells that he rode out from Aleppo in company with some forty other Englishmen and that a tent was pitched in a pleasant valley beside a river where 'wee had severall pastimes and sports, as duck-hunting, fishing, shooting, handball, krickett'.

If cricket had become the sport of Englishmen abroad by the middle of the seventeenth century, it had long taken root in the south-east of England. As he journeyed through Kent in 1723, the Duke of Portland recalled how, upon the heath outside the town of Dartford, 'the men of Tunbridge and the Dartford men were warmly engaged at the sport of cricket, which of all the people of England the Kentish folk are most renowned for, and of all Kentish men the men of Dartford lay claim to the greatest excellence.'

The Men of Kent were unquestionably the dominant cricketers of the first half of the eighteenth century, but in or around 1750 a club was formed in a remote village in Hampshire whose deeds and players shine like a beacon from the darkness of the middle ages of cricket.

Hambledon was neither the birthplace nor the cradle of cricket; the game was already a lusty infant when Hambledon came into existence. The great days of Hambledon lasted barely twenty years, yet the club has earned a place of importance and affection in the memory of the game which few other clubs can boast.

This stems from the fact that, more than a generation after Hambledon had played its last match of note, a book was published which set down in lyrical freshness the events and characters of the club's great days. The book was *The Young Cricketer's Tutor*, and it was written by Charles Cowden Clarke from the reminiscences of John Nyren.

Nyren was sixty-nine when the book was published. It contains an account of the Hambledon club and its players in the time of Richard Nyren, the father of the man whose voice we hear passionate and true throughout *The Young Cricketer's Tutor*, with which cricket's oral tradition really begins.

John Nyren was fourteen when he joined Hambledon as a sort of 'farmer's pony', and he remained with the club until 1791, by which time its great days were drawing to a close. He believed that Hambledon, his birthplace, was 'the Attica of the scientific art' he celebrated and that no team in England could compare with the Hambledon club. 'The whole country would flock to see one of their trial matches.'

The two principal bowlers in my early days were THOMAS BRETT and RICHARD NYREN of Hambledon; the *corps de reserve*, or change-bowlers, were BARBER and HOGSFLESH. Brett was, beyond all comparison, the fastest as well as the straightest bowler that was ever known: he was neither a thrower nor a jerker, but a legitimate downright bowler, delivering his ball fairly, high, and very quickly, quite as strongly as the jerkers, and with the force of a point blank shot. He was a well-grown, dark-looking man, remarkably strong, and with rather a short arm. As a batter,

[4]

he was comparatively an inferior player – a slashing hitter but he had little guard of his wicket, and his judgement of the game was held in no great estimation. Brett, whose occupation was that of a farmer, bore the universal character of a strictly honourable man in all his transactions, whether in business or in amusement.

Richard Nyren was left-handed. He had a high delivery, always to the length, and his balls were provokingly deceitful. He was the chosen General of all matches, ordering and directing the whole. In such esteem did the brotherhood hold his experience and judgement, that he was uniformly consulted on all questions of law or precedent; and I never knew an exception to be taken against his opinion, or his decision to be reversed. I never saw a finer specimen of the thorough-bred old English yeoman than Richard Nyren. He was a good face-to-face, unflinching, uncompromising, independent man. He placed a full and just value upon the station he held in society, and he maintained it without insolence or assumption. He could differ with a superior, without trenching upon his dignity, or losing his own.

Nyren had immense advantage over Brett; for, independently of his great knowledge of the game, he was practically a better cricketer, being a safe batsman and an excellent hitter. Although a very stout man (standing about five feet nine) he was uncommonly active. He owed all the skill and judgement he possessed to an old uncle, Richard Newland, of Slindon, in Sussex, under whom he was brought up – a man so famous in his time, that when a song was written in honour of the Sussex cricketers, Richard Newland was especially and honourably signalized. No one man ever dared to play him. When Richard Nyren left Hambledon, the club broke up, and never resumed from that day. The head and right arm were gone.

Barber and Hogsflesh were both good hands; they had a high delivery, and a generally good length; not very strong, however, at least for those days of playing when the bowling was all fast. These four were our tip-top men, and I think such another stud was not to be matched in the whole kingdom, either before or since. They were choice fellows, staunch and thorough-going. No thought of treachery ever seemed to enter their heads.

Upon coming to the old batters of our club, the name of JOHN SMALL, the elder, shines among them in all the lustre of a star of the first magnitude. He was the best short runner of his day, and indeed I believe him to have been the first who turned the short hits to account. His decision was as prompt as his eye was accurate in calculating a short run. Add to the value of his accomplishment as a batter, he was an admirable field's-man, always playing middle wicket; and so correct was his judgement of the game that old Nyren would appeal to him when a point of law was being debated. Small was a remarkably well-made and well-knit man, of honest expression and as active as a hare.

The name and figure of TOM SUETER first comes across me — a Hambledon man, and of the club. What a handful of steel-hearted soldiers are in an important pass, such was Tom in keeping the wicket. Nothing went by him; and for coolness, and nerve in his trying and responsible post, I never saw his equal. As a proof of his quickness and skill, I have numberless times seen him stump a man out with Brett's tremendous bowling. Add to this valuable accomplishment, he was one of the manliest and most graceful of hitters. Few would cut a ball harder at the point of the bat, and he was moreover an excellent short runner. He had an eye like an eagle — rapid and comprehensive. He was the first who departed from the custom of the old players before him, who deemed it a heresy to leave the crease for the ball; he would get in at it, and hit it straight off and straight on; and, egad! it went as if it had been fired. As by the rules of our club, at the trial-matches no man was allowed to get more than 30 runs, he generally gained his number earlier than any of them. I have seldom seen a handsomer man than Tom Sueter, who measured about five feet ten. As if, too, Dame Nature wished to show at his birth a specimen of her prodigality, she gave him so amiable a disposition, that he was the pet of all the neighbourhood: so honourable a heart, that his word was never questioned by the gentlemen who associated with him: and a voice, which for sweetness, power and purity of tone (tenor), would, with proper cultivation, have made him a handsome fortune. With what rapture have I hung upon his notes when he has given us a hunting song in the club room after the day's practice was over.

GEORGE LEAR, of Hambledon, who always answered to the title among us of 'Little George', was our best long-stop. So firm and steady was he, that I have known him stand through a whole match against Brett's bowling, and not lose more than 2 runs. The ball seemed to go into him, and he was as sure of it as if he had been a sand bank. His activity was so great, and besides, he had so good a judgement in running to cover the ball, that he would stop many that were hit in the slip, and this, be it remembered, from the swiftest bowling ever known. The portion of ground that man would cover was quite extraordinary. He was a good batsman, and a tolerably sure guard of his wicket; he averaged from 15 to 20 runs, but I never remember his having a long innings. What he did not bring to the stock by his bat, however, he amply made up with his perfect fielding. Lear was a short man, of fair complexion, well-looking, and of pleasing aspect.

At a time when a wicket-keeper wore none of the protection that a keeper wears today and when he stood up to all bowlers on wickets which were rough, the position of long-stop was a most important one, so that it is not surprising that John Nyren drew attention to Lear's prowess. Indeed, he remembered with pride the quality of the Hambledon fielding as a whole, and Edward Aburrow, known as Curry, Peter Steward, who went under the name Buck, and Tom Taylor were members of the eleven mainly on the strength of their ability to stop and throw.

The matches were generally played for large stakes and excited much gambling on the result, which is why honesty and integrity were counted as important qualities in a player.

The bowling was under-arm, and the early bowlers seldom practised spin. If there was a twist on the ball, it was from leg to off. John Nyren claimed that Hambledon produced the first off-break bowler. He was known as 'The Little Farmer', but his name was Lamborn, although Nyren inadvertently called him Lambert.

He was a bowler – right-handed, and he had the most extraordinary delivery I ever saw. The ball was delivered quite low, and with a twist; not like that of the generality of right-handed bowlers, but just the reverse way: that is, if bowling to a right-handed hitter, his ball would twist from off stump into the leg. He was the first I remember who introduced this deceitful and teasing style of delivering the ball. When All-England played the Hambledon Club, the Little Farmer was appointed one of our bowlers; and, egad! this new trick of his so bothered the Kent and Surrey men, that they tumbled out one after another, as if they had been picked off by a rifle corps. For a long time they could not tell what to make of that cursed twist of his. This, however, was the only virtue he possessed, as a cricketer. He was no batter, and had no judgement of the game. The perfection he had attained in this one department, and his otherwise general deficiency, are at once accounted for by the circumstance that, when he was tending his father's sheep, he would set up a hurdle or two, and bowl away for hours together. Our General, old Nyren, after a great deal of trouble (for the Farmer's comprehension did not equal the speed of lightning), got him to pitch the ball a little to the off-side of the wicket, when it twist full in upon the stumps.

Nyren was jealously proud of the deeds of the Hambledon team of his youth and, in particular, of their performances against All-England, which was not, in fact, quite what it sounds, but an eleven made up from some of the best of Hambledon's opponents. Of these, one of the most notable was Edward Stevens who was known as Lumpy.

Born in Surrey in 1735, Lumpy was hailed by Nyren because he 'would bowl the greatest number of length balls in succession', and at a brisk pace. His accuracy was such that, in a single wicket match between Five of Hambledon and Five of Kent in 1775, he three times bowled right through John Small's wicket. Hambledon needed 14 runs to win, and Small, the last man, scored them.

It was conceded that this was a great misfortune for the bowler, and soon after the third stump was added so that never

[8]

again was a bowler to be made to pay for his accuracy as Lumpy had done. Nyren believed that it was the ability to bowl straight and quickly that gave the famous man his greatest pleasure and was also the source of a weakness.

In those days it was the custom of the party going from home to pitch their own wickets; and here it was that Lumpy, whose duty it was to attend to this, always committed an error. He would invariably choose the ground where his balls would *shoot*, instead of selecting a rising spot to bowl against, which would have materially increased the difficulty to the hitter, seeing that so many more would be caught out by the mounting of the ball. As nothing, however, delighted the old man like bowling a wicket down with a shooting ball, he would sacrifice the other chances to the glory of that achievement.

Frame, Shock White and John Wood were other bowlers who presented Hambledon with formidable opposition, and there were batsmen of strength, too, like Minshull, 'conceited as a wagtail', and Miller, 'steady as the pyramids', yet Nyren would allow the men of Hambledon to bow to none of them.

Quiddington was a long-stop, and an admirable one; not, however, so implicitly to be depended on as Lear, whose equal in that department of the game I never saw anywhere.

For the same cause, too, I must place our Sueter above Yalden, who was their best wicket-keeper, and he would have been highly prized anywhere; but neither he nor Quiddington ever had to stand against such steam-engine bowling as Brett's; and yet Lear and Sueter, in their several departments, were safer men than their opponents. Yalden, too, was in other respects an inferior man to Sueter. His word was not always to be depended on when he had put a man out — he would now and then shuffle and resort to tricks. In such estimation did the other stand with all parties — so high an opinion had they of his honour — that I firmly believe they would have trusted to his decision, had he ever chosen to question that of the umpire!

[9]

The 'grand' matches were played for five hundred pounds a side so that honesty and honour, as we have indicated, were of paramount importance. Nyren boasted that the Hambledon men were true Englishmen who would give an enemy fair play, and he recalled with warmth and joy the scene on Broad-Half-penny Down when one of the important matches was in progress.

There was high feasting held on Broad-Halfpenny during the solemnity of one of our grand matches. Oh! it was a heart-stirring sight to witness the multitude forming a complete and dense circle round that noble green. Half the county would be present, and all their hearts with us. Little Hambledon, pitted against All-England, was a proud thought for the Hampshire man. Defeat was glory in such a struggle – victory, indeed, made us only 'a little lower than angels.' How those fine brawn-faced fellows of farmers would drink to our success! And then, what stuff they had to drink! – Punch! – not your new *Ponche a la Romaine*, or *Ponche a la Grosielle*, or your modern cat-lap milk punch – punch be-deviled; but good, un-sophisticated, John Bull stuff – stark! – that would stand on end – punch that would make a cat speak! Sixpence a bottle.

There would this company, consisting most likely of some thousands, remain and anxiously watching every turn of fate in the game, as if the event had been the meeting of two armies to decide their liberty. And whenever a Hambledon man made a good hit, worth 4 or 5 runs, you would hear the deep mouths of their whole multitude baying away in pure Hampshire – 'Go hard! go hard! – *Tich* and turn! – *tich* and turn!'

Hambledon attracted many of the finest players of the age, and a second generation arose which included such men as Noah Mann, a severe hitter and fine fielder from Sussex – 'He was short, and black as a gypsy, broad chest, large hips, and spider legs. He never played with a hat; *his* complexion *benefited* the Sun' – Richard Francis, who had played for Surrey against Hambledon and later played in Essex and many other counties,

Richard Purchase, James Aylward, Tom and Harry Walker, John Wells and the fearsome bowler David Harris.

Responding to Nyren's recollections of the Hambledon men, the Reverend John Mitford painted his own picture of Harris with unfettered enthusiasm.

Who knows not David Harris? the finest *bowler* whom the world ever rejoiced in when living, or lamented over when dead. Harris was by trade a potter, and lived at Odiham in Hants, an honest, plain-faced (in two senses), worthy man. 'Good David Harris' he was called; of strict principle, high honour, inflexible integrity; a character on which scandal or calumny never dared to breathe. A good cricketer, like a good orator, must be an honest man; but what are orators compared to the men of cricket. There have been a hundred, a thousand orators; there never was but one David Harris. Many men can make good speeches, but few men can deliver a good ball. Many men can throw down a strong enemy, but Harris could overthrow the strongest wicket. Cicero once undermined the conspiracy of Catiline; and Harris *once* laid prostrate even the stumps of Beldham.

It is said that it is utterly impossible to convey with the pen an idea of the grand effect of Harris's bowling. His attitude, when preparing to deliver the ball, was masculine, erect, and appalling. First, he stood like a soldier at drill, upright. Then with a graceful and elegant curve, he raised the fatal ball to his forehead, and drawing back his right foot, started off. Woe be to the unlucky wight who did not know how to stop these cannonades! his fingers would be ground to dust against the bat, his bones pulverized, and his blood scattered over the field.

Harris's bowling was described as one of the grandest sights in the universe, 'simply and severely great', but, as Mitford indicates, the finest bowler of the age was not without human frailty.

Harris was terribly afflicted with the gout; it was at length difficult for him to stand; a great armchair was therefore always brought into the field, and after the delivery of the ball, the hero sat down in his own calm and simple grandeur, and reposed. A fine tribute this, to his superiority, even amid the tortures of disease.

Mitford then offered a comparison between the merits of Harris and Lumpy.

Harris always chose a ground when pitching a wicket where his ball would *rise*. Lumpy endeavoured to gain the advantage of a declivity where his might *shoot*.

Harris considered his partner's wicket as carefully as his own. Lumpy attended only to himself.

Lumpy's ball was as well pitched as Harris's, but delivered *lower*, and never got up so high. Lumpy was also a pace or two slower.

Lumpy gained more wickets than Harris; but then fewer notches were got from Harris's bowling: and more players were caught out. Now and then a great batter as Fennex, or Beldham, would beat Lumpy entirely; but Harris was always great, and always to be feared.

Mitford uses Beldham as the yard-stick by which batsmen should be measured. There were, in fact, two Beldhams, George and William, and they were farmers. George was a competent player, but he made infrequent appearances; and it was his brother, 'Silver Billy', who was regarded as the best batsman of his time. He was the last survivor of the great cricketers of the Hambledon era.

William Beldham was born near Farnham in Surrey in 1766, and he died in Tilford in Surrey shortly before his ninety-sixth birthday. His last match of importance was played at Godalming in 1821 by which time he was fifty-five years old. He was known as 'Silver Billy' because of his light-coloured hair and handsome, fair complexion. Nyren asserted:

No one within my recollection could stop a ball better, or make more brilliant hits all over the ground. Wherever the ball was bowled, there she was hit away, and in the most severe, venomous style. Besides this, he was so remarkably safe a player; he was safer than the Bank, for no mortal ever thought of doubting Beldham's stability.

> Beldham was a young man when he joined Hambledon, and his potential was quickly recognized, and Nyren believed that he had never seen a youngster with such a command of batting.

With the instruction and advice of the old heads superadded, he rapidly attained to the extraordinary accomplishment of being the finest player that has appeared within the latitude of more than half a century. There can be no exception against his batting, or the severity of his hitting. He would get in at the balls, and hit them away in gallant style; yet, in this single feat, I think I have known him excelled; but when he could cut them at the point of his bat, he was in his glory; and upon my life, their speed was as the speed of thought. One of the most beautiful sights that can have been imagined, and which would have delighted an artist, was to see him make himself up to hit a ball. It was the beau ideal of grace, animation, and concentrated energy.

> Beldham lived revered in his old age. His home near Farnham was a shrine visited by Mitford and by the Reverend James Pycroft who, in 1837, interviewed the veteran and set down his memories of the game.

When I was a boy (say 1780), nearly all bowling was fast, and all along the ground. In those days the Hambledon Club could beat All-England; but our three parishes around Farnham beat Hambledon.

The first lobbing slow bowler I ever saw was Tom Walker. When, in 1792, England played Kent, I did feel ashamed of such baby bowling; but, after all, he did more even than David Harris himself. Two years after, in 1794, at Dartford Brent, Tom Walker, with his slow bowling, headed a side against David Harris, and beat him easily.

Kent, in early times, was not equal to our counties. Their great man was Crawte, and he was taken away from our parish of Alresford by Mr Amherst, the gentleman who made the Kent

[13]

matches. In those days, except around our parts, Farnham and the Surrey side of Hampshire, a little play went a long way.

We used to go as eagerly to a match as if it were two armies fighting; we stood at nothing if we were allowed the time; from our parish to Hambledon is twenty-seven miles, and we used to ride both ways the same day, early and late. At last I and John Wells were about building a cart, you have heard of tax carts, sir; well the tax was put on then, and that stopped us. The members of the Hambledon Club had a caravan to take their eleven about, and used once always to play in velvet caps. Lord Winchelsea's eleven used to play in silver-laced hats, and always the dress was knee-breeches and stockings. We never thought of knocks; and I remember I played against Browne of Brighton too. Certainly you would see a bump heave under the stocking, and even blood come through; but I never knew a man killed, now you ask the question, and I never saw an accident of much consequence, though many *all but*, in my experience. Fancy the old fashion before cricket shoes, when I saw John Wells tear a finger nail off against his shoe-buckle in picking up a ball.

I remember when many things first came into the game which are common now. The law for leg-before-wicket was not made, nor much wanted, till Ring, one of our best hitters, was shabby enough to get his legs in the way, and take advantage of the bowlers, and when Tom Taylor, another of the best hitters did the same, the bowlers found themselves beaten, and the law was passed to make leg-before-wicket out. The law against jerking was owing to the frightful pace Tom Walker put on, and I believe that Harry also tried something more like the modern throwing-ball, and caused the words against throwing also. Wills was not the inventor of that kind of round bowling; he only revived what was forgotten or new to the young folk.

Tom Walker was the most tedious fellow to bowl to, and the slowest runner between wickets I ever saw. I have seen, in running a four, Noah Mann, as fast as Tom was slow, overtake him, pat him on the back, and say, 'Good name for you is *Walker*, for you never were a runner.' It used to be said that

David Harris had once bowled him 170 balls for one run! David was a potter by trade, and in a kind of skittle alley made between hurdles, he used to practise bowling four different balls from one end, and then picking them up he would bowl them back again. His bowling cost him a great deal of practice; but it proved well worth while, for no man ever bowled like him, and he was always first chosen of all the men in England.

In our days there were no padded gloves. I have seen Tom Walker rub his bleeding fingers in the dust! David used to say he liked to *rind* him.

'Drawing' between leg and wicket is not a new invention. Old Small, of 1750, was famous for drawing, and for the greater facility he changed the crooked bat of his day for a straight bat. There was some fine cutting before Saunders's day. Harry Walker was the first, I believe, who brought it to perfection. The next genuine cutter, for they were very scarce (I never called mine cutting, not like that of Saunders at least), was Robinson. Walker and Robinson would wait for the ball all but past the wicket, and cut with great force. Others made good off hits, but did not hit late enough for a good cut. I would never cut with slow bowling. I believe that Walker, Fennex and myself, first opened the old players' eyes to what could be done with the bat; Walker by cutting, and Fennex and I by forward play: but all improvement was owing to David Harris's bowling. His bowling rose almost perpendicular: it was once pronounced a jerk; it was altogether most extraordinary. For thirteen years I averaged 43 a match, though frequently I had only one innings; but I never could half-play unless runs were really wanted.

Beldham touches upon the changes in bowling style that had taken place and upon the succeeding debate. The old type of fast underhand bowling gave way to high lobs, and men like Beldham and Fennex savaged such bowling by moving down the wicket. The dominance of bat over ball became so common as to raise concern over the length of time that was required to bring a result in matches in which the best players were involved.

[15]

Legislation was brought in to outlaw 'throwing' actions, but the style was revived by John Willes of Kent who was said to bowl 'straight-armed'. Others followed his example, but batsmen, unable to cope with such bowling, objected. On 15 July 1822, Willes played for Kent against MCC at Lord's and was no-balled by umpire Mann. The bowler threw down the ball, mounted his horse and rode out of Lord's and out of cricket history.

The cause of the new style of bowling was taken up by William Lillywhite, the Nonpareil, who, in conjunction with James Broadbridge, raised Sussex's position of eminence. In 1827, they were deemed worthy of facing All-England in three 'experimental' matches.

With William Lillywhite and James Broadbridge bowling round-arm, Sussex won the first two matches with considerable ease. The professionals on the England side stated that they would not play the third match unless the Sussex bowlers bowled fairly. A compromise was reached in that the England side was strengthened and triumphed by 24 runs. They were indebted not only to better batsmen, but to the bowling of G. T. Knight, an influential member of MCC, who himself bowled round-arm.

Knight was an advocator of the legalization of the high delivery form of bowling, entered into strong debate on the subject and exerted pressure on the MCC.

The Marylebone Club had been formed in 1787 and had made their first revision of the laws a year later. The first match between Gentlemen and Players took place at Lord's, then on the site of Dorset Square, in 1806, and in 1814, the famous ground, named after its founder, Thomas Lord, moved to its present location in St John's Wood. The MCC were, by then, the accepted law-makers of the game, and in 1828 they authorized that the bowler could raise his hand level with the elbow. It was to be another thirty-six years before 'over-hand' bowling was legalized.

In the debate about the varieties of bowling action, which

was, in effect, a debate as to how to achieve an acceptable balance between bat and ball, Alfred Mynn, 'the Lion of Kent', was held up as the model of the older style of bowling. Mynn, a gentle giant of a man, was the most revered and best-loved cricketer in England before the advent of W. G. Grace. Richard Daft, the Nottinghamshire professional, played with Mynn towards the end of his career and remembered him as

. . . by far the biggest man I ever saw. He stood well over six feet, and must have weighed, at the time I knew him, twenty-three or twenty-four stone; nor was there anything clumsy or awkward in any of his movements, which were, on the contrary, stately and dignified at all times. He was a fine batter against fast bowling, but was not so good against slow. He was a first-rate fast round-arm bowler, and his delivery was a treat to witness. He walked a few paces up to the wicket, and delivered the ball like a flash of lightning, seemingly without effort.

Mr Mynn was one of the kindest-hearted men I ever met, and was as gentle in his manners as he was strong in person. I have often felt glad that I was not born ten years later than I was, for in that case I should not have had the pleasure of knowing one of the most famous cricketers and good-hearted fellows of his or any other generation. He was once terribly punished on one of his legs during a very long innings, but stood up for several hours at the wicket, making a great many runs before he would retire; but he was compelled to do so at last when his leg was found to be dreadfully injured. He was confined to his bed for a long period, and it was thought his surgeon would be obliged to take the leg off; but happily this extreme measure was not resorted to, and Mr Mynn was afterwards quite sound again.

The incident to which Richard Daft refers was the North v. South match at Leicester in 1836. The first meeting of these two sides came at Lord's in mid-season, and the North won. The return match, for £500 a side, excited tremendous interest. There was a huge attendance which included the dignitaries of

[17]

MCC who had made a special journey by coach. In practising before the match, Mynn was badly hit on the leg. It must be remembered that he played in the days before batsmen wore pads. Against the advice of his friends, Mynn insisted on playing although he could not bowl. He made 146 without being dismissed and won the match for the South, but he was dreadfully hit about the leg by the quick bowling of Redgate.

Eventually, Mynn was taken into a tent where he showed his injuries to Lord Frederick Beauclerk. His lordship immediately ordered a carriage to take Mynn from Leicester to London, but so badly injured was he that he had to be laid on the roof of the coach for the journey. He was laid up for many months and there was grave concern for him, but he was eventually able to return and reclaim his title of Champion of England in 1838.

William Caffyn, the Surrey cricketer, confirmed Daft's opinion of Mynn and was able to give a greater insight into the big man's constitution and character.

He had an affectionate regard for his old fellow-players who had fought shoulder to shoulder with him through his brilliant career, and there are many players who were just becoming known to him in his latter days who could bear witness to the kindness and encouragement he showed to them. As a bowler, he was very fast, with a most stately delivery, bowling level with his shoulder. As a batsman he was a fine powerful hitter. He played a driving game, setting himself for this and not cutting much. Against fast bowling he was magnificent, and against slow of an inferior quality he was a great punisher. Against the best slow bowling of the day he did not show to so much advantage. He had not that *variety* of play which enables a batsman to deal with this sort of bowling to the best advantage. His pluck and gameness were something wonderful, and were shown in every department of the game. He had an iron constitution which nothing seemed to upset. He liked good living, and seemed especially to enjoy his supper. I have often seen him eat a hearty supper of cold pork and retire to bed almost directly afterwards! A curious custom of his was taking a tankard of light bitter to bed with him to drink during the night. 'My boy,' he once said to me when he saw me taking a cup of tea, 'beef and beer are the things to play cricket on!' He was a fine single-wicket player, and was never beaten. His batting and bowling were both eminently adapted for success at single wicket, as he got nearly all his runs in front of the wicket, and his bowling was rather on the 'short' side and not easy to drive.

> Mynn was one of the mainstays of the 'Good Old Kent Eleven' which dominated cricket during the first years of Queen Victoria's reign. Fuller Pilch, Nicholas Wanostrocht, known as Felix, Billy Hillyer and Ned Wenman were the other outstanding members of this great side. Caffyn played against all of them and believed Pilch to have been among the best batsmen he ever saw.

There have been few, in my opinion, to surpass Pilch as a batsman with style and effect combined. His attitude at the wicket was perfect, keeping both legs very straight. He played forward a great deal, and his bat went down the wicket like the pendulum of a clock. He not only utilized his forward play for defensive purposes, but scored from it very frequently as well. His best hit was one in front of cover-point. I do not think that anyone ever excelled him in this stroke. He was a powerful driver when the ball came to him, but did not leave his ground much.

Pilch was a Norfolk man by birth, but receiving £100 a year to live in Kent, he took up abode there in 1835. He was a tall man, just over six feet, and was powerfully made. He was exceedingly good-tempered, and very kind to all young players with whom he came in contact. He was a remarkably quiet man, with no conversation, and seemed never happier than when behind a churchwarden pipe, all by himself.

> Felix was a schoolmaster, a musician and an author whose knowledge of the science of cricket was unequalled by any other man of his day. He was a left-handed batsman, and his

career lasted from 1834 until 1857 when he was smitten by paralysis. The Reverend James Pycroft recalled playing with him in the early part of his career.

I played with him in 1838, the left-handed men of England against the Marylebone Club, with Cobbett, Pilch and Wenman given. This was the last time the Left-hands attempted an eleven. They had once numbered men strong enough to beat the Right, however small the choice of Left-hands.

Felix was a most brilliant hitter. His cut sent the ball like a shot through the fieldsmen, but the style of it was peculiar. He never shifted his pivot foot (the left to him, remember; the right to another), but always crossed his right foot over.

William Caffyn supported Pycroft's assessment of Felix's hitting and, in particular, his brilliant cutting.

I have seen no batsman from W. G. Grace downwards who could excel him in this particular. Being a left-handed bat, he had ample opportunities of indulging in this favourite hit of his, as most of the bowlers in those days did not change sides of the wicket when bowling to a left-handed man; and as they bowled round the wicket in most cases with a break from leg, a batsman like Felix had only to wait for a slightly over-tossed ball to punish it severely. He once told me that he learnt this stroke by suspending a ball from the ceiling with a piece of string and hitting it with a bat as it swung towards him (an old-fashioned method practised by many enthusiasts anxious to improve their batting in those days).

Felix and Mynn were regular members of the Gentlemen's side against the Players who had Pilch and Wenman in their number. In the fixture at Lord's in 1833 and 1834, Herbert Jenner played alongside Felix and Mynn, but the Gentlemen were heavily beaten in both years even though they batted sixteen men in 1833. This was the year that Jenner was President of MCC, although only twenty-seven, and he was the last president to appear in the Gentlemen and Players match during his year of office.

Born in London on 23 February 1806, Jenner, who later changed his name to Jenner-Fust, was educated at Eton and Cambridge. He was one of the great amateur players of his day, a brilliant wicket-keeper, very good batsman and useful bowler. His life was long – he was in his ninety-fourth year when he died – but his cricket career was relatively short. His last game was for the Gentlemen of Kent in 1838 when he was only thirty-two years old.

He played in the first Varsity match, at Lord's, 4 June 1827, and he was one of those responsible for establishing the fixture. He hit 47, which was more than the rest of the Cambridge side put together, and took 5 wickets. Bad weather prevented the game from being completed. At the end of the century, he spoke to A. W. Pullin about the birth of the Varsity match and the cricket of his day.

I am not quite clear whether we challenged Oxford first or they challenged us. I do know, however, that the idea of a match was quickly taken up. I either proposed or seconded the resolution that the match should be arranged, and I know the idea was accepted with alacrity, and there was very little discussion about it. The second match was not played until 1829, and that took place on the Magdalen ground at Oxford.

I often played in a white beaver hat, but people used to call those of us that did so postboys, and that caused us to drop the practice. At Eton and Cambridge we wore pretty much what we liked, but fancy jackets were not favoured. Knee-breeches, and thin gauze silk stockings doubled up at the ankles, formed a popular costume.

I kept wicket without pads or gloves; in fact, pads were not heard of in my young days, and the player would be laughed at who attempted to protect his shins. When the ball was wet I occasionally used a kid glove, but that was all. It should be remembered, too, that we often had to play on very rough grounds, which made the task of the wicket-keeper all the more difficult and dangerous. Yet I never met with a serious accident. The worst was a fracture of the middle finger of the right hand, and the dislocation of the forefinger.

I used to keep wicket to Alfred Mynn. He could get a very nasty spin on the ball. I stood up to him without gloves or pads, as I have stated, but I don't mind confessing that I was sometimes glad when the umpire called 'over'. A very fine and manly fellow was Alfred Mynn, and all that has been said and written of his great qualities does his memory no more than justice. He was as large in heart as he was great in cricket. It is indeed hard to say what he was and what he was not. In his day he was tremendously popular.

One of the best wicket-keepers Kent ever produced was E. G. Wenman. He was better than old Tom Box. I liked Wenman the better because you could always depend upon him, and you could not do the same with Box. Old Lillywhite used to say the same. Box used to keep too stiff at the wicket, and could not get out to reach the ball as Wenman did. Poor Box! He had a tragically sudden death at the post of duty at the finish.

The best bowler of his day was old W. Lillywhite, the first of the cricketing family of that name. 'I bowl the best ball and Harenc the next,' was a favourite remark of Lillywhite's. No doubt Harenc was a first-rate bowler, and with a side-hill, as at Harrow, was irresistible. His deliveries imparted far more twist than Lillywhite's, but the latter bowled more with his head, and on that account his saying, 'I bowl the best ball and Harenc the next,' was quite justified.

I once arranged (1834) to take a team representing West Kent to play Norfolk, at Elmham, a return match for the game they had played at Chiselhurst. I got promises for a full team, but when the day came those who had promised had all cried off, except a man who was subject to fits, and not good enough for a run. However, I was determined to fill the engagement, so in company with the fits subject I set off to play the county match, determined to make up a team on the way as best I could. At one place where the coach stopped I came across three young men who seemed nice fellows, and as they said they could play cricket I pressed them into my service for the match. Then we went on to Cambridge, and I ransacked King's College, and found four more men to join me. Two others were met on the ground in Norfolk, and with this strange combination – as it may seem to you – we won the match. There was not the keenness and partisan spirit in cricket in my days that you see now. If a man wanted to play out of his county he could do so. All that was wanted was an agreeable company and a pleasant match.

The structure of cricket changed considerably in the years that separated Jenner-Fust's playing career from this interview with Pullin. The lackadaisical regulations which governed qualification were brought to an end in 1873 when it was agreed that at the beginning of each season a cricketer should state which county he would assist, the county of his birth or the county of his residence. A cricketer was no longer allowed to play for more than one county during the season. The county championship as we know it today began to take shape. In Jenner-Fust's day, as he indicates, men played for whom they pleased.

Tom Box whom he mentions was the Sussex wicket-keeper for thirty years, but during that time he also played for Hampshire and, in 1849, he appeared twice for Surrey as a 'given man', or special guest player included to balance the sides in strength. He retired in 1856 and looked after the Brunswick Cricket Ground in Brighton. He later became ground-keeper at Prince's which was Middlesex's home for five seasons, 1872–76.

Prince's was a lovely ground situated in the middle of a fast-growing district at the back of Harrods. It fell victim to the property developers, and Middlesex moved to Lord's. The last game to be played at Prince's was between Middlesex and Nottinghamshire, and, needing 55 to win, the visitors were 10 for 1 when Box, who was attending to the scoreboard, dropped dead of a heart attack.

The earliest county clubs were not formed in order to field

[23]

sides in county competition. They were intended primarily as practice clubs for their members, and professionals were employed to bowl, advise and give strength when needed.

William Caffyn's first appearance in first-class cricket was for the Players of Surrey against the Gentlemen of Surrey in June, 1849. The Surrey Club had been formed in 1845 and had quickly become a power in the land, but Caffyn's father, a hairdresser and musician, saw no future in cricket as a profession.

My father was much averse to my taking up cricket as a profession, and when I was selected to play for the Players v. the Gentlemen of Surrey at the Oval, he refused point-blank to supply me with any money to get there. I managed to borrow half-a-crown, however, and received ten shillings and my expenses for playing in the match, so I felt quite rich when I returned home. In 1849, I was engaged by Captain Alexander of the 'Auberies' in Suffolk to play in all his matches. He was a very keen cricketer, and had a ground in the park at his house. Wisden had been engaged there the previous year, and had, I believe, spoken a good word for me to Captain Alexander. A number of capital matches were played at the Auberies, and very pleasant they were. The MCC and the I Zingari both visited us while I was there; and I thus had to encounter such players as F. W. Lillywhite, W. C. Morse, the Hon. Robert Grimston (who sometimes played with us as well as against us), the Hon. F. Ponsonby, and others. Often while the gentlemen were at dinner in the evening I used to sit in the park and give them a solo on the cornet. While I was engaged at the Auberies I played with eighteen of Suffolk against the famous All-England Eleven at Bury St Edmund's; and in this, to me, most important match, I had the misfortune to make a pair-of-spectacles! I was consoled somewhat with what I did with the ball, and obtained 5 wickets for 39 runs in the second innings of England. The wickets I took were those of Messrs A. Mynn, Guy, Pilch, Box and Hillyer. Martingell, I remember, was missing from his hotel one evening, and old Clarke for a joke sent the crier round Bury to call out,

'Lost, a Martingell!' I was so proud of being seen with the All-England Eleven that, although I was not on their side, I rode to London with them on the coach when they went away, for no other purpose than to be in their society.

> Caffyn was to become a member of the All-England XI a year later, 1850.

I took part in a North and South match this year, which was one of the most remarkable I ever played in, made so by the fact of Wisden *bowling* all our wickets down in the second innings for 76 runs, of which I was top scorer with 24. Wisden's performance was indeed a remarkable one when one considers that it was a first-class match. Of course he was helped a good deal by the wicket, which was generally all in favour of the bowler at Lord's in those days. I may add that in our *first* innings we were all disposed of for 36 (W. Clarke taking 6 wickets), and here again I was top scorer with 9 runs! The reason of Wisden's playing for the North was owing to his owning (in conjunction with George Parr) a cricket-ground at Leamington.

After this match I was engaged by William Clarke (always known as 'Old Clarke') to play for his All-England Eleven at Cranbrook.

> Born at Nottingham in 1798, William Clarke was eighteen when he first played for his native county. In 1838, having acquired the inn by his second marriage, he founded the famous Trent Bridge ground. Successful as he had been as a bowler, he did not appear at Lord's until 1836, and he was forty-seven before he was selected for the Players against the Gentlemen. He took 5 for 30 in the first innings and was recognized as the finest slow bowler in the country.
>
> Richard Daft who, like Caffyn, was to play for Clarke's All-England XI, recalled the veteran's bowling action.

Clarke's delivery was a peculiar one. He came up to the crease with the usual 'trot' which nearly all slow under-hand bowlers adopt, but instead of delivering the ball from the height of, or between, the hip he at the last moment bent back his elbow, bringing the ball almost under his right armpit, and delivered the ball thus from as great a height as it was possible to attain, and still be underhand. He was by this delivery able to make the ball get up higher and quicker from the pitch than he would have done if he had delivered it in the same way as other lob bowlers. I have often heard old cricketers say that they have received many balls from Clarke which got up quite 'nasty' from the pitch, with a lot of screw on them. He seldom bowled two balls alike, and could vary his pace and pitch in a wonderful manner. He was able to detect the weak points of a batsman quicker, perhaps, than any bowler that ever lived.

> Clarke's first appearance for the Players against the Gentlemen at Lord's was in July 1846, and George Parr made his debut for the Players in the same fixture. Like Clarke, Parr was a Nottinghamshire man, born and bred in Radcliffe-on-Trent; and, also like Clarke, Parr became closely associated with the All-England XI. Known as the Lion of the North, he accomplished many wonderful feats with the bat and was recognized as the greatest batsman since Fuller Pilch in his prime. Caffyn played both with him and against him and remembered him with admiration and affection, for George Parr

... was a well-known figure on the old cricket-fields, and easily spotted out among his fellow-players. He was rather over medium height, with round shoulders and powerful arms. He stooped slightly and limped somewhat in his walk, seeming to have a fagged and tired appearance. He had a florid complexion, large blue eyes, auburn hair, and thick chestnut-coloured moustache and whiskers.

George Parr never received any 'coaching' at cricket. He had a *natural* gift for batting excelled by no one. He always played with a straight bat, and with a certain amount of wrist-work, but his body seemed so to smother his hands as it were (especially in his back-play) that this was not particularly noticeable.

At the time that I joined the All-England Eleven in 1850 there is no doubt that Parr was the most dangerous bat in England. He gave one the impression that he was able to deal with all kinds of bowling on all kinds of wickets. When one has said that he played thoroughly *sound* cricket, one has given a general outline of the play of George Parr. He certainly played a different game to any one who had preceded him, using his feet and going out to drive straight balls far more than anyone else. His style of defence was 'low down', both in playing forward and back, and in this he presented a strange contrast to Pilch. When in attitude at the wicket he bent his left knee and arched his back a good deal; still, he did not crouch down so low as some other players we have seen. He cut hard and well in front of the wicket, with the right foot advanced, but required a ball a good way from the wicket to make an effective cut. His late cut was a hard chop striking the ground at the same time as he struck the ball. This stroke was the best he had, barring of course his leg-hitting. He drove hard and well, and often left his ground to do so. As a leg-hitter he will always be best known. The great secret of his success in this respect was that he hit *more* balls to leg than anyone else.

His method was to reach out with the left leg straight down the wicket, bending the knee, and to sweep the ball round in a sort of half-circle behind the wicket.

There seems to be an idea sprung up of late years that Parr was in the habit of hitting *straight* balls to leg, but this is a mistake. In Parr's day it would have been considered decidedly bad form to have even pulled a short ball round in that direction, and to have attempted to make a deliberate leg-hit from a ball on the wicket would have been unpardonable.

It is true that he ran it very fine, especially with a ball breaking in from leg, and when bowling against him I used always to remember this, knowing that if he hit round to leg and missed the ball I should most likely bowl him off his pads. I was attempting this when he hit me over the tavern at Lord's in the England and United match in 1860. This ball pitched outside his leg-stump and did not break in at all as I meant it to do, and it was promptly hit out of the ground.

If Parr's genius was instantly acclaimed – he was nineteen when he first played for Nottinghamshire and twenty when he first appeared for the Players – Clarke's recognition came late, but Old Clarke was one of the most important figures in cricket history.

In the 1840s England had entered into a period of prosperity and social change. For certain there were 'two nations', but the wealthier of the two began to enjoy greater leisure, and cricket was being more widely played and arousing greater public interest than ever before. The advent of the railways reduced the barrier of distance, and it needed only a man of vision to realize the opportunities that were now available for the popularization and commercial advancement of cricket. William Clarke was that man, and however great his prowess on the field, he claims immortality for his formation of the All-England XI in August 1846.

Clarke gathered together the finest players in England, and they travelled the length and breadth of the country playing against Twenty-two's or Eighteens of local sides. In *The Cricket Field*, Pycroft reported a conversation between Clarke and James Dark, the proprietor of Lord's.

'I heard', said Dark, 'of Clarke having made a match against some side at Newcastle, where, as I told him, there were no players at all fit to stand against him.' 'Never you mind,' replied Clarke, 'I shall play sides strong or weak, with numbers or with bowlers given, and shall play all over the country too – mark my words – and it will make good for cricket, and for your trade too.' And sure enough the increase in my bat-and-ball trade bears witness to Clarke's long-sighted speculation.'

Caffyn commented on how exhausting he had found a season with the All-England XI, but he was quick to acknowledge how successful had been Clarke's venture.

It will be seen how successful Clarke had been with his travelling eleven in a short time. Two years before the idea of starting such

[28]

an organization had never entered his head, and now he found himself overwhelmed with letters requesting him to take his team to almost every corner of the United Kingdom.

> Richard Daft remembered vividly the strains and stresses of playing for the All-England XI. The railways were developing rapidly, but they were still in their infancy, and although the main towns were linked by rail, there were still journeys to be made by coach to and from the venues at which matches were played.

We were very hard worked at the time the All-England Eleven was in full swing, as the matches began early in the season and finished late; and having other important fixtures besides, we were continually on the move. Travelling during the night was every week indispensable, and travelling in those days was not what it is now.

I remember once having to drive over a moor in the dead of night after playing at Redruth, in Cornwall. It was pitch dark, and we had a deep ditch on either side of us, and as we were driving a coach-and-four this was not very pleasant. To make matters worse, a dreadful thunderstorm came on. We were most of us rather nervous, for there was not a house about for miles round. Poor old George Parr, I recollect, was in a terrible way.

There sat next to him an officer who had ridden in the charge at Balaclava, on which occasion, he afterwards told me, he was not nearly so frightened as he was when on the top of this coach. His nervousness, however, took a different form to that of poor George; for he continued all the way to pour forth a volley of imprecations on the road, the weather, and on our situation generally. George entreated him almost with tears to moderate his language, or he was sure, he said, we should all be killed.

Well, after a long time we came to an isolated cottage, where we determined to stop and get something to eat, for we were nearly famished. For some time we could make nobody hear, but at length an old fellow in a nightcap put out his head and a blunderbuss from an upper window. The latter he appeared to be levelling at the head of George Parr, who was nearest to him. The old man was as deaf as an adder, and it was a difficult matter to make him understand that all we wanted was something to eat and drink, and that we were quite willing to pay for all we might have. On hearing this he slowly descended the stairs, unbarred the door, and in we all went.

> If the travelling was arduous for the accomplished professionals, the standard of cricket could be most testing for many of those against whom they played. In continuing his reminiscences of Clarke's side, Daft recalled the fears of one opponent at facing the bowling of R. C. Tinley, yet another Nottinghamshire cricketer.

Many of our All-England Eleven matches were the pleasantest I ever took part in, for in all cases we were made much of by the supporters of the teams we played against, who generally did everything in their power to make us comfortable. The rough wickets were often the most disagreeable item in the matches; but at many places we had nothing to complain of. We generally had to face some good bowling, for mostly a crack professional or two assisted the twenty-twos and eighteens we were opposed to. But some of the batting of the local cricketers was of a very second-rate character. There was one gentleman whom we met more than once who always went in last or last but one, but who never failed to get his pads on before the first wicket fell.

I remember once playing in one of these matches, and a gentleman came in whose bat literally shook as he took his guard. Tinley was bowling at the time; but before he began to play this batsman turned to the fielders who were nearest to the wicket, and said: 'Well, gentlemen, you see the form I am in. I have been through the Crimea, and never knew then what fear was; and here I am shaking in my shoes at a little fellow like that [pointing to Tinley] for I *know* he'll get me out!' – which Tinley did with the very first ball he sent him.

When playing in Cornwall, we got the twenty-two out in three-quarters of an hour in their first innings; and I remember that when playing against England at Sheffield, Tinley, with his slows, took in one innings the whole of the 17 wickets.

[30]

Whatever the strength or weakness of the opposition, the achievements of William Clarke and his eleven were mighty, their contribution to the growth of cricket incalculable. It has been estimated that in the seven seasons between 1847 and 1853 Clarke took 2,385 wickets. He never took less than 222 wickets in a season, and, in 1853, he was said to have captured 476 wickets. Having obtained a wicket with the last ball he ever bowled, he died in 1856, some four months short of his fifty-eighth birthday by which time he had given over the captaincy of the All-England XI to George Parr who also became manager.

Caffyn was to pay tribute to Clarke in his reminiscences at the end of the century:

Whatever may have been the slight failings as a man of this truly great cricketer (and I am bound to confess that he and myself did not get on too smoothly together), on looking back across a space of nearly half a century one is lost in admiration for this glorious veteran, who did perhaps more than anyone else ever has done to popularize our great national game throughout the length and breadth of this country.

Caffyn touches upon Clarke's failings as a man, and it was these failings which were to cause a split in the All-England XI. He was said to pay his men between six and four pounds a match depending upon the length of the journey, which was not generous, and he was generally known as being tight-fisted in his business dealings.

He gathered together the leading cricketers in the country – Pilch, Mynn, Felix, Parr, Martingell, Box, Hillyer – and recruited others over the years. One of his earliest and most notable recruits was John Wisden. We have already referred to Wisden's feat of taking all ten wickets for North against South in 1850, a match in which Caffyn played, and Caffyn believed Wisden to have been one of the best all-round cricketers he ever saw.

Wisden was the best fast bowler I ever saw for so small a man. His height was said to be 5 feet 4 1/2 inches, but I should not think he stood even as high as that. When I knew him he would weigh perhaps a little under ten stone. He was a remarkably good-tempered little fellow, with a most comical expression of face. He was a grand bowler, with, I think, the easiest delivery I ever saw. In the days when the bowler was compelled to bowl level with the shoulder, Wisden was always spoken of as being remarkably 'fair'. Indeed I think he never gave the umpire any trouble as to the doubtfulness of his delivery at any time. He had a great command of 'pitch', was very straight, and likely to slick a batsman out even on a good wicket, however well set, as his ball came in quick off the pitch, and he bowled many shooters.

As a batsman he was first-rate. He played with a beautifully straight bat, which he appeared to hold very lightly, but nevertheless he could hit hard and clean. In 1849 he scored exactly 100 in the Sussex and Kent match, and in 1855 his score of 148 for Sussex v. Yorkshire was much talked about. There is no doubt that if Wisden had less bowling to do he would have been still-more famous as a batsman.

Wisden was also a shrewd businessman, the famous annual which still bears his name is testimony to that fact, and he became less than satisfied with the payment and the treatment that he was receiving from Clarke for playing for the All-England XI. He and James Dean senior, another Sussex man, led a break-away group from Clarke and established the United England XI in August 1852. The following month, in a match at Sheffield, the members of this new team drew up a manifesto in which they stated that none of them would appear in any game, with the exception of county matches, which were under the control of William Clarke.

Not until after Clarke's death did the United England XI and the All-England XI meet each other in a contest, and then, at Lord's in June 1859, the United XI won a low-scoring match by 37 runs. Caffyn had match figures of 11 for 63, and he and Atkinson bowled unchanged throughout the match.

For the All-England XI, John Jackson took 14 for 61 in the match. Richard Daft remembered Jackson as

. . . one of the best fast bowlers we ever had. His delivery was very fine, as he stood straight up and delivered exactly level with his shoulder. He stood over six feet, and was a very powerful man. In the field he somewhat resembled Dr W. G. Grace. He was a very good bat, too, and often made a lot of runs. I remember his getting exactly 100 for Notts v. Kent at Cranbrook in 1863, on which occasion his hitting was tremendous.

He was born in Suffolk, but had lived in Notts ever since he was a few months old. He had a peculiar habit of blowing his nose with a loud report whenever he got a wicket. Carpenter used to call him the 'fog-horn' on this account; he was a rough-and-tumble sort of fellow in these days, and often got into scrapes of some kind or other, much to the annoyance of George Parr. I shall never forget George's anger when he kicked a cup of coffee over his new flannel trousers one morning at breakfast.

Some thirty years on, A. W. Pullin was to track down Jackson in Liverpool.

A bent and grisly man of sixty-seven, with the remnants of a fine presence, subsisting on a pittance of five shillings and sixpence a week, willing to work but elbowed out by younger and more vigorous competitors in the battle of life, having no permanent address, and always hovering on the threshold of the workhouse.

This is the John Jackson of today. Jolly game, cricket!

Jackson himself commented upon the payments he had received as a player.

We old cricketers made but a very poor living by our occupation, and sometimes we had to stick up for our rights. I remember once going from Uppingham to London. Some of our fellows had an agreement to play for four pounds or five pounds under a hundred miles, and five pounds or six pounds over that distance. I had made no agreement. At the close of the match old Mr Dark, who used to almost run Lord's ground, offered me four pounds. 'What's that for?' I asked. 'Four pounds for playing,' he replied. 'Keep it until it's five pounds,' I retorted, and left it. I had to go up to Lord's soon after for the Gentlemen v. Players' match, and then I said I wanted ten pounds, including the five pounds owing to me. Mr Dark gave me three packages. 'There's a mistake here,' I said, on glancing at their contents. 'There is no mistake,' he curtly replied. I took the packages away, and on examining them found they contained in all forty-three pounds. Of course I took the money back. Mr Dark saw his error, paid me my full fee, and for some years afterwards always gave me a bat.

Of course, you will know I went with the first English team to Canada and the States in 1859, and with George Parr's team to America and Australia in 1864. We did not lose a match on either the American or the Australian trip, but we ought to have been beaten in Sydney. Chris Tinley had to go in last when it required 1 to tie and 2 to win. He hit a ball straight into a fielder's hands, but the man dropped it and a run was scored for the stroke. During this tour E. M. Grace and I played an eleven of Castlemaine ourselves and defeated them, too.

My career with Notts closed in 1866 owing to an injury I received in the match with Yorkshire at Trent Bridge. I was fielding at very long slip, and in running after the ball I fell and ruptured a blood-vessel in my leg. I was laid up twenty weeks after it, but got well. I think I ought to have been played again for my county, and that I should have been had it not been for the fact that I was not strictly Notts born, though as other cases have passed muster I don't see why mine should not.

> Jackson is referring to the fact that it was not until 1873 that it was decreed that a player could not appear for more than one county and that there should be rules of qualification by birth or residence. Before that time, things were rather lax.

People are strict now, and rightly so, about county qualification. I wonder what they would think if a county was given three men for a match. That happened on one famous occasion, I being one of the given men, and Parr and Caffyn the other two. It was England v. Kent at Lord's (5 July 1858), and the match was all over in one day. England got us out for 33 and 41, and won by 10 wickets. I think I did my share, though, for in England's first innings I took 9 wickets for 27 runs. In our second innings H. H. Stephenson did the hat trick with the last three balls, the victims being myself, Mr B. Norton, and W. Baker.

As he recalls, Jackson was one of the party of twelve led by George Parr which toured Canada and the United States in September and October 1859. The tour was organized by W. P. Pickering, an old Cambridge Blue and an original member of the Surrey CCC, who had emigrated to Montreal. He arranged sponsors and the fixture list of eight matches. Among the twelve were Wisden, Caffyn, Alfred Diver, Robert Carpenter, Stephenson and John Lillywhite. Fred Lillywhite also accompanied the team as reporter, and he took along his printing-press and scoring-tent.

Fred Lillywhite was one of cricket's early historians. He went into business with John Wisden, but the partnership split after the tour to North America in 1859. Lillywhite had been preoccupied with *Scores and Biographies*, but he fell foul of the MCC who believed that it 'exceeded fair limits of criticism upon cricketers', and, following his split with Wisden, he was based at the Oval where he was a supplier of cricket clothes and equipment and printed score-cards. As reporter of England's first tour abroad, he left a vivid picture of the trials, tribulations and successes of the trip.

The agonies of the journey out, which took just over a fortnight, were forgotten when the party encountered the hardships of the homeward voyage. The tour itself was a huge success, and Lillywhite recorded the first day's play in Montreal. Many of the spectators had waited in the city for more than a week excitedly awaiting the delayed arrival of the cricketers.

[35]

On 24 September, Fred Lillywhite set up his tent. The weather was not very fine but cleared up towards midday.

At about eleven o'clock, the British Eleven were on the ground, and the natives seemed very much amused at seeing them at practice. The company soon became very large, and by the time 'play' was called there were not less than three thousand spectators. The large stand on the right-hand side of the gateway was soon filled with ladies; on the left there were a great many carriages. On the lower part of the ground a tent was erected to supply refreshments to the public, close to which was a smaller one for the English only. Soon after twelve o'clock the Eleven were seen on the field. Every man knew his place. Jackson and Caffyn started bowling, Lockyer at the wicket, Parr point, Diver long-stop, Stephenson middle-wicket, Caesar cover-point, Lillywhite long-leg, Grundy short-leg. G. Swain, Esq. and Lieutenant Surman took the bat first and played very steadily, but could not make many runs, the ground being very dead. The bowling of the Eleven was anything but good; the sea voyage seemed to have taken effect on all the bowlers. No stand was made until Mr Pickering went in. He played very well and reminded the Englishmen of what he was when he played at Lord's. His forward play and cutting were the same as in former days. He, with Mr Daley, displayed some first-class cricket. Mr Daley is a young player, with a good defence, and can hit well all round. His 19 was the largest score. He made two splendid cuts for 3 each, one good drive for 3, and two twos at the leg. These two gentlemen caused a change in the bowling; Stephenson was put on at Caffyn's end, but he, like the others, was not up to the mark; nor Wisden, who was tried at Jackson's end. At last Parr went on at Stephenson's end, and it was soon found that the Canadians were not up to the slows, for Parr made sad work with them. No other double figure was made than that of Mr Daley. At half-past four the Twenty-two were all out, with a score of 84 runs – by no means a bad one, considering the state of the ground.

After the usual time allowed between the innings, the Eleven sent Wisden and Grundy, to the bowling of Harding and Fisher. It was very bad light; the sun was going down behind the mountains, and that caused a particular glare, which the 'John Bulls', as the Canadians called them, were not used to; and it was well there was so little time to play, or they would probably have lost 2 or 3 wickets. Hardy bowled Grundy off his legs in his second over. Hayward went next, and with Wisden, stayed until time was called. This ended the first day's play.

Eventually, the England XI won the match with considerable ease as they did all their other fixtures. They were enthusiastically received wherever they went and regally entertained. In all, the party travelled nearly 7,500 miles in little more than two months, beginning and ending the journey in London and sailing from and to Liverpool. Caffyn reported that each of the players cleared about £90, with which they were well satisfied.

The tour to North America opened up lucrative possibilities for the top cricketers, and the catering firm of Spiers and Pond offered each player £150 plus first-class travelling expenses to tour Australia in 1861–62. George Parr and the Notts players considered the offer not good enough, and they refused to make the trip, but the leading Surrey cricketers, under H. H. Stephenson, accepted. This was to cause a north and south rivalry which became heated and lasted for some time.

Stephenson's side was enthusiastically received and was highly successful. Large crowds attended their matches, and so popular were the cricketers that Spiers and Pond offered them £1,200 to stay another month. Many of the players had other commitments and the offer had to be declined.

Two years later, another England side went to Australia under the captaincy of George Parr, and the men he took with him were fully representative of the best in England, with only Caffyn of the 1861–62 side retained. The side included a little-known Gloucestershire amateur by the name of E. M. Grace. He had made over 1,000 runs in all matches in 1863, and Caffyn had played against him in the Surrey v. England match at the Oval that summer.

Mr E. M. Grace's play is difficult to describe. Quickness of eye and hand were the secret of his success as a batsman. He could detect the length of a ball to a nicety, and was able to make up his mind what to do with it in less time than most players. He was a tiresome bat to bowl against, for one never knew what he would do with the best ball one could send up to him. A really good-length ball on the middle stump he would despatch to the on boundary without the slightest regard to the feelings of the poor bowler. He was one of the few bats I have seen who could hit with as great a certainty when he first went in as when he had got well set. When occasion required, however, he could defend his wicket as well as anyone. Had Mr Grace never got 10 runs in an innings, he would have been worth playing in any team for his unique fielding at point. Such a point had never been seen before, and perhaps never will be again.

> Parr's side went through Australia unbeaten, and each man cleared about £250 from the trip, after paying all expenses. William Caffyn, one of the first great all-rounders of English cricket, remained behind in Australia, having accepted an engagement with the Melbourne Club. He did not return to England until 1871 by which time much had changed, and his best days were behind him.

2

FAR TOO MUCH OF
THE BUSINESS ELEMENT

Richard Daft

V. E. Walker to A. W. Pullin

George Anderson to A. W. Pullin

W. G. Grace

Ted Pooley to A. W. Pullin

C. I. Thornton to A. W. Pullin

C. W. Alcock

Hon. R. H. Lyttleton

Lord Harris

A. E. Knight

C. B. Fry

Lord Hawke

George Giffen

The Gentlemen during the earlier part of my time were no match for the Players, though in subsequent years, when the Messrs Grace were in their prime, they were certainly their superiors. While the Gentlemen improved, the Players fell off, for they had not, in my opinion, such good men as when I first began to play; when Parr, Carpenter, Hayward, Stephenson, Caffyn, and others ceased playing, their places were filled by batsmen who, though good men enough, were not quite in the same class as their great predecessors.

So wrote Richard Daft in his *Kings of Cricket*. His assessment of E. M. Grace echoed the assessment that Caffyn had made.

He must always have possessed a marvellous eye to have made with safety the strokes he did. He was as quick as lightning in all his movements, both with the bat and in the field. He was, I consider, *the* best point that has yet been seen.

I had the pleasure of knowing both the mother and father of this famous player. The former knew ten times more about cricket than any lady I ever met. As an instance of this, I will here mention a circumstance often talked of by George Parr. During the time of the palmy days of the All-England Eleven, Mrs Grace wrote to Parr, asking him to play her son (Mr E.M.) in some of his matches, as she was sure, she said, he had the making of a fine player; and, amongst other things, said she had a younger son who would in time make a better batsman than any of his brothers, for his *back play* was superior to theirs. I never saw this letter, as George had either lost or destroyed it, which in after years he greatly regretted. Subsequent events proved how correct Mrs Grace had been in her prediction in this case, for the younger son she alluded to was Mr W.G.

W. G. Grace first appeared at Lord's in July 1864, playing for the South Wales Club against MCC. The following year, he was in the Gentlemen's side against the Players both at the Oval and at Lord's, and the greatest of cricket careers was launched.

[41]

His astounding feats with the bat could have been accomplished by no man, however good a player, who was not possessed of great physical advantages, an iron constitution, and who did not live temperately. He has altered but little in his style of play since I first knew him. There has never been any show about his play, and it is only the best judges who can most fully appreciate his great abilities. His defence has always been perfect, his hitting powerful and clean, and the way in which he is able to *place* a ball for runs is truly marvellous.

In my opinion, the two great secrets of his success have been his great self-denial and his constant practice. He never, I believe, until he had reached the top of the ladder, neglected any opportunity of improving himself in every department of the game. In all this he has been a model to young cricketers. Everyone is, no doubt, anxious to succeed at the profession he takes up; but how many, whose profession is cricket, really make it their first consideration?

> Not only was Daft full of praise for Grace's dedication, but he was at pains to point out the size of the man's achievements in comparison with others.

There have been batsmen lately who have almost equalled some of Dr W. G. Grace's best efforts as far as the number of runs goes; but when the bowling he obtained his scores against and the wickets he played on are taken into account, I fail to see how their performance can be compared with his; for many of his large scores have been made not against the weaker counties of England, but often against the finest combined talent of the country.

> One of the greatest of all-round cricketers to precede W. G. Grace was V. E. Walker, one of seven brothers who lived at Southgate and were instrumental in the formation of the Middlesex Club in 1864. In conversation with A. W. Pullin, Vyell Walker touched upon some of the changes in cricket which took place at the outset of Grace's career. The most significant was undoubtedly the change in the law governing bowling

action. On 10 June 1864, following the match between Oxford University and MCC at Lord's, the MCC members met in the tennis court and passed a new law which abolished the restriction on the height of the hand at the point of delivery. This change had been brought about by events at the Oval two years earlier, although the debate had been going on for some time. Vyell Walker recalled the rumpus concerning umpire John Lillywhite and bowler Edgar Willsher.

It seems ages since that row that led to the change in the law as to over-arm delivery. The matter has often been referred to, and has now long since passed into history. Well, I was the England captain, and the match was England v. Surrey at the Oval on August 25, 26, 27, 1862. The only amateurs in the England team were Lord Cobham, then the Hon. C. G. Lyttleton, and myself. We led off with a score of 503, towards which Tom Hayward made 117. Surrey went in towards the close of the second day, and Edgar Willsher was no-balled six times by Lillywhite for having his arm too high. Willsher was savage, and threw the ball down in disgust, after which he and his brother professionals marched off the field in high dudgeon. Lyttleton and I lay down on the grass, while the Surrey crowd looked on and admired us in their own peculiar way. Finally, as it was late in the day, we went into the pavilion too, and it was arranged that the game should be continued next day with a fresh umpire. This was done, the new umpire being G. Street.

I was told afterwards that Lillywhite had hinted to Willsher that he should no-ball him if he did not alter his mode of delivery. I did not know anything of the coming trouble at the time, or I should not have put Willsher on to bowl at the end at which Lillywhite was umpiring. That, I think, is self-evident. Willsher and Lillywhite were really very great chums, and they soon made up the little difference which this scene caused.

The matter did not end quite as simply as Vyell Walker suggests, for George Anderson, the Yorkshire cricketer, told Pullin that the northern professionals believed that Lillywhite had been prompted beforehand to no-ball Willsher. Anderson was one of those who refused to play against Surrey for some seasons because of this.

Anderson also drew attention to the quality of wickets that the All-England XI and cricketers of their time had had to play on.

The first time we went to Glasgow, before we could begin to play, old Fuller Pilch had to borrow a scythe and mow the wicket. It was like playing in a meadow. Then once at Truro one of our men, in fielding a ball, actually ran into a covey of partridges!

Vyell Walker was adamant that the game had changed so much by the eighteen-nineties that it had become impossible to draw comparisons between individual players.

In the first place, the wickets at Lord's, oh dear! In old Dark's days the ground was all ridge and furrow, and you had to consider yourself lucky if you did not get two shooters in each over and one on the head.

Walker bowled lobs round the wicket because he knocked his knuckles on the stumps when he bowled over the wicket. He took all 10 wickets in a match on two occasions, and for some time it was believed that he had done it three times. In Middlesex's first county game, against Sussex at Islington in 1864, he claimed 9 wickets, and the tenth man was run out when the ball beat the batsman and rebounded off the wicket-keeper's pads into the stumps with the batsman out of his ground. As the batsman had touched the ball on its way to the keeper, the dismissal was later deemed to be run out.

For England against Surrey at the Oval in 1859, Vyell Walker took 10 wickets for 74 runs and then hit 108. Pullin reminded him of the occasion, and he commented:

The curious part of the bowling feat was that when the last man came in, Julius Caesar, who was ninth on the list, he was missed off my bowling. I thought at the time that I was just going to miss the

10 wickets' feat, but I got the other fellow, Granny Martingell, caught by Wisden, and thus accomplished the performance I wanted to do. My success struck me as singular at the time, because the bowler at the other end was far greater than I – namely, John Jackson. Bickley also had a few overs. In the next innings Jackson had satisfaction, for he took 6 wickets for 21 runs, while I obtained 4 for 67 runs.

I used to bowl lobs, and it was with lobs that this feat was recorded. Lob-bowling was to me an acquired art, adopted through the exigencies of school cricket. I used to bowl round-arm, with a medium pace. The Hon. Robert Grimston and Lord Bessborough, who used to coach us at Harrow, got me to take up lob-bowling for the good of the school team. I used to bowl rather fast lobs, too, with a high delivery. I had a habit of running well up the pitch after the ball, and that got me a number of wickets.

> Lob-bowling went out of fashion although Digby Jephson, the Surrey captain, bowled lobs at the beginning of the twentieth century. Simpson-Hayward of Worcestershire bowled under-arm until the outbreak of the First World War, and played five times for England against South Africa, 1909–10.
>
> Vyell Walker was invited to take a side to North America in the autumn of 1868, but he was unable to make the trip. He agreed to go there in 1872, but he was forced to drop out at the last moment because of business commitments, and the side was led by W. G. Grace. Walker was far from happy with the changes in cricket that he saw in the latter part of his life.

I am sorry to say that I do not think the game has improved. There is more self now than there used to be. Men do not play as much for their side as they might do, and as they did in my younger days. 'Average hunting' and record beating have done something to bring this unwelcome change about. I also think that too serious attention is paid to the game, and this is good neither for the pastime nor for those who play in it. In short, there is far too much of the business element in it all round.

I have always thought it a thousand pities that runs could not be run out as they used to be, though I confess I do not see how the difficulties in the way of abolishing boundaries are now to be overcome. By the present system of boundaries a great deal of the beauty of the game in the field, particularly in the art of throwing in, has disappeared. The endurance of the batsman is also not what it had to be formerly. W. G. Grace could not have made anything like so many hundreds as he has done in the more recent part of his career had the runs been actually run out, as in his younger days. His weight would not have allowed him to get over the ground in time.

Vyell Walker gave this interview in 1899 by which time W. G. Grace's great and glorious career was nearing its end. Grace himself echoed Walker's criticism of the wicket at Lord's in the first half of the century:

Wickets at the Oval were always much better than at Lord's, where the clay in the soil has always handicapped the ground men. It may surprise some people who admire the existing green sward at Marylebone when I say that within my recollection I could go on to the pitch at Lord's and pick up a handful of small pieces of gravel. That was very detrimental to the wickets, as a ball would sometimes hit one of the small stones and fly high in the air.

To show how crude the arrangements at Lord's were in the old days, I may mention that it was not until 1865 that the scorers were provided with a covered box in which to do their work. Up to that year the two unfortunate men had been perched high on seats without any protection whatever from sun or rain.

It was about this time, too, that boundaries came into being, and Grace tells of an incident that helped to bring about their introduction.

There were no fixed boundaries at Lord's when I first played there. If the ball struck the pavilion railings a four was allowed – although even that rule was suspended one year – but every other hit had to be run out. The institution of boundaries came about in a curious way. As interest in cricket extended and deepened the crowds attending the matches increased rapidly. Occasionally a ball would be hit among the spectators, who would open to let it pass through them, but often close again immediately. Fieldsmen frequently found it difficult to get through the crowd to the ball. On one occasion Mr A. N. Hornby was out in the long-field at Lord's, when a ball was driven among the spectators. As everybody knows, the Lancashire amateur was a very energetic fieldsman, and as he dashed after the ball he scattered the crowd in all directions. One poor old gentleman, not being sufficiently alert to get out of the way, was thrown on his back and rather severely hurt. The incident opened the eyes of the authorities to the necessity for better regulations, and as the result a boundary line was instituted.

Richard Daft emphasized the dedication with which Grace applied himself to practice and to the game and, in his own memoirs, *The Champion*, gave evidence of this:

I cannot remember when I began to play cricket. Respect for the truth prevents me from saying I played the first year of my existence, but I have little hesitation in declaring that I handled bat and ball before the end of my second.

If I was not born a cricketer, I was born in the atmosphere of cricket. My father, who was a keen sportsman, was full of enthusiasm for the game, while my mother took even more interest in all that concerned cricket and cricketers. When I was not much taller than a wicket I used to wonder what were the hard-cuts, leg-hits, and long-drives, about which my father and brothers were constantly talking. As far back as I can remember cricket was a common theme of conversation at home, and there was great excitement in the house when some big match was coming off in the neighbourhood.

If Mrs Grace is generally seen as the inspiration behind her cricketing family, the most famous and talented of her sons did not forget the maxims given him by his father.

When my father became a medical student, it was impossible for him to get away in the afternoon or evening, as most students do in the present day, and if he had not resorted to extraordinary hours he would have been compelled to give up playing. Two or three days a week throughout the cricketing season, he and a number of companions were in the habit of going to the Downs and practising between the hours of five and eight in the morning. In that way only could he continue the game he loved so well; and I remember we tried to follow in his footsteps in after years, at not quite so early an hour. He had the great qualities of perseverance and concentration, and he diligently impressed upon us the need for cultivating them.

I can remember his words now:

'Have patience, my boy; where there's a will there's a way; and there is nothing you cannot attain, if you only try hard enough.'

> W. G. maintained his father's principles, as Daft testified, and his first opportunity to play in an important match came about because his elder brother, E. M., stayed longer in Australia in the spring of 1864 than had been anticipated.

My brother Henry and I were invited to join in the annual tour of the South Wales team. I do not know what was my qualification for playing for South Wales, but we didn't trouble much about qualification in those days.

Most of the players came from the West Country, and, after all, my brother and I were only divided from Wales by the Severn.

We came to London to play, and I made my first appearance at Kennington Oval on July 12, 1864. I secured four wickets in the first innings, and made 5 and 38 with the bat. After the Kennington match the captain of the South Wales told my brother that he didn't want me to play in the next match, which was at Brighton. Then, as now, it was always easier to get men to play at seaside resorts than in the provincial towns, and the Hove ground has always been very popular. But my brother Henry would not have me left out of the Brighton match, and insisted that I should play. I did, and went in first wicket down. When I had made 170 in the first innings and not-out 56 in the second, the captain did not repent that I had been included in the team. That was my first notable achievement away from home.

Grace led a side to North America in 1872, and in 1873–74 he took a party to Australia. He was somewhat surprised by the standard of the Australians who had benefited greatly from the tuition that they had received from such men as Caffyn. Grace was disappointed in the quality of the pitches and later claimed to have given his hosts much needed advice on the preparation of wickets.

Four years later, James Lillywhite took a side to Australia, and the two matches that were played at Melbourne in March and April 1877 have since been recognized as the first Test matches. The wicket-keeper in the party of twelve was Ted Pooley, but he was arrested in New Zealand following an argument over a bet and was not released until it was too late for him to play in the games in Melbourne.

Pooley, who played for both Middlesex and Surrey, had started his career as a bowler, but he succeeded Tom Lockyer behind the stumps at the Oval, and he was considered the greatest wicket-keeper of his time, although he never was to appear in a Test match.

A. W. Pullin interviewed Pooley at the end of the nineteenth century and found that the old 'keeper had hands that were merely 'lumps of deformity'.

Every finger of the two hands had been broken; so have the two thumbs. The joints are knotted and gnarled in a way that suggests the thumbscrew rather than the stumper's gloves. The writer suggests that some of the deformity might be due to rheumatism. 'Not a bit of it,' replies Pooley, bringing a maimed fist down with a heavy thump on the table. 'There's no rheumatics there; it's all cricket.'

Pooley told Pullin of his encounter with the famous prize fighter Jem Mace, the champion of England.

I was keeping wicket at a match at Lord's – on a pitch which at the time was so bad that you could put your finger between the cracks on the surface. A ball shot up and knocked out three of my

[49]

teeth. At lunch-time I was going to wash my damaged mouth when I was told a gentleman wanted to be introduced to me. He proved to be Jem Mace. 'Pooley,' said he, 'I would rather stand up against any man in England for an hour than take your place behind the wicket for five minutes. I heard that ball strike you as if it had hit a brick wall.'

> Pooley's injuries, and there were many, were sustained because he played on poor wickets, stood up to the fastest of bowlers and wore only scant protection in the form of the gloves and pads. C. I. Thornton, whom Pooley and many others regarded as the hardest hitter the world has seen, always batted without pads. Pooley claims that he and Thornton hit in excess of 130 in half an hour at Canterbury on one occasion.

Mr Thornton hit one ball over a tree into the hop-gardens, after which I remarked to him, 'I'll give you the belt, sir.' I tried to throw a ball over that tree afterwards and could not manage it.

> Thornton was never able to take part in any cricketing tours because of his business commitments, and it is remarkable that a man who played the game only occasionally and always purely for pleasure should have retained such a permanent place in cricket lore as one of the game's greatest hitters.
> Grace felt that . . .

It is superfluous to say that he was the hardest hitter – he has sent balls out of the Oval on three sides of that gigantic ground – and the most speedy run-getter I ever saw in the cricket-field. A hundred runs an hour was about his normal pace. He stands quite alone as the hitter of my time, and will never be excelled, even if he is equalled. Without pads – which he said interfered with his running – and without gloves, he forced the fastest bowling, apparently without any fear of injury. Once he paid the penalty for disregarding the precautionary batting gloves by having a finger-nail ripped off by a ball from S. M. J. Woods, but even then Mr Thornton seemed to care less about his injury than about the fact that the same ball disturbed his bails. The secret of Mr Thornton's hitting power was his eyesight and timing the ball correctly.

[50]

Thornton was the founder of the Scarborough Festival, and it was at Scarborough, in 1886, that he gave what his contemporaries considered the most sensational display of hitting ever seen in England.

It was in the match Gentlemen of England v. I Zingari, and among I Zingari bowlers was Mr A. G. Steel. I went in for the Gentlemen in the second innings when the score was 133 for 4 wickets. In seventy minutes the score was exactly doubled, and I had made 107 out of 133, all other wickets having fallen and I being not out. There were eight 6s – one being attributed to an overthrow – and twelve 4s in my score, and one of the 6s went through an open window in the houses on the Square side of the ground. Probably Mr Steel had never had such rough punishment before.

Thornton's claim is probably true, for Steel was an all-rounder of high quality who captained England on four occasions and had an excellent record in thirteen Test matches against Australia. Thornton's 107 was comprised of only 29 scoring strokes.

As we have mentioned, he was never able to tour, although tours were now proliferating. An Australian Aborigine side had toured England in 1868, and an American baseball team came in 1874. Four years later, the first Australian side was in England. The party was captained by David Gregory, and it included men like Murdoch, Spofforth and Blackham who were to become legends in the history of the game.

No Test matches were played during the season, for the first Test match in England did not take place until 1880, and then it was only a hurriedly arranged affair towards the end of the tour.

Lord Harris had taken a side to Australia in 1878–79, and there had been an ugly incident in the game against New South Wales at Sydney. There had been heavy betting on the match, and when Murdoch was given run out in the second innings the home supporters invaded the field and menaced the

Englishmen. Lord Harris himself was allegedly struck across the body with a stick.

The decision by the Australians to visit England in 1880 was made late, and the tourists discovered that the counties had already arranged their fixtures and found it difficult to accommodate the visitors.

The Australians had been exceedingly popular on the 1878 tour and had drawn large crowds to the Oval, but the Surrey secretary, C. W. Alcock, one of the great figures in the history of sport in Great Britain, tells of the problems which attended Murdoch's side of 1880.

Events had occurred during the visit of Lord Harris's team to the Colonies, in the previous winter, which had seriously affected the friendly relations hitherto existing between English and Australian cricketers. Under the circumstances it was felt that the tour might well have been deferred. But besides this, the Australians were so late in deciding to come that most of the principal clubs had already completed their programme when James Lillywhite was authorized to act on their behalf. Derbyshire, Gloucestershire, and Sussex were, indeed, the only counties able to arrange matches, for the fixtures with Yorkshire were not under the auspices of the County Club. As it was, the team was not seen at Lord's, and it was only at the last moment that matters were arranged for them to appear at the Oval. It was a happy thought of the Surrey authorities to suggest a match against a representative team of England at the end of the season. To consult Lord Harris was the first step, and the promise of his hearty co-operation removed one of the two principal difficulties. The other was to find a suitable date, and here they were again lucky in having the way smoothed for them. The only suitable days were September 6, 7 and 8, and then Sussex had fixed to meet the Australians at Brighton. To the credit of the Sussex Committee, be it said, they readily agreed to alter the dates so as to allow England and Australia meeting on the days named.

As it was my mission to interview the Committee of the Sussex

County Cricket Club as well as Lord Harris, I can speak feelingly of the ready response given by both to the suggestions which emanated from the Surrey Committee. Lord Harris was playing at Canterbury during Canterbury week, and a kindly welcome he gave me. It was indeed his ready and cordial promise of assistance of the request given him on behalf of the Surrey executive which brought the first test match into the regions of possibility.

Another member of the aristocracy was also instrumental in bringing the event to pass.

The Earl of Sheffield, then, as for many years, President of the Sussex County Cricket Club, presided at the meeting, which was held in the pavilion at the county ground at Brighton. I can recall well even now the hearty reception he gave to the proposal we had to make. It certainly smoothed the way for us, and it is pleasant, as an actual witness, to be able to record this, the first of a long list of kindly offices rendered by Lord Sheffield to Australian cricket.

So the first Test match to be played in England came about on 6, 7 and 8 September 1880. Lord Harris captained the England side; W. L. Murdoch led Australia.

The great Australian all-rounder George Giffen echoed the beliefs of his team-mates when he asserted that Murdoch was the greatest of Australian batsmen. Murdoch was captaining Australia for the first time at the Oval, and he had not hit a first-class century before this match. Giffen said of him:

Whenever I have played with him he has been the captain, and one has therefore appreciated the more his courage in trying circumstances. No matter how tight the hole we were in, Billy, with a smile of assurance and a cheering word, would go in himself and often master the bowling with his splendid defence. He has all the attributes that go to make a great batsman – keen eyes (he is a capital pigeon-shot), a thorough mastery of the science of the game, rare coolness, and the patience of Job. He batted as artistically as one could wish, and it was an education to watch how he drove or cut the ball along the sward, seldom mistiming the stroke one iota.

[53]

Alcock's efforts in bringing about the first Test match in England were well rewarded. There were three of the Grace brothers in the England side.

The Australians were singularly unlucky in having to play without their great bowler, F. R. Spofforth, who had injured his hand rather badly just before. Even in his absence the Australians proved themselves worthy opponents of the pick of English cricketers. What a wonderful sight the Oval presented during the whole three days! The public interest in the match took curious forms. The supply of score-cards gave out towards the finish, and the spectators were seen at the printers' box presenting envelopes and leaves out of note-books to ensure a copy of the official record. With glorious weather over forty thousand persons paid during the first two days. And which of us can forget the memorable scores of W. G. Grace and W. L. Murdoch? W. G. Grace's first innings of 152, to be overshadowed by the Australian captain with his even more brilliant second innings of 153 not out! How well and pluckily the Australians played, too, right up to the bitter end. England with only 57 to get to win, lost five of their best batsmen for 36, and but for the free hitting of Frank Penn, who had W.G. in with him at the finish, might have lost some more wickets. And how well I can remember that wonderful catch of G. F. Grace at long-on which got rid of the great Bonnor in the Australians' first innings. It was one of the best if not the very best I have ever seen. Fred Grace declared that his heart stopped, he had to wait for it so long. G.F., by the way, was unlucky enough to get a pair, but the two good catches of his were some compensation. Poor dear old Fred! It was his last big match, and within a fortnight he was dead. He died from the effects of a chill taken during a railway journey. Peace to his memory! A keener sportsman or a better fellow never lived.

The premature death of his younger brother, who had appeared in the Canterbury week before his sixteenth birthday, shocked W.G., for, apart from the natural feeling of family loss and the sadness of losing a young man in his prime, he considered G.F.

a brilliant all-round cricketer and the finest fielder of his day.

W.G.'s century at the Oval was the first by an English batsman in a Test match. He was already 32 years old by the time of his Test debut, and he was able to play Test cricket in Australia only once, 1891–92, when he led Lord Sheffield's side, yet he dominated first-class cricket until the end of the century.

The Hon. R. H. Lyttleton expressed the view that this dominance

. . . somewhat spoilt the excitement of the game. His side was never beaten. Crowds thronged to see him play, all bowling was alike to him, and the record of Gloucestershire cricket, champion county for some time through his efforts, is the only instance of one man practically making an eleven for several years. The other Gloucestershire players will be the first to acknowledge the truth of this. Gloucestershire rose with a bound into the highest rank among counties when W. G. Grace attained his position amongst batsmen, a head and shoulders above any other cricketer.

As Lord Harris pointed out, W.G. never lost his vital enthusiasm for the game. This was an important ingredient in his success.

W.G. was desperately keen for his side to win, and consequently was led, in his excitement, to be occasionally very rigid in demanding his full rights, but he was so popular, and had the game so thoroughly at heart that such slight incidents were readily forgiven him and indeed more often than not added to the fund of humorous stories about him. When the luck of the game went against him his lamentations were deep, and his neighbourhood to be temporarily avoided, except by the most sympathetic.

Albert E. Knight, a Leicestershire professional batsman and a lay preacher, believed that in W.G. cricket past and present had blended into one mighty stream. Knight played against the old man only late in his career, and his reverence for the great

[55]

player was augmented by a sharp perception of character and technique.

I well remember, some five or six years ago, the tall and heavy figure of W.G. fielding at point in an MCC v. Leicestershire game. A constant stream of comment flowed from his lips in a high-pitched, rather amusing tone, but he stroked his beard thoughtfully, and his watchful eyes betokened a wisdom greater than his speech conveyed.

'Eh, give me the ball; I can get this young man out,' he exclaimed at length. There were none to say him nay, and he took the ball. A few heavy strides, a slight rotary action of an arm just raised above the shoulder, and the right hand seemed to come down the pitch, a slow straight ball accompanying it, while the big beard and the bigger body shuffled away in the direction of mid-off. The first ball hit the batsman upon the leg, there was a quick turn round, a half-raised hand, and an excited ''s that?' (the 'how' was lost in the beard). The umpire blushed, but said 'Not out.' One subsequently found that there were umpires who found it very hard to say 'Not out' to the appeal of so venerable an authority. If mumbling mutterings may indicate dissatisfaction, the great champion was rather hurt by the continuance of this boy's innings. It was not much prolonged, however, for the boy rambled forward and his leg stump was disarranged. He retired wondering why and how he was so simply defeated. As one watched him baffling many a subsequent batsman, the question repeated itself. Was its length so wonderful? One ball just a trifle faster or slower? Was it the feint of a break that never was? Or was it the worrying tenacity of the bowler which overawed these batsmen and probed them to mental unrest? I rather think it was the latter.

Something of the same feeling of wonder has always been suggested to me in watching the batsmanship of Dr Grace, or in reading of the wonderful physique and endurance which, even almost to his fiftieth year, made him so supreme a batsman. That long and eventful career, embracing an extraordinary record of more than two hundred centuries, is never seen in its right proportion until by a circuit of thought we have realized the greatness which characterized the elite of generations bygone. One thinks it is the tenacity added to his style, the mentality which never sleeps, which is most characteristic of him.

The possibilities of beauty which may fly forth from the 'lyre' of the bat have seen a more finished expression and a greater symmetry than W.G. has given them. There is no stroke exploited by him which older and younger players did not possess. In the warp of his great natural gifts, of mental and physical endurance, and in the woof of his long experience, he has woven a more enduring web, a more permanent material fabric, than any other cricketer past or present, or perhaps to come. Untwine the fabric here and there, lay out the variegated filaments – the drive, the cut, the leg glance – and each stroke may more brightly gleam in the garment of a particular player who monopolizes one or other of them. Dr Grace sums up cricket ... he incorporates its massive splendours, its persistence, its marvellous endurance. In the sum of his achievements, in the *impersonal* greatness which characterizes his ability, in the large time-view which is his possession, we feel how great is the measure of his superiority.

> If Grace was the unchallenged king of cricket in the second half of the nineteenth century, he was quick to acknowledge Arthur Shrewsbury of Nottinghamshire as the greatest professional batsman of the age. He toured Australia four times, and he was a model of consistency for a long period. He first appeared for the Players against the Gentlemen in 1876, and twenty-three years on Grace could say of him:

His hand has lost none of its cunning, and his defence is as fine today as ever. Batting is as a science to Shrewsbury, who possesses all the nerve, patience, eyesight and strength which are the essentials of the ideal batsman. His coolness is remarkable, so remarkable that it is impossible to tell from his play whether he has been batting five minutes or five hours. His caution never relaxes, and his judgement is seldom at fault. Every hit is timed to a nicety, and a lofty stroke is a thing he very seldom indulges in. He cuts

[57]

with singular dexterity, and the wrist action which he brings into play when blocking a ball is a point young cricketers should observe and study. At one period of his career he showed a tendency towards stonewalling, and scored so slowly that spectators found that with all his stylish form his batting was tedious, and when Scotton and he were partners their displays were, I must confess, more scientific than exciting. In later years he has returned to his earlier and rather freer form.

> If Shrewsbury's batting exemplified the studied care of the dedicated professional, then Ranjitsinhji, the Indian prince who honed his game at Cambridge, was the supreme amateur, exotic in character, extravagant in technique.

How a man of his slender physique and apparently delicate constitution has so completely mastered the art of batting as to score with astounding rapidity and ease off all manner of bowling upon every variety of wicket is simply wonderful.

> Yet in singing Ranjitsinhji's praises, Grace also touched a cautionary note.

'Ranji' is unique as a batsman. Most batsmen have one or two favourite strokes of which they are masters. 'Ranji' has half a dozen strokes, which he plays with perfect ease and almost mechanical precision. Some of them are what one may call 'unorthodox'. I am afraid that when he gets older his habit of stepping in front of his wicket to play straight balls to leg will often cost him his wicket. Even with his wonderful, almost hawklike, eyesight he frequently gets out leg before wicket in trying to play a ball to leg which keeps lower than he expects. He hits all round the wicket with extraordinary skill, but is seen at his best in a leg-glance, which with him is an exceedingly pretty stroke. This is his favourite hit, and always delights onlookers.

> Ranjitsinhji played his county cricket for Sussex who could also boast the great Corinthian C. B. Fry in the last years of the century. In 1896 Ranji was the outstanding batsman of the

[58]

season, but he was not chosen for the Lord's Test. There were three Tests against Australia that year, the other two being at the Oval and Old Trafford. Fry explained why Ranji was not chosen for the Lord's Test.

Ranjitsinhji, the phenomenally successful batsman of the year, was included in the teams selected by Lancashire and Surrey, but omitted from the team chosen by the MCC. As there was no doubt of Ranjitsinhji's merit, clearly the MCC had decided that an Indian ought not to play for England, while Lancashire and Surrey had decided that he ought.

In 1906 A. E. Knight expanded upon these hints of racial prejudice.

Ranjitsinhji, quite apart from his unique place among batsmen, has demonstrated the fact that English birth is no essential for success upon the cricket field. There is indeed an extraordinary suppleness in many of the coloured races which predisposes them for excellence in such a game as cricket, whenever mental capacity is high enough to adequately supplement the purely natural physical facilities. Even in the West Indian Ollivierre, far removed as he is from this prince of batsmen, there is a certain allusive *nuance*, suggestive of a far-away glamour which no English player possesses. It is, I think, very unfortunate, writing purely from the cricket point of view, that racial caste should mar the progress of the black races, and, incidentally, of ourselves too, in the game. In places, however, and particularly is this the case in Africa and Australia, the black man plays cricket upon sufferance.

Ranjitsinhji's entry to the game was made easier by his social standing and his Cambridge education; Ollivierre, on the other hand, was a professional. He had toured England in 1900 with the first West Indian side to visit this country and had been the outstanding batsman. He remained in England to qualify for Derbyshire which he assisted until 1907.

By the time that first West Indian side arrived, England had already been visited by teams from South Africa, Canada, India and Philadelphia as well as by several Australian sides. Following the success of teams going to Australia and North America, there were tours of South Africa, India and West Indies, although only on the trips to South Africa were matches played which have since been recognized as Test matches.

The third of the tours to South Africa, 1895–96, was under the leadership of Lord Hawke, and he had with him a strong side, as he also had when he returned to the Cape three years later.

The first of Hawke's tours of South Africa was managed by George Lohmann, the great Surrey bowler. As Hawke recalled, the first trip was not without its problems.

Twice I have taken teams to South Africa, and both have left me the pleasantest memories. But whereas in the second there were no adverse exterior influences, the first was obscured by the political crisis, for we were actually playing cricket at the time when the country was convulsed over the Jameson Raid and when rumours of the wildest kind permeated even our dressing-rooms in the pavilion.

My side was a really good one, useful in every department, and I have always thought that the experience he gained on matting wickets made C. B. Fry the great bat he subsequently proved to be. It was the reverse with me, for I have never been comfortable batting on matting. George Lohmann not only managed the tour but bowled so phenomenally well that he took 157 wickets for less than seven runs each. We lost only two matches, both against odds, and won seven of our sixteen engagements, including all three representative matches.

. . . South Africa was entirely outplayed, losing at Port Elizabeth by 288 runs, at Jo'burg by an innings and 197 runs, and at Cape Town by an innings and 33 runs. In the first match they were helpless against Lohmann, who had the extraordinary average of eight wickets for 7 runs. Tom Hayward and A. J. L. Hill each made a century in the subsequent games, but J. H. Sinclair with 40 was their highest scorer. The bowling was better than the batting, G. A. Rowe and Middleton being the cleverest. The finest feature, of course, was the magnificent wicket-keeping of E. A. Halliwell — the Blackham of South Africa.

> John McCarthy Blackham was known as the 'prince of wicket-keepers', and he was behind the stumps for Australia in each of the first seventeen Test matches. He went on the first eight tours to England and captained the 1893 side. His team-mate George Giffen was fulsome in his praise.

During the whole of his first-class career he was peerless as a wicket-keeper. One could not help admiring him as he stood behind the stumps at a critical period of a game. With eyes keen as a hawk, and regardless of knocks, he would take the fastest bowling with marvellous dexterity, and woe betide the batsman who even so much as lifted the heel of his back foot as he played forward and missed the ball. I have seen him do some marvellous things. For instance, when the 1884 Australian Eleven defeated the Gentlemen of England by 46 runs, he stumped the last three batsmen. He was never a particularly reliable run-getter, yet few great batsmen have pulled a side out of a tight place more frequently than he has with his unorthodox batting. And how he could demoralize the bowling! Let him get a start and it was difficult to place the field for his strokes.

Being of a highly-strung temperament, 'Old Jack' could never bear watching an exciting finish. Instead he would with clenched hands and chin on chest pace up and down the dressing-room in a way which earned for him many years ago from one of the earlier Australian Elevens the sobriquet, 'The Caged Lion'. He always was a grand judge of the game, and few men could more quickly detect a weakness in a batsman. Nevertheless, he made far from an ideal captain, on account of his tendency to worry and magnify temporary misfortunes. In fact during the three months which elapsed between the first and the last of the test matches with Lord Sheffield's Eleven, Blackham, who was captain of the Australians, lost a stone in weight, which he attributed to worry and anxiety.

[61]

The elevation of South Africa to Test status, and tours by West Indians, Philadelphians and Parsis did nothing to diminish the fact that England's principal opponents were Australia. It was these two countries that vied perpetually for supremacy, and it was these two who produced the greatest players. One of the most feared of fast bowlers was Spofforth who had missed the first Test match in England through injury but whom Giffen considered

... absolutely the greatest bowler of my time. Turner may have been as deadly on sticky wickets – to have been more venomous was impossible – but he had not the same command over the ball that Spofforth had. The Demon, who had made a deep study of the art of bowling, had a wonderful control over his pitch, and he seldom turned the ball unless, if it were allowed to pass the bat, it would hit the wicket. On a batsman's wicket he was not so fine a bowler, perhaps, as Palmer or Boyle, but let the pitch give him the least help, and his breakbacks became unplayable. What a sight it was to see Spofforth bowling when a game had to be pulled like a brand from the burning! He looked the Demon every inch of him, and I verily believe he has frightened more batsmen out than many bowlers have fairly and squarely beaten. When the Demon meant business, the batsman had to look out for squalls. His pitch would be perfect, and it was almost impossible to get the ball away – save, of course, on the truest of wickets. His feat against England at the Oval in 1882 is, perhaps, the finest bowling performance on record. Besides this, he has three times done the hat-trick in first-class matches. The unfortunate accident to his finger in 1886 disabled him for some time, although I believe in London club matches he bowls well now. I often thought what a pity it was that he and Turner had not been in the 1888 team together, when the English wickets in the main were suitable for both of them. 'The Demon' at the one end and 'The Terror' at the other would have been a deadly combination.

Giffen himself was a great all-rounder and was considered the

W. G. Grace of Australia. He captained Australia on four occasions, but it proved to be a position he did not relish. The bowling performance by Spofforth the Demon at the Oval in 1882 to which Giffen refers saw the great Australian fast bowler take 14 for 90 in the match, the first instance of a bowler taking 14 wickets in a Test match.

England needed only 85 to win in their second innings, but in his last eleven overs Spofforth took four wickets for two runs, and at one time three wickets went down in four balls. Spofforth ended with 7 for 44, and England were bowled out for 77, giving Australia victory by seven runs. It was following this match that the mock obituary appeared in *The Sporting Times* which brought about the term 'The Ashes'.

Giffen stood down as captain after the 1894–95 series in Australia, and Harry Trott led the team to England in 1896.

He was a distinct success, his genial nature – I doubt whether any one ever knew him to have a downright quarrel with another player – helping him to gain that ascendancy over his men, without which no captain, however skilful, can secure the best play of his team.

> Australia won five of the eight Test matches against England in which Harry Trott was captain, and his own contributions were significant, both with bat and ball.

His great strength is, of course, in batting, and under all conditions he has not many superiors. On a good wicket I have seen him adopt forcing tactics worthy of a big hitter, and in the very next match play keeps on a difficult pitch with wonderful skill. His 143 at Lord's in 1896, when he thumped the mighty Richardson as though the bowling were the most ordinary stuff in the world, must rank as one of the finest innings contributed in test matches.

The greater the match, the better he plays.

> Harry Trott's younger brother Albert had astonishing success on the occasion of his debut against England in 1894–95, taking

8 for 43 in the second innings, but he was not selected for the tour of England the following year. Disgruntled, he came to England and qualified for Middlesex, giving immense pleasure for some years as a big hitter, fine bowler and great entertainer. Lord Hawke took him to South Africa in 1898–99, and he played in both Tests, so becoming one of the five cricketers who have represented both England and Australia. Hawke had a soft spot for Trott whom he believed had 'quaint ways'.

Trott was rather like Tom Emmett, full of drollery and apt to take his batting lightly. Indeed, towards the end, he degraded his magnificent hitting powers into blind swiping. Alas! he was one of those who through too short a life could not resist temptation. A wit once said: 'It is not a temptation if you resist it.' *Alberto* resisted none. At one time he was the best all-round cricketer in the world.

Trott took nine wickets in the first Test in Johannesburg to play a vital part in England's dramatic victory by 32 runs. He also played a significant part in an even more dramatic victory in the second Test, as Hawke related:

I won the toss – 'as per usual' was a comment – and it did us no good, for we were all out for less than a hundred.

J. H. Sinclair bowled really beautifully, and followed this up by a superb century. Not only was his hitting splendid all round the wicket, but the cleverness with which he managed to get all the bowling when the tail were with him was uncanny in its success. He smashed his bat in trying to hit Trott out of the field, and then smote the next delivery miles high full-pitch into the pond, one of the biggest strokes I ever witnessed. He was finally out to a huge on-drive splendidly judged and held almost on the ropes by Tyldesley. The batsman shook the fieldsman's hand in frank admiration, certainly reciprocated, for a spectacular and admirable innings.

A minority of 85 was no light matter in a match of this description. But it did not worry Frank Mitchell, though both he and

[64]

Warner were given several lives. This excellent start was followed by a perfectly model exhibition by Johnny Tyldesley, his three-figure exhibition not possessing a faulty stroke. It was 'a regular Coo Palairet effort', delightful to watch. Albert Trott opened his shoulders to the tune of a couple of sixes, and Frank Milligan hit clean and hard. On one occasion he was racing to pile up runs from an overthrow, only to find the umpire had called 'over'. Our big score of 330 had been thoroughly well made.

Two hundred and forty-six to win, and it did not seem a very onerous task for South Africa. But in twenty-two overs Haigh and Trott had dismissed the whole side for 35 runs. 'Sinclair let drive at Haigh's third ball, and Milligan, leaning over the ropes, made a magnificent one-handed catch just when everybody thought the ball was over the ropes behind the bowler. One of the catches of a lifetime of cricket.' The crowd gave the bowlers a most sporting ovation, but were crestfallen at the unexpected collapse of their representatives. Murray Bisset, the South African captain, remarked:

'It's not only a licking you have accomplished, but your two bowlers have rubbed it in.'

In fact, when England next toured South Africa, 1905–06, under Pelham Warner, they were beaten by four Tests to one, so quickly had South African cricket developed. The England sides that toured abroad were never as strong as the sides which competed in Test matches at home when all the leading amateurs were available. Of Lord Hawke's side which beat South Africa at Cape Town in April 1899 only Johnny Tyldesley, the Lancashire batsman, was selected for the first Test match against Australia at Trent Bridge two months later. This was to be W. G. Grace's last Test match.

The social divisions of the age had kept Grace from the captaincy of the England side until 1888 by which time he was forty years old. He had not been to public school or to Oxford or Cambridge and, accordingly, he had had to play under Lord Harris, Hornby and Steel, all of whom had those qualifications.

[65]

By 1888, however, his rivals had disappeared and he was undisputed leader of England in the last thirteen Tests in which he played. By the time he played against Australia at Trent Bridge in 1899 he was nearing his fifty-first birthday. He hit 28 and 1 and did not take a wicket. C. B. Fry, as one of the leading amateurs in the country, was a member of the selection committee which met on the Sunday after the Nottingham Test and he told how the end of the great man's Test career came about.

I was a few minutes late. The moment I entered the door W.G. said, 'Here's Charles. Now, Charles, before you sit down, we want you to answer this question, yes or no. Do you think that Archie MacLaren ought to play in the next Test match?'

Now, Archie MacLaren had in the winter of 1897–8 been the most successful batsman in the team taken to Australia by A. E. Stoddart. He had scored two centuries in Test matches and had divided a thousand runs with Ranjitsinhji with an average of 54. He had played Jones with great success. He was on top of the Australian bowling as a whole. Our batting had not shown up well at Nottingham. In our summer of 1898, however, he had not played nor in the early matches of 1899. It happened that I had been thinking about Archie MacLaren so I answered without hesitation, 'Yes, I do.'

'That settles it,' said W.G.; and I sat down at the table. Then, and not till then, did I discover that the question W.G. had asked me meant, 'Shall I, W. G. Grace, resign from the England Eleven?' This had never occurred to me. I had thought it was merely a question of Archie coming in instead of one of the other batsmen, perhaps myself. I explained this and tried to hedge, but the others had made up their minds that I was to be confronted with a sudden casting-vote. So there it was. I who owed my place in the England team to W.G.'s belief in me as a batsman gave the casting-vote that ended W.G.'s career of cricket for England. Consider that W.G. was a greater name in cricket in those days than Don Bradman is now. Consider, too, that he was still one of the best change-bowlers in England – about as good then as C. V. Grimmett is now – and consider, too, his tremendous personality.

Fortunately for my peace of mind I found out afterwards that W.G. felt that he ought to retire, not because he could not bat or bowl to the value of his place, but because he could not move about in the field or run his runs. At Nottingham he had missed a catch at point which he could have taken with ease if he could have bent. This gave Clem Hill a crucial second chance. I was in with W.G. while we put on 75 runs for the first wicket. Had I been in with Joe Vine of Sussex the score would have been over 100. We lost innumerable singles on the off-side, and I never dared to call W.G. for a second run to the long-field. When we were walking out from the pavilion as the first pair for England in my first Test the Old Man said to me, 'Now Charlie, remember that I'm not a sprinter like you.' There is no doubt that it was best for W.G. to retire. But I still think that some other instrument of his fate might have been chosen.

> Grace had the highest admiration for MacLaren who had scored a century for Lancashire against Sussex on the occasion of his county debut in 1890 when just down from Harrow. Five years later, he hit 424 for Lancashire against Somerset at Taunton, a world record at the time. Grace believed him to be among the most stylish of batsmen:

He has fewer 'showy' strokes than Ranjitsinhji, but he plays every variety of stroke with wonderful precision, times every ball with marvellous exactness, and hits all round the wicket with perfect confidence. His hard cutting and clean driving are, perhaps, his finest strokes, but his wrist-play is very pretty to watch. Though by no means a tall man he is muscularly powerful, and puts plenty of power into his strokes. In the field he can hold his own with anyone, being especially good as third man, and in the long-field the number of runs he saves in a long innings is simply wonderful.

> C. B. Fry pointed out that, however successful MacLaren had

been in Australia, he should not have succeeded Grace as captain of England:

By order of seniority and on the score of at least equal merit, F. S. Jackson ought to have had the reversion of the captaincy, even if Archie MacLaren was brought in to raise the batting strength. It was true that Archie possessed a full knowledge of the Australian personnel owing to his recent experience in Australia, but I do not believe that any of those present at the Selection Committee realized that in bringing him in place of W.G. they were going over the head of F. S. Jackson.

Stanley Jackson . . . though recognized as a batsman of outstanding class, as well as the best all-rounder in English cricket since the prime of W.G., did not play very regularly for Yorkshire and never went to Australia. His success was registered in Test matches in England. It was accidental that up till 1899 Archie MacLaren had figured in the public mind as an established captain, whereas Stanley Jackson, playing under Lord Hawke in the Yorkshire eleven, had not.

MacLaren was not a success as captain. Australia won at Lord's in 1899 and took the series, and in Australia, 1901–02, MacLaren's side was beaten by four Tests to one. In 1902 Australia won by two to one. In 1905, however, F. S. Jackson, a man of many talents, led England to victory over their oldest rivals and enjoyed a wonderful series as an all-rounder.

A. E. Knight said of him:

Mr Jackson's all-round play is altogether delightful. On every kind of wicket MacLaren seems determined to force the game, to dominate the bowler; while Jackson's attitude to bowlers always reminds me of the French nobles about to face the guillotine – a kind of divine challenge to powers which even in their triumph are beneath him.

With the passing of Grace, however, the English supremacy was challenged by the Australians through the all-round cricket of Noble and Armstrong, the fast bowling of Ernest Jones, and the batting of Hill, Darling and Victor Trumper.

Albert Knight played in three Test matches in Australia, 1903–04, when Pelham Warner's side took the series by three to two. He recalled Trumper's innings in the first Test of the series at Sydney when Australia began their second innings 292 runs behind England, for whom R. E. Foster had hit 287 on his Test debut.

In Victor Trumper we have seen the very poetry and heard the deep and wonderful music of batsmanship. Not the structures of a great mentality, nor the argument of logic, but a sweet and simple strain of beauty, the gift of the gods alone. Stylish in the highest sense, orthodox, yet breaking all canons of style, Trumper is just himself. On the occasion of a great Test match at Sydney, the Englishmen had built up a colossal score after a relative Australian failure in the first innings, Mr R. E. Foster playing the record innings of his life and of these great contests. The Star of Australia seemed fast setting, but a couple of tail-end batsmen played out the last hour of the day with a quite heroic barndoor performance of exasperating correctness. The morrow dawned, and faint hopes glimmered in forty thousand minds, when, with the dismissal of one of these monuments of scientific patience, the young Australian champion emerged on to the green.

A slender figure, wan and drawn of face, cadaverous, but spiritualized with the delicacy of ill health, glides to the wicket. Nor ornament nor colour marked his featureless attire, the personality was all-dominating. He took guard quickly, more quickly took a glance round the field, and received his first ball. 'Dreams of summer dawn in night of rain' presented no fresher vision than this boy's play to that black sea which hid the blistered grass of the Sydney hill. Not in his fascinating collection of strokes, nor in their frank and open execution merely, lay the charm; it was man playing away a power which was himself rather than in him. With luxuriant masterfulness, yet with the unlaboured easy naturalness of a falling tear, or rather of showers from the sunny lips of

[69]

summer, he diverted the ball in every conceivable direction which his genius willed. Not violently nor recklessly, like his comrade Duff the revolutionary slashing with his pike, not with the careworn, anxious deliberation of Noble, does he reach the heights, but, insensibly and unconsciously, lifts us with him to where winds blow cool and the outlook is infinite. Can the force of consolidated mass, a record of two hundred centuries, convey the power of high elevation? Perhaps so, at least we glorify the former more. Aglow with instinctive inspiration, this young prophet played with the world's greatest bowlers, played as men play when 'time and hour' bring out the man and persuade us he is as the gods.

With bat whipping like a flail, he drove the fastest swervers of Hirst, and jumped in with fearless precision to the tempting slows of Rhodes, hooked the dropping 'googlies' of Bosanquet, and alternately late cut or pushed to square leg the pace-making deliveries of Arnold. One by one his colleagues fail and pass before an attack of magnificent precision and persistence. 'Our Vic' remains, and when a partner's lazy incompetence rendered his last effort to secure the bowling futile, with his colleague's loss, he left the field still undefeated. He had given to his country at least an outside chance of victory, and the glow of a hope once seemingly impossible. Nothing akin to jugglery or contemptuous languor mars the incomparable grace and simplicity of this perfect batsman. His greatness is of that high kind which appeals to the technical no less than to the more human critic. His simplicity has no faintest touch of *simplesse*, he convinces the onlooker and the bowler that the stroke he executes is precisely what should be done. There is no subtlety, no show of miracle, but the perfect openness and the direct simplicity of a master.

Trumper made 185 out of 294 scored while he was at the wicket, but Australia were beaten by five wickets. The partner guilty of 'lazy incompetence' was Jack Saunders, a very fine left-arm spinner, but a natural number eleven as a batsman.

Trumper played his last Test match against England in February 1912, and he finished his international career with 50, but his side was beaten by an England team which included batsmen like Hobbs, J. W. Hearne and Woolley, and bowlers of the calibre of F. R. Foster, Sydney Barnes and Johnny Douglas.

Victor Trumper died at Sydney on 28 June 1915. He was in his thirty-eighth year. A. E. Stoddart, a great batsman who had led England with distinction in Australia, had committed suicide a month earlier; and W. G. Grace, 'The Champion', died four months after Trumper. Most assuredly, a golden age of cricket had come to an end.

3

A LOVELY LIFE

A. E. Knight

Prince Ranjitsinhji

William Woof to A. W. Pullin

Lord Hawke

H. W. Lee

Jack Hearne jnr

Sir Jack Hobbs

It was professional cricketers who travelled the length and breadth of Great Britain and spread the popularity of cricket. It was a professional combination that undertook the first overseas tour; and it was an all-professional side that took part in the first Test match. But with the coming of W. G. Grace the amateur dominance began, and it became unthinkable for a professional to captain a county side, let alone the England side.

A. E. Knight, himself a professional, reasoned in 1906:

Our captain is an enthusiast who has kindly consented to undertake that most onerous and honourable position. We are glad that he is an amateur, because in the interests of pure sport we think it preferable for the ruling genius of a team to be one apart from the paid player, and one, in a financial sense, independent of the governing committee.

It is simply impossible under the social conditions of present-day cricket for a professional to be fairly considered as a captain.

A decade earlier, Ranjitsinhji had commented upon the increasing number of professional players. Of cricket, he said:

From being a recreation it has become an occupation. A man nowadays cannot play first-class cricket and do much else. And many people regard this as not quite as it should be. They cry out against the present state of things, because men are taken away from trades and useful occupations in order to play cricket for some fifteen years of their lives, and the very best years into the bargain. They point out, also, that though a professional cricketer may lead a very pleasant and harmless life as long as he is young and fit to play, the profession he adopts ceases with his youth, so that he is left stranded at an age when most men are just beginning to be successful, and are ensuring the position of themselves and their families.

Ranjitsinhji refuted all arguments regarding taking up cricket as a profession, and he believed that a cricketer would always find employment after his years of active service.

He can always obtain a berth either as a school coach or as a club bowler, the duties of which he can fulfil adequately until he is practically an old man. And all this time his wages are good enough to enable him to put by a sufficient provision for his old age. As a matter of fact, the demand for players who have been first-class to fill posts at clubs and schools is far in excess of their supply. A first-class cricketer, whose character is good, can rely with certainty upon obtaining on his retirement from county cricket a suitable and well-paid berth, which he will be capable of filling for many years. Frequently, too, their fame and popularity help cricketers to find good businesses upon their retirement, when usually they have a certain amount of money, gained from their benefit match, to invest. Certainly, from a material point of view, a successful cricketer's career is by no means unprofitable. More than that, it is far better than those followed by most men in the class from which the majority of professional cricketers are drawn.

> This is a rosy picture, but it was not always concurrent to the facts as is evidenced by A. W. Pullin's meeting with Ted Pooley, and by the comments made to him by William Woof, the slow left-arm bowler who played for Gloucestershire from 1878 to 1894, and then spasmodically until 1902. He became chief coach at Cheltenham College while still at the height of his powers.

You ask me why I have not had a benefit from the Gloucestershire Club. Frankly, I don't know. I should like to know. I assisted them for eleven years, and a benefit was promised to me by Mr W. G. Grace. It has been stated that I absolutely refused to play with the county team, but that is simply not true. Last year they had me down twice as reserve, but I was not called upon to play. When on the Bristol ground ready to play, a gentleman told me that he was glad I had reconsidered my resolution not to play again for Gloucestershire; but I told him I had never refused to play, and the idea that I had refused at any time to play when asked was entirely wrong. I cannot understand how it originated.

I know that Mr W. G. Grace was greatly offended at my acceptance of the chief berth at Cheltenham College, which prevented me playing with the county team before the vacation. The County Committee once wanted me to sign an agreement to leave my situation here and play regularly with the team. I asked them if they would give me a term of years as an engagement, but Mr Beloe, who was in the chair, stated that they could not do it. I then told the Committee that they could not expect me to leave a certainty for an uncertainty. They therefore left me out of the team, though I was at the top of my form. Perhaps it is only natural that I should consider myself rather badly used in the matter.

> There were tensions between professionals and amateurs over payments. Indeed, before the Oval Test match between England and Australia in 1896, five professionals threatened to strike over match fees, believing that the amateurs were being more generously reimbursed over 'expenses' than they were being paid in wages. Abel, Hayward and Richardson relented, but Lohmann and Gunn did not. Lohmann never played Test cricket again. In 18 matches, he had taken 112 wickets at 10.75 runs each.
>
> One thing that rankled with the professionals was that their Australian counterparts were accorded amateur status although, as A. E. Knight related, they were paid quite handsomely, at least in terms of expenses.

In Test games £25 and travelling expenses are granted. The players as a rule come together from their far-away homes for preliminary practice with each other, and as the match may last for the better part of a week, a South Australian coming up to Sydney would be absent from his home for well-nigh a fortnight. The fee cannot therefore be termed an extravagant one. Transactions such as theirs, not dissimilar, save in their greater duplicity, have marked our own cricket. The late Arthur Shrewsbury has told me that in his early days he has often played in matches for a fee of £10, and an amateur in the same game has received £50. Not until we have a real and vital principle underlying our own amateurism – in lieu of grotesque semblances fostered by an amiable laxity and shuffling expediency – can we fairly rebuke Australian practices.

> No man did more to raise the lot of the professional cricketer than Lord Hawke, who captained Yorkshire from 1883 until 1910. He was, in fact, the first *amateur* captain of the White Rose county, and he set about a reformation which was to make Yorkshire supreme in England. He was determined to rid the county of unruly and intemperate elements, and he took the bold step of dismissing the great Edmund Peate, a slow left-arm bowler who had no equal in England.
>
> Hawke had the greatest admiration for Peate as a bowler and recalled that in his first season as captain of Yorkshire he saw Peate produce the finest achievement of his career.

We were playing Surrey at Leeds, and, thanks to Billy Bates's plucky hitting, just exceeded the century, which we thought equal to a normal three hundred, so dead was the wicket. Our visitors had a good side, but seven of them failed to score, and the wretched total of 31 was due to Peate, whose analysis actually read eight wickets for 5 runs, these all being singles made in different overs. This was the very best bowling feat to which I ever fielded out. Peate was blessed with the most perfect action of any man I have ever seen deliver the ball.

He had no theories. Nobody ever bowled more with his head, but his only principle, with all his variations, was always to bowl with a length – a golden rule he acquired from watching Alfred Shaw. He was a really charming fellow. One of my saddest tasks was to dismiss him from the Yorkshire eleven.

> Four years after his outstanding performance against Surrey, Peate was dismissed by Hawke, for he was a man who enjoyed life a little too well, and unwisely. Nor was he to be the last great player to be sacked by Hawke.
>
> Peate was succeeded in the Yorkshire side by another of cricket's finest left-arm slow bowlers, Bobby Peel. There were

many who considered Peel to be the best of all, but Yorkshire had a happy knack of unearthing cricketers of great quality.

It has often been observed that one of the reasons for the success of Yorkshire is that no sooner has a big cricketer fallen out of the side than another newcomer has been found to take his place who proved equally useful. Certainly nothing in cricket was more fortunate than the way in which Wilfred Rhodes came in to replace Peel in 1898, and no other bowler ever leapt into the forefront of cricket so instantaneously or maintained his command over the ball in the best company for such a protracted period.

> Peel had suffered the same fate as Peate. He arrived on the field the worse for drink, allegedly urinated, and was taken by the arm by Lord Hawke, led off the field and out of the Yorkshire side.
>
> It must not be thought that Hawke was an enemy of the professionals, however; far from it. He fought for the introduction of winter pay, and he introduced a system of bonus payments which was much appreciated by the Yorkshire players, for whom he had the greatest affection. He knew well the plight of the professional when he first became captain of Yorkshire, and, in commenting on the life of Tom Emmett, the professional who had preceded him as captain, he was quick to point out the change of status that he had helped to bring about for the county cricketer.

In 1883 . . . life was not so comfortable then as it is for a modern county professional. Not only was the pay less, but the benefit smaller. Tom Emmett was quite content with receiving £620.

I can remember the day when people were so proud to be seen speaking to a great cricketer that professionals were beset by spectators, asking them to have drinks. But nowadays, if a professional wants a drink – after a day's play – he pays for it himself and resents pressing offers from admiring strangers. Look, too, how neatly and smartly the professionals turn out both off as well as on the ground. They live soberly and thriftily, they are good citizens, good husbands and good fathers, and they are the best company in the world.

> Lord Hawke was writing in 1924, and he was to continue to hold sway over Yorkshire cricket until his death in 1938.
>
> One of the professionals who became a county player in the wake of Lord Hawke's reforms was Harry Lee who batted and bowled for Middlesex from 1911 until 1934. He joined the MCC ground staff at Lord's in 1906, and he recalled the hierarchy that existed within a county side during his early years in the game. The senior professional in the Middlesex side of the time was J. T. Hearne, a great bowler and a considerable character. He was known as 'Tireless'.

His second-in-command was Frank Tarrant, an Australian who spent most of his playing life in England, and therefore missed the highest honours, but he was before the First World War one of the greatest all-rounders in the game. At the time of which I am writing, he was a mature man in his thirties, famous as a cricketer, and the idol of the Lord's crowd.

When we were on tour, the amateurs stayed at one hotel, the little band of professionals at another. J. T. Hearne was in charge of us, and there was a set hour for us to be at meals or in bed. When we came to sit down, the juniors stood back until the seniors had chosen their places. Then J. T. would take his seat at the head of the table, and carve the joint, handing round the plates in proper order of seniority, and giving himself the carver's portion last of all.

One morning I reached the dining-room just before nine o'clock. Tireless was there, looking slightly put out. Every second or two, he took the big gold watch from his waistcoat pocket, examined it anxiously and tucked it away again. Finally, when he was near boiling point, he said to me, 'Where's Frank Tarrant this morning?' I said I had not seen him.

J. T. looked at his watch again, clicked his tongue, and said, 'Go up and tell him it's five to nine. Breakfast's at nine sharp, tell him.'

I went upstairs and found Frank still in bed.

'J. T.'s looking for you,' I said.

Frank shot out of the bed-clothes. 'It's not nine yet, is it?' he asked anxiously.

'No, but it's three minutes to.'

'Good Lord!' said Frank (or words to that effect). 'Tell him I'll be down by nine.'

And down he was, washed, shaved and in parade order, by one minute past nine exactly. I have never known how he did it; but even that feat did not save him from J. T.'s reproachful look and mild rebuke.

It might seem that this atmosphere was trying for the young professional. But it was not. It seemed to weld the team together into a whole. There was no grabbing or backbiting, and we were a happy side. This may have been due to our good fortune in possessing a captain and a senior professional whose personalities and skill could be whole-heartedly respected. Certainly I noticed in later years a change for the worse in the smooth running of the machine, when newcomers, fully conscious of their cricketing brilliance, showed little respect for the older traditions. One well-known professional came on tour with us for the first time, sat down to dinner without waiting for anyone else, grabbed his knife, and reached across to help himself to butter. 'You pig,' said Young Jack Hearne. 'Are you so hungry you can't even wait for the soup?'

It was a small incident, and I don't know why it has stuck, except that it seemed to represent many changes in the approach to cricket, both on and off the field.

> J. W. Hearne had been on the Lord's ground staff when Harry Lee arrived in 1906. He was always known as 'Young' Jack to distinguish him from the veteran J. T. By the outbreak of the First World War, he was regarded by the public much as Denis Compton was to be regarded nearly forty years later. He was a classic bat, and

... He had scored hundreds for Players against Gentlemen and for England against Australia before he was 21, and until the late twenties he was considered by some a better bat than Patsy Hendren. Between, say, 1913 and 1930, Young Jack was almost

[81]

certainly the greatest all-rounder in England. He was shy and reserved, and had to be pushed forward in company. He was neat in dress, as in play.

On the field his concentration was intense, and I believe he could literally read the letters on every ball bowled to him.

Before the First World War, Frank Tarrant and Young Jack put up several huge scores for Middlesex. Against Worcestershire at Lord's Frank scored 200, Jack 104, and each took 5 wickets in the Worcestershire second innings. Against Lancashire, Tarrant had 198, Jack 204. But their best achievement was against Essex. Mr J. W. H. T. Douglas won the toss on that occasion, and, expecting a sticky wicket, put Middlesex in. Middlesex scored 464 for one wicket declared, Tarrant not out 250, Hearne not out 106. Essex were put out for 173 and 235, Hearne taking 14 wickets for 146 runs.

> Jack Hearne played for Middlesex from 1909 until 1936, and between 1911 and 1926 he played 24 times for England. His first Test match was against Australia at Sydney in December 1911. Pelham Warner, the captain of the MCC party, fell ill after the opening match of the tour, and Johnny Douglas led the side in the Tests. Jack Hearne died in 1965, but his son, also Jack, has vivid memories of his father's career.

He was very fond of Johnny Douglas. I think that there was something similar in their characters, and that's why Douglas was such a favourite. I know that when Douglas was drowned at sea my father said, 'I bet he died trying to look after his father. He was that sort of man.'

Dad was really at his best before the First World War and just after. When he was picked to go to Australia, 1911–12, Middlesex didn't want him to go. They didn't think it was going to do him any good. All right, he was a good player, but he was very young. You know, unless you're very careful, you can kill somebody off, and Middlesex thought in an old-fashioned way that that would happen to Dad. I don't think it would have done. Anyway, he went, and he got a hundred in his second Test, and he wasn't twenty-one. And they brought back the Ashes.

Dad had always wanted to be a professional cricketer. They didn't earn a lot of money then, but he didn't do badly when he was on tour. All the cricketer Hearnes were from very humble backgrounds, but they were all good sportsmen, and they knew how to behave themselves as cricketers and as men. They'd have been horrified at some of the things that go on today.

Patsy Hendren was, of course, his great friend. Patsy played soccer for Brentford, and my father and he used to go there training before the cricket season began. My father was a good footballer, but he never earned a living at it. He used to work for my grandfather during the winter because he had been brought up as a wheelwright. At least, he used to work when he was shooting or fishing – he loved that.

His father and his grandfather were wheelwrights, all the family were for many generations past. It didn't mean just making wheels. It meant building the whole of farm carts and vans, making doors, wheelbarrows and ladders. I would have been a wheelwright. I didn't have to learn it because from a very early age I could handle a paint brush, a hammer and a spokeshave.

I don't know what took my father into cricket, but it was part of a family tradition. They were all so good at sport. He was a natural. There are a lot of people who can't understand that, or they refuse to believe it, but it's true – he was just a natural sportsman. My grandfather was a keen sportsman, although he was not outstanding at anything, and he must have encouraged my father and given him every opportunity to play cricket.

My father had a good pedigree. He came from a family that was well established in the game. There was a talent running through the Hearnes. It ended with my brother and me. I often wonder whether it will surface again. There may be a little boy somewhere – there are a lot of us in South Africa and Australia. My grandson has got some talent. He's not afraid of a hard ball, and he's got the eye.

My father had so many friends through cricket. Douglas, as I've said, was one of his great favourites, and there was 'Chubby' Tate. He could sink them. A lot of these friendships came from the drinks they had together at the bar, and from the fact that they played against each other and had respect for each other. I don't think many appreciate that. I think it was a much more friendly game than it is now. In those days you were a professional playing with a rapport and a respect for other chaps, that's not to say there were not a few bad apples in the barrel.

He was never worried about the distinction between amateurs and professionals. His favourite picture was one he had taken with Bob Wyatt, and another was of he and 'Gubby' Allen going out to bat together at Lord's. He had a great respect for those amateurs who deserved it and a great contempt for those who didn't. It didn't worry him in the slightest. If he had been a lesser player, it might have done. He was so far above most of them. He could almost look down on them if you like. I don't think that they pulled rank on him much after he'd become established.

I always remember one story he told me about an amateur, the sort of chap he couldn't stand. I won't tell you his name. He came in to bat, this chap, with a real autocratic manner, but it was well known that he didn't like a short ball on his body because he would very likely just cock it up to backward short-leg. The lad round the corner just where he didn't want a fielder was a raw youngster, and the amateur came in and looked at him contemptuously and said, 'If I offer, I shall offer bloody hard, you know.' Of course, the poor confused boy didn't know what to do. That was the sort of amateur the old man couldn't stand – ones who try to take advantage of a youngster and pull rank – but generally he was very pally with most amateurs.

As I have said, he and Hendren were great friends. They had their differences. You don't spend as much time on tour together as they did without having them, but of all the players, old Patsy was the closest to us. He was 'uncle' Pat. He used to delight in teasing us children, telling his daft stories. He was great fun. He was a joker who never had any children of his own, and I think that that was why he was so good to us.

Probably second only to Patsy Hendren my father's other great pal, on and off the field, was dear 'uncle' Joe Murrell who kept wicket for Middlesex when J. W. was at the height of his bowling career. Joe would forever remind young players in later years of the vicious leg-breaks and unplayable googlies that he had to gather from 'J. W.'. 'Uncle' Joe was a frequent visitor to our home where he would make himself comfortable and, sucking on the pipe protruding from his rather comical face, would always like to know how stamp collections were progressing. *Wisden* gives a brief account of the famous tie between Surrey and Kent at the Oval in 1905 when Joe, fielding for Kent at third man, caught a high, skied ball to dismiss the last Surrey batsman. I have that ball with an attached silver inscription safely locked away with my father's trophies.

Dad got on very well with 'Gubby' Allen. He could see potential in people when they were young, and he saw it in 'Gubby'. If a player fulfilled the promise that he could see was there, that was it as far as Dad was concerned. And I think a lot of them responded. He enjoyed the coaching when he went back to Lord's after the Second World War. That was his reunion with Middlesex. I think it was Walter Robins' idea, and he was a man who didn't allow people to mess about.

My father never said much about Frank Mann. He wasn't very close to him. He had played with Plum Warner so long. Old Plum was his favourite. He was my godfather, and Dad was always keen to keep us up to the mark. 'You're seeing Mr Warner today. So just you remember.' Nigel Haigh was a bit of a character. He was Lord Harris's son-in-law.

People today could not imagine the crowds and the reception that the players used to get in the Middlesex and Surrey matches. Whatever happened, we had to beat Surrey. The old enemy. He took me to see a match after the war, and we sat in the pavilion, up at the top. The old man never used to say a lot, but he saw Jack Robertson stroking the ball all over the place, and when he'd got to about eighty Dad turned to me and said, 'You know, he's got a damned good bat there.'

I wondered what he was talking about. You never knew with him whether he was pulling your leg or being serious. So I didn't say anything. He thought the world of the lads, but he always thought they should have done better than they did. During the lunch-break we went down to the dressing-room, and there was Jack Robertson putting on his pads again. The old man said to him, 'Oh, by the way, Jack, that's a damned good bat you've got there.'

Jack smiled and said, 'Yes, it's the best I've ever had.' I didn't know who was pulling whose leg. Jack Robertson had perfect timing, and the ball was going off the bat so sweetly. I'll tell you another thing. He played shots just like my father. He even walked to the wicket just like the old man.

Of course, Middlesex beat Surrey at the end of the 1920 and 1921 seasons to win the Championship each time. My father thought it was a great feat, first under Warner, then under Mann. He'd played a large part in the successes, but he had so many great moments that he was never one to talk about his own success. I suppose an innings against Yorkshire on a foul wicket when the ball was doing everything was one he was most proud of, and he said, 'I didn't do so badly.' Runs against Yorkshire were always important to him.

He thought much about the young players who followed him and was always sad if they didn't realize their potential. He rated Denis Compton very highly from the outset of his career.

My mother never went with him on tour. That was the way in those days. The only time she ever went with him was when he went to India, to Patiala, on a coaching engagement. It was at the end of the 1914 season. They thought the war was going to be over in six weeks – they always do. He went with Frank Tarrant who had big connections there and had much to do with horse racing.

He was in his element in India. He went tiger shooting, but you couldn't shoot until the Maharaja of Patiala had his shot first. That was a different generation. I was nearly born in India, but Mum couldn't stand the heat. Dad loved it there. There were no pressures, and there was the long sea voyage to get there. He enjoyed his travels, and he became quite a connoisseur of wines and spirits. He sampled plenty of them in all the towns he visited and at the functions he attended.

They played a lot of cricket in those days, usually only a break on Sunday. 'I'm sick of the sight of grass,' he used to say toward the end of the season.

My mother and we boys used to go to Birmingham when Middlesex were playing Warwickshire. We all used to stay with 'Tiger' Smith who was another of those friends Dad made on the 1911–12 tour of Australia. Smith was a fine wicket-keeper, and a great character.

My father's bowling declined somewhat after the First World War. He broke his wrist roller-skating, which was all the rage at the time, and he could never turn it over to bowl his leg-breaks and googlies as he had done before, but he still took a lot of wickets. As I say, roller-skating was a mania at the time, and he never did it again after he broke his wrist.

I don't think he ever really wanted my brother and myself to become cricketers. He had seen so many promising youngsters fall by the wayside, and he thought it was only a good career if you reached the top. There were parts of him most folk never reached. Probably only his immediate relatives really knew him.

The younger generation – Hutton, Compton – sent their sons to public schools. I sometimes wish we had been sent, too. You acquire a certain self-confidence, and you're better able to deal with situations when they arise. We went to a private prep school and could have sat the St Paul's entry exam, but we didn't.

My father remained concerned about Middlesex all his life. He always looked at their score, and he enjoyed the time he was coaching. He got a lot out of it. I suppose when you've played all your life it comes as a terrible break when you stop. He enjoyed the company of the younger players, especially Jim Sims.

One of the things he found it difficult to come to terms with in later life was the fact that there were no longer any amateurs. They had played such an important part in his life. They were the leaders, and we're still looking for them. They don't make them now. It's no longer a game. It's a business.

The professionals of my father's generation did not have the influence that players have today. He couldn't get me a ticket for the 1948 Test against Australia at Lord's, but I was told to be at an entrance near the old main gates by the shop, and I got in there. One of our ancestors, Thomas Arthur Hearne, used to live in a house there when he was groundsman.

Harry Lee was another man for whom my father had a lot of time. He was a very good pro, but he never had much luck. He only had one son, and he lost him in the war; and his brother Jack, who played for Somerset, was killed on D-Day. Harry himself had been wounded in the First World War.

The most troublesome bowlers my father ever reckoned to have faced were Gregory and McDonald on fiery wickets. He wore no helmet nor protection of that kind.

I asked him once how fast Larwood was, and he thought for a moment and said, 'Well, he bowled a short one from the Nursery End that would have knocked my head off, but it brushed the peak of my cap and went one bounce to the boundary.'

Bill Bowes worried him a bit. He was deceptive, quicker than he looked. Dad rated that Yorkshire side of the thirties very highly. He had a great respect for all Yorkshire sides. It might have been due to the fact that he lived in Yorkshire during the First World War. He always rated them.

He was unsettled for some time after his retirement as a player. He joined the police during the war, and then for a while he took over the Bricklayer's Arms public house on the Bath Road, a short distance from the entrance to London Airport. It was later known as The Air Hostess, and it has now been demolished. My parents were never really happy there, and when the opportunity came to go back to Lord's after the war he could not get there fast enough. In some way I feel this sort of rounded off his life-long association with cricket, fulfilled him if you like, for he became a contented man again.

J. W. Hearne's career ran almost parallel to that of Jack Hobbs, considered by the majority to be the greatest opening batsman the cricket world has known. It is reported that George Macaulay, one of Yorkshire's finest medium-pace bowlers, bowled to Hobbs on a treacherous wicket at Sheffield and saw the Surrey man make 76 in 48 minutes. When he was out Macaulay remarked, 'Well, they tell me he's The Master. But I think he's God Almighty.'

Hobbs opened for England from 1908 until 1930, and his Test career ended with what was, at the time, a record, 5,410 runs and 15 centuries. In all first-class cricket he hit 197 centuries, which remains unapproached. This would certainly have been more had he not had to spend two years qualifying for Surrey by residence.

'For Hobbs, cricket even at its most serious, remained a game, to be enjoyed in the spirit of a game. He scored centuries and broke records because he could not help it.'

He was introduced to Surrey by Tom Hayward, and, on the occasion of his eightieth birthday, Hobbs recalled how he first joined Surrey.

I should say cricket was in my blood. I always wanted to be a cricketer as far as I can remember. I suppose I had a lowly upbringing, and I thought at that stage, boyhood, it was a chance of making money, earning a living.

My father was a groundsman at Jesus College, Cambridge, and I used to see a lot of cricket. I went for a couple of seasons to help him, to do odd jobs, and fielding and things in the nets and so on. I can honestly say I was never coached at all. All I can remember is Dad having me out in the nets a couple of times at college, and he bowled to me without pads on. When he bowled a straight one – and he had this spinner – I used to nip back. I could sense the break coming, and, with no pads on, I drew away from the wicket a bit, and I remember him trying to put me right. It was very difficult for me to explain to him why I did that although he was censuring me for it.

Tom Hayward was a fellow Cambridge man, and I used to see him going about the streets, and I revered him, but I never knew him before he came to Surrey. I was a great admirer of him when I was a boy, and I used to think what a great thing it must be to play for Surrey.

In 1903, I suppose he'd been told about me, and he arranged a little practice game on Parker's Piece – Parker's Piece being our playground in Cambridge – I suppose to see what I was like. I remember Gilbert Reese was one of the bowlers, and Tom came and bowled at me. I had my knock, and I think I played pretty well. They seemed to be impressed, and Tom Hayward recommended me to the Oval. I went up there, and Tom looked after me for a bit. He had my interests at heart.

I remember the first good deed he did. He approached the secretary, who was Mr Allcock in those days, and he was instrumental in getting me a ten pounds bonus at the end of the season to help my weekly wage along. Ten pounds was a lot of money to me in those days.

I came down to London, and I think was paid 30s. a week, and I had to find my lodgings and keep myself. I was very satisfied with the way Surrey treated me over the years. They were very good to me. I don't think I had any difficulty – with the bonus Tom got me. I lived quite close to the Oval in good digs, and I joined a youth club at Camberwell. I used to go there every evening.

Looking back, I wish I'd have made better use of it, going to school or something like that. I had absolutely nothing in the winter. I wasn't allowed to go home to Cambridge in the winter. I had to keep my digs on, because I was qualifying. In winter I think we only got a pound a week, and I did nothing else. Occasionally I went to have a net at Camberwell baths.

I played for Cambridge before I met Tom, as an amateur. I was a club player and was invited to play. I think I got thirty – thirty-two in my first knock, and made a good stand for the seventh or eighth wicket; did pretty well. I didn't get many in the other games. That didn't happen until 1904 when I was qualifying for Surrey, and they approached me and asked if I'd like to play for Cambridge. I could as it was the county of my birth, and I did very well, and that helped me get in the Surrey side as soon as I was qualified, I think. I never played for Surrey second eleven.

The first game I played, strangely enough, Tom Hayward was captain because there was no amateur in the side, and he took me

in first with him. He was a very great player, very great indeed. It
surprises me when I look back that his name's not mentioned
more. He was extremely good against fast bowling. His weakness,
as far as I could see, was against leg-break and googly bowlers, but
the googlies would have worried anyone at the end of his career.
They did all the elderly players of the time, but had they
experienced them earlier in their careers, when younger, they would
have mastered them as later players like Washbrook and company
did.

W. G. played against me in the first first-class game I ever
played. He was captain of Gentlemen of England. It was run from
the Crystal Palace. It was a great event for me, of course. I think it
was Easter Monday 1905. We won the toss, and I went in and got
18, and Ernie Hayes and I, I think, were the top scorers. We were
all out very quickly, and then we got the other side out pretty
quickly. We went in before the close of play, and at the close I was
44 not out. Well, 44 not out was a big score for me then. I
remember going along to the Tivoli, the old Tivoli in the Strand,
the Tivoli Music Hall, and standing outside there waiting to get in,
and the papers came along, the evening paper, ha'penny a time,
and I read all about Hobbs' innings. The reports came in very
quickly in those days. I was very pleased with myself. I may sound
conceited, but it wasn't conceit. My lowly upbringing guarded me
from conceit.

I never regretted being a professional cricketer. I was very proud
to be a professional cricketer. There is no hesitation that I would
do it all over again. I could never have been an amateur – it wasn't
in me. As the years went by, I enjoyed it to the full. The distinction
between amateurs and professionals never worried us in those days.
We just accepted it.

It was my ambition when I was young to play for Surrey. The
thought of England never entered my head. To play for Surrey was
more than a great event.

I watched other cricketers play, the university players, and I
suppose I copied them, that was how I learned technique. When I'd
played first-class cricket for a couple of seasons, it's only then that

[91]

you just realize what you've still got to learn. It's only from experience of playing the first-class game that you improve.

My first season I began in a blaze of glory. I told you I was 44 not out, and I ended with 88. That was a good score for a side as famous as Surrey. The first month was fine. Then it went that I couldn't get a run – and then it started to come back again. I got runs. The next season the bad patch lasted a bit longer. I should have got away from the game for a while. You get stale on occasions, and you need to get away from it for a bit.

I never had a really long spell of failure, though. I kept myself fit, and I was always keen. If I got a hundred one day, I never rested on it. I had the next innings on my mind. The nice thing about getting a hundred is that it pleases your friends. I don't know – great times.

> One of the first problems that Hobbs had to face when he entered first-class cricket was the googly, the off-break with the leg-break action, which Bosanquet had developed at the turn of the century and which caused something of a revolution in cricket in the Edwardian period. The South African side of 1907 and 1908 contained four googly bowlers, and Hobbs made the first Test century against them in 1909–10. Hobbs described his experiences of playing against them and other googly bowlers.

I said that I could sense the break when my father bowled to me in the nets at Cambridge, but really I could see him spinning the ball. When we came across these South African googly bowlers it was very difficult in the early stages, out on that matting in South Africa. I didn't really know what the googly was. Occasionally I could find there was something wrong with them, but for the most, in the early stages, I played the ball on its merits. I smothered it, covered the break. In the very early stages, I couldn't tell which way it was turning, that very early tour. I did afterwards. I was looking for it. It was very easy.

It's really very easy to spot the googly with nine bowlers out of ten. You get the odd one who mystifies you a bit – strangely

[92]

enough I think it was Walter Robins. Other people found him easy.
Just as I remember Tom Hayward had great difficulty in spotting
the first googly bowler we had to contend with in first-class
cricket, that was Mr Carr of Kent. He was the easiest thing in the
world to me. As a matter of fact that particular bowler showed you
the ball as he was coming up to bowl, so it was easy. Even then
some people had difficulty in playing the googly.

Mr Schwartz was playing for South Africa in 1907. We knew he
couldn't bowl the leg-break so that they'd all be googlies, but even
then we had difficulties really in playing them as off-breaks.

> Hobbs believed that he was a better batsman before the First
> World War than he was in the nineteen-twenties although it
> was in the second half of his career that he established his
> major records and accomplished the feats for which he is best re-
> membered.

In those early days, I didn't know so much about defence and
things, but I had more strokes and I wasn't afraid to produce them
when the occasion arose. I could hit all round the wicket, had all
the strokes. I hadn't the same fear of getting out. I had the joy of
life, whatever it was. It pleased me, and it suited my vanity, I
suppose. I hadn't the figures to play to.

After the war, when they started talking about W. G., and I
started really making a name for myself, it was figures that counted
all the time. Unless I'd got so many runs, I'd failed. I was cautious.
I didn't get myself out so much. In those younger days I got myself
out a lot playing shots I ought not to have done. I suppose I was at
an experimental stage, and I was taking a risk.

There were always certain days you felt top of the world; other days
the same ball could prove difficult. I can't say that I didn't really feel I
had a weakness. That's not to say there weren't players better than
me. There were so many good players throughout the world. It seems
to me that you're not a really famous player until you retire from the
game. I had pleasure in getting a hundred in a Test match, and I
suppose I was the first cricketer to get the publicity treatment when
the press and film men followed me to see if I'd get W. G.'s record.

The season in question was 1925 when Hobbs was the first batsman to reach two thousand runs in first-class cricket, a feat he accomplished on 20 July. As century followed century there came the realization that W. G. Grace's record number of centuries in first-class cricket, 126, was about to be equalled. It must be remembered that Grace had set a standard which lingered in the minds of many as being invincible.

I believe I got twelve 100s pretty quickly in that 1925 season. I'd come back from Australia, and I'd done pretty well out there, and I was at the top of my form. I must have been because I kept getting 100s, and I hit my twelfth of the season when we played Kent at Blackheath.

We came to Brighton to play Sussex, and, of course, all the press men came down and expected me to get 100. I failed, and dear old Maurice Tate had me l.b.w. to one that nipped back very quickly off the pitch. And that started it, and after that I went on and on. Tom Webster would draw a cartoon in the *Daily Mail* every day, and it got rather humorous. Then it got beyond that stage and got rather worrying. Even Tom got a bit annoyed, going round and finding I didn't make this hundred. I got 70s and 80s. At that time, placards came out several times every afternoon, and they would say 'Hobbs Fails Again' even if I got 60 or 70.

At Brighton, the press wanted me to do all sorts of things for publicity. One chap wanted me to go for an early-morning bathe. I didn't have to swim, just put a swimming costume on and have my picture taken, and I had all sorts of offers. I was even offered quite a good fee to appear at the Coliseum. But that wasn't for me. I don't know what they expected me to do, and fortunately I turned it down.

They were all waiting for the 100 that would equal W. G.'s record, and we went down to Taunton in the middle of August, and I got a little bit edgy when I was 91 not out on the Saturday night. I got the runs on the Monday, and I was very relieved and very happy. In the second innings, when I made the next 100 which broke W. G.'s record there was hardly anybody there – no press men.

They were great days. P. G. H., Mr Fender, came running out with a glass to give me. It wasn't champagne. I think it would have been the wrong time to have champagne. It was ginger ale. It didn't get me out. I got myself out.

The last time I had met W. G. was in 1915 when I was playing in a charity match at Catford, and he went out of his way to speak to me, and I was very flattered.

> One of the most remarkable things about Hobbs' career was that he continued to prosper as a batsman until his last season, 1934, when he hit the last of his 197 centuries. It was against Lancashire, the County Champions, at Old Trafford in George Duckworth's Benefit Match, and it was the only hundred hit against the Champions during the season.

I got big scores after I was forty because I was solid, and perhaps there weren't the great bowlers about that there'd been in my younger days.

I think I'm right in saying that you should always play back if you can because you can watch the ball right onto the bat. When you play forward there must be a split second when you lose sight of the ball. If I was in trouble I had a tendency to play back. But batsmen on the whole had a more difficult job in those days.

As I got older it became more difficult to hit the ball on the off, and I developed my on-side play. I found it easier to get behind the ball.

I came relatively late into the first-class game and had to qualify. I kept myself fit most of the time. I never really liked drink, just a glass of wine with my dinner, and I used to play badminton in the winter.

But the 100 against Lancashire was a great struggle. I suppose I was a little bit beyond it. I needed more net practice, but I had a lot on my plate at the time. I was very pleased for George Duckworth who'd asked me to go up there, and I think George was pleased, too. It was a struggle. Lancashire were a good side in those days. I felt fit. I certainly didn't feel fifty-one, but I matured late in the game.

In the course of his career, Hobbs' name was associated with four other batsmen with whom he formed opening partnerships which were among the most illustrious that the game has seen. For Surrey, his name was linked first with Hayward and then with Sandham; for England, he joined first with Wilfred Rhodes and then with Herbert Sutcliffe, both Yorkshiremen.

I had a very happy association with Wilfred. It was the beginning, and we gained the reputation for being great short runners. He ran many short runs for me. He was always backing up and came when I called. Old Tom would never have had Wilfred as a first wicket batsman. It all depends how you describe a great batsman whether it's the runs he gets or the way he gets them.

Archie McLaren wouldn't consider a batsman unless he was one who scored brilliantly, was a stylist. He would prefer him against one who scored more runs.

Herbert was a great runner and a great player. He seldom said no. We had some happy times together. Right from the start we settled down.

Sandy I grew up with. I had some great times with him, too.

Tom Hayward was not a quick runner. When he got out and Ernie Hayes came in I enjoyed the short runs. I used to love it. As I have just said, Bert was a great runner — Sutcliffe, our names were always linked together — but there was never anyone better than Wilfred Rhodes. We started in South Africa and continued in Australia. You could put Wilfred and Herbert on a par. Andy Sandham wasn't so quick.

There was one occasion when Herbert would never forgive me. It was at Melbourne in 1925. We'd batted all day on the Saturday. We had the Sunday rest and came in on the Monday and we'd got 283. And Herbert was desperately keen, and, of course, I was, too, that we'd beat the record which Wilfred and myself held of 323. I think it was the second ball Arthur Mailey bowled to me was a full toss, and I tried to play it just wide of mid-on quite safely, but I made a yorker of it, and I was bowled.

I think the best games I played were both with Herbert. One

was the famous one at the Oval in 1926, and the other was at Melbourne when we had to wait, and it was another sticky wicket. Hugh Trumble, one of the very greatest of bowlers, thought we would get no more than 70, but we struggled on, and I got 100 before I got out.

It was in Melbourne, and I can remember it as if it were yesterday, that drinks were always supplied in the dressing-room, and we could help ourselves ad lib, but for some reason, we'd been drinking too much or they were cutting down on expenses, they cut this out so drinks were only out for an hour or two. Dear old Percy Chapman, I know he'll forgive me, at lunch time, just before the drinks stopped, he'd put a little gin in a ginger beer bottle and hide it some place in the dressing-room. He was saving it for tea time. I watched him do this once or twice, and I changed his gin for water while he wasn't looking. And we came in from fielding two hours in the hot sunshine, and Percy rushed to his bottle. He took a sip, and said 'That b———, Jack Hobbs.' He got it right straight away. Dear old Percy.

He was captain at the Oval in 1926, of course, when we won back the Ashes. Herbert and I got 100s in the second innings. It was a difficult wicket, and there were fielders clustered round close to the bat on the leg side, and you had to play the ball on its merits. I think that that was one of the best games I ever played in.

> Hobbs played against some of the greatest bowlers the game
> has known, and he gave an assessment of their speed and
> quality.

Byrne, who played for Warwickshire, was very fast, and I once tried to hook him. The ball hit the edge of my bat, hit me a tremendous whack on the front of my cap and went up in the air, and I was caught. Larwood, Gregory, McDonald, Neville Knox were all very fast, but 'Tibby' Cotter of Australia was very fast indeed. He was a bundle of energy, but really it all depends on how the batsman and the bowler feel on the day.

Johnny Douglas was a great fast-medium bowler. He was a

wonderful bowler. He gave me as much trouble as anybody, for he could make the ball swing both ways. I remember on one occasion I was set to cut a ball, and it moved in the air and bowled me; and another occasion I was set to drive a ball that seemed well up to me, and it was an away swinger and I was caught in the slips.

Maurice Tate was a great player. He bowled so well in Australia, beating Herbie Collins and Ponsford time after time. He was almost too good for them. I'd always have him on my side.

Syd Barnes, S. F., I've always put right at the top. He was the best bowler ever. I don't think even now there was anybody better, although I admit there were others almost his equal, like Bill O'Reilly. Syd hated batsmen. He had the leg-break, the off-break, and he was fast, tall and made the ball get up to unpleasant heights. He was lethal on matting in South Africa, and in Australia, 1911–12, he was marvellous.

'Charlie' Blythe was one of the loveliest slow left-arm bowlers I ever saw. He was prepared to bowl on a hard wicket as well as on one that helped him. One day, he took something like 8 for 40, and his captain came to him and said, 'Well bowled indeed, Charlie.' But Charlie said, 'I don't want you to say well bowled when I've taken 8 for 40. I want you to say well bowled when I've bowled all day and got 1 for 90.' That was his attitude. You got him on a sticky wicket, and he really gave you problems.

Then there was Wilfred Rhodes and Charlie Parker, but Blythe was a little bit quicker and a vicious spinner. Perhaps Wilf was a little past his best when I faced him so it must be 'Charlie', or Colin, to give him his real name.

I bowled a bit for Cambridge and in club cricket, but not very much after that, although I did once open the bowling for Surrey against Warwickshire when one of our players hadn't turned up for some reason. I opened the bowling with Bill Hitch and got five wickets. I bowled away-swingers and an occasional off-break.

Hobbs played many great innings, but his selection of the finest innings he ever played was something of a surprise.

Strangely enough, the best innings I ever played was on a sticky wicket, and it was for Archie McLaren's XI, but it wasn't a first-class match. I think the best first-class innings I ever played was for Lionel Robinson's XI against the Australians at Attleborough in Norfolk in 1921. I made 80-odd. I played really well, as good an innings as I ever played, against Gregory and McDonald. I had made 80-odd when I strained a muscle in my thigh, and that put me out for a few weeks. Then I came back and got 172 not out against Yorkshire. That was to be my last game. I was picked for the third Test, fielded and went down with appendicitis. I have often wondered if I would have made 200 centuries if I had not missed that 1921 season.

I used to like to play the wristy square-cut and the off-drive through the covers. A six always pleases you – however you hit it.

People want to see players get on with it, play their strokes. That's why Denis Compton was always worth watching since the war, and Ted Dexter and Jim Parks. What a lovely player Peter May is. You can go back as far as you like, and he'd hold his own in any company. Colin Cowdrey is another.

It's been a lovely life. I've enjoyed it to the full, and it's made me many, many hundreds of friends all over the world. I've thoroughly enjoyed it.

4

THEY WERE ALL
GOOD CRICKETERS
IN THEM DAYS

M. J. C. Allom

H. G. Owen-Smith

T. B. Mitchell

Jack Hobbs's Test career stretched from 1907–8 to 1930. He played sixty-one times for England, and forty-one of those Test matches were against Australia. He appeared eighteen times against South Africa and twice against West Indies in 1928. This was in the first series in which West Indies had been accorded Test status. In January 1930 New Zealand became the fourth nation to enter the Test arena. India followed in 1932.

In the winter of 1929–30 MCC sent parties to both New Zealand and West Indies so that Test matches were being played concurrently by England in different parts of the world.

The England side in New Zealand was led by Harold Gilligan who made his Test debut in the first game at Lancaster Park, Christchurch. Others who made their debuts in that Test were 'Tich' Cornford, the fine Sussex wicket-keeper; Stan Worthington, the Derbyshire all-rounder; Morris Nichols, another all-rounder from Essex; Maurice Turnbull, later to be captain of Glamorgan and a Test selector; and Maurice Allom, a pace bowler from Surrey, who recalls the start of his career and that first Test match in Christchurch.

I never had any idea of playing cricket seriously until, I suppose, my second year at Cambridge when I had a good seniors' trial, and I played twice for the university – that was in 1926 – I think mainly because a lot of the regular side were taking exams. I remember I had a successful match against the Army and then went on with the Cambridge side up to Old Trafford. It rained, of course, and we played one afternoon, that's all, but then the next year was when I got my blue – that was 1927. I suppose my father was rather proud, and he was kind enough to let me go up a fourth year as a Bachelor of Arts to play cricket, and then I had some success.

I first played for Surrey in 1927 after the University match, and then again in 1928. Then, in 1929, I played virtually a full season, really playing whenever I wanted to. Then I got picked for the MCC team to New Zealand, and I think that my father thought, 'Well, damn it all, we'd better let this young man do a bit of this if he wants to do it.' So I went on playing until 1933, that was the last time I played any number of matches for Surrey.

I went with the 1930–31 side to South Africa and played in one Test, but I played in all four Tests in New Zealand, 1929–30. I did fairly well in New Zealand. I took four wickets in five balls, including the hat-trick in the first Test, which is still a record. It was a good side.

I got Stuart Dempster, as I remember, on the second ball of the over. It was then Tom Lowry, Ken James and a fellow called Badcock. That was the only time I ever took a hat-trick in the whole of my cricketing life. The interesting thing was that I'd bowled, I think, as well as I'd ever bowled for an hour without any result at all, and afterwards, Harold Gilligan, who was skippering the side, told me, 'You know, I'd decided to give you one more over, and if you didn't get anybody out I thought, well, the thing to do is to give him a rest and to bring him on the other end.' And that was the one.

I was very lucky to be allowed to play by my dear old papa, but I was lucky also in having some success when I did, and therefore one really crowded an awful lot of cricket into six years.

Jack Hobbs was at the end of his career when I came into the Surrey side, but I think you've got to put Jack Hobbs on a pinnacle by himself. He wasn't the run machine that Don Bradman was, but he was an artist of the greatest magnitude. Of course, I only played with him in the autumn of his career. He was getting on when I first played for Surrey in 1927, and he gave up in 1934, just after I did, and he was fifty-two then.

I always remember a typical example of his artistry in the match Surrey against South Africa – I can't remember which year that would have been – but Dennis Morkel was their quick-bowler. I can remember Dennis Morkel bowling Jack a ball about six inches outside the off-stump, and Jack going across and hitting it for four past the square-leg umpire with an absolutely straight bat. He just turned. Morkel then bowled the next ball about nine or ten inches outside the off-stump, and Jack played exactly the same stroke. Then Dennis Morkel bowled the ball even further outside the off-stump, and Jack stood still, and it was a wide. Jack stood there and roared with laughter. He had an intense sense of humour. He was a great artist. I think he was one of the nicest men I ever met on a cricket field.

I'll tell you an interesting thing about the amateurs and professionals. When I came into that side as a youngster there was Jack Hobbs calling me 'sir' or 'Mr Allom', and then, in after years, we served on the Surrey Committee together by which time he was Sir Jack Hobbs, but it wasn't really until he had served on the Committee for a number of years that I could get him to call me by my Christian name. It was so inbred into people like that, and I think that Andy Sandham until his dying day never called me anything but 'Mr Allom', which a modern cricketer wouldn't understand.

If I had been playing today, I don't think I would like to have played all the time, like a professional. It is such a different game now. It puts tremendous pressures on cricketers, especially from the media. In my day, on the South African tour, there were only two reporters, one for Reuters, the other for Exchange Telegraph. They were two terribly nice South African chaps who became great pals of ours, and they would never have disclosed any confidences, would never have thought of it. They took part in a lot of our fun and games together, but when it came to cricket they only reported the match and were told anything the skipper wanted to tell them, and that was the end of it.

Maurice Allom played in an age which was rich with famous names and players who have become legends in the history of the game.

I played against some of the great players of the time. I can't think there has been anything more difficult than bowling against Ponsford, Woodfull, Bradman, McCabe and Kippax. They were tremendous players. I always think that Bill Ponsford was really as difficult to bowl to as anybody. He made an enormous number of runs. He didn't have quite the same dramatic results as Bradman, but very nearly. The runs he made in Australia were fabulous, and he scored runs in England. He was a wonderful player.

South Africa had one or two very good players – Herbie Taylor, Cameron, Nourse – the younger Nourse. I'm not certain we didn't play against the father, too.

Perhaps one likes to think it, but we had many more good players in this country. When I went to New Zealand another side went to West Indies to play some Tests, and they were both good sides.

Wally Hammond was our best bat at that time, I think. He was a majestic player. Gracious me! Wally was absolutely unbelievable on the off-side. He wasn't a hooker. He never really hooked the ball very often, but his off-side play was marvellous. He had such strength off the back foot, you know. He could hit the ball through the covers off his back foot like a rocket. He was a great player, Wally, and, of course, quite a character. He was a playboy to start with, but he was, I would have to say, at that period in the early thirties, head and shoulders above the other England players.

Herbert Sutcliffe was rather an extraordinary type of player. I don't know what it was about Herbert, but, in fact, I say it myself because he wrote it in his book, he was my rabbit. He was the first pro I ever got out, playing for Yorkshire against Cambridge, and you know, I got Herbert out so many times that I think he must have had a fixation. It's funny, but he was a good chap to have as a rabbit.

His method was rather unusual. He was much more of a glider of the ball. You very seldom saw Herbert drive the ball through the covers. He was much more of a placer on the leg side. Of course, his record was tremendous.

I played against Jack Hearne, 'Young Jack', as they called him. He was still playing for Middlesex, and Hendren went on until after I gave up because he was quite a bit younger than Jack

Hearne. He was a lovely character, Patsy Hendren, always behaving like a sort of clown.

> Maurice Allom played under and against some of the most successful, and controversial, captains the game has known – Percy Fender of Surrey, Brian Sellers of Yorkshire, and Douglas Jardine, who led England on the much documented 'body-line' tour of Australia, 1932–33. In Harold Larwood, Jardine had at his disposal the best fast bowler in the world at this time, and he evolved a form of leg-theory attack which temporarily blunted Bradman's prolific run-scoring and put the Australians to flight. It was a form of attack that caused bitterness and debate, and which, sixty years on, still raises the heat of conversations.

When I came into the Surrey side Fender was skipper, and I think he taught me more about first-class cricket in a short space of time than I would have learned from anybody else. He was a great student of the game. Tremendous captain. He was always thinking. You could see him standing in the slips, his old brain-box going round. He never let things get bogged down. He knew the weaknesses of most batsmen in England.

Then Jardine took over. The true story of that was not told in Fender's biography. Richard Streeton talked about this time when the Surrey Committee got rid of Fender. He said that they had a row of some sort, and they appointed Jardine as captain. What he didn't say, because he would have had no reason to know this, was that they wanted a change in captaincy. I don't know why they did, but they did. I suppose it's like all these things when people have been there long enough you want to change them. They asked me to captain the side, and this would have been in 1931, I suppose, and I said certainly.

I can remember 'Shrimp' Leveson Gower calling me into the Committee Room and saying, 'Look here, Maurice, I think they want Douglas Jardine to come back and captain the side to Australia in thirty-two, and he's agreed to play through this season and lead up until then. Would you mind if he captained

[107]

the side for a season or two, and then perhaps you'll take it on afterwards?'

Well, of course, I agreed. In the event, I had to give up cricket so I never did captain the side, but it wasn't just a straight swap with Jardine for Fender. They wanted me to do it.

Jardine was a good county captain, but I led the side an awful lot because he was playing in the Test matches and the representative matches that summer, the summer of '32. He played little for Surrey really, and they had, in fact, appointed me officially vice-captain so I led the side a lot that year.

I think he was a rather unrelenting, dour character. I got to know him quite well. He was what I would call a typical Wykehamist – there is a certain something, I think, about Wykehamists. He was an intellectual, you see. I used to spend a lot of time with him when we were playing at the Oval. We used to take a taxi to Westminster and get out and walk across Green Park to his club, and we used to talk about all kinds of things. I got to know him very well. He was a very likeable person, although he was rather cynical.

I can understand him being unpopular in Australia because he gave the impression of being rather stuck up, and they didn't like that sort of thing. Of course, the body-line, compared with what we've seen in recent years, was not as dangerous. The thing about it, which the laws of the game prevent now, was that in those days you could have as many short-legs as you wanted, in front of the umpire or behind him, so that there was this ring of short-legs and two men on the boundary so there was really no shot to play. It was the astonishing accuracy of Harold Larwood which made it possible.

I can remember Fender, who reported that tour for one of the newspapers, telling me he'd seen the whole series and, as far as he could remember, it wasn't until the second innings of the fourth Test match that Larwood bowled a ball on the off-side when he had a leg-side field, which was an extraordinary bit of accuracy.

I think the objection to it was that it spoilt the game of cricket.

It wasn't all that dangerous compared with what we've seen in recent years because he didn't bowl at people's heads. He bowled at chest height so that either they had to hook the ball or play it down with those sharks hanging around there.

It was interesting that 'Gubby' Allen refused to bowl the leg-theory. 'Gubby' would have told you that quite definitely he considered it to be detrimental to the game of cricket, which I suppose it was.

Harold Larwood was tremendously fast. I remember playing in the Folkestone Festival just before he went to Australia. It had been a very hard August, and the Folkestone ground was just like a bit of iron. The England team had to go from Folkestone to the Scarborough Festival overnight, a hell of a long way, and they could catch an earlier train to get up there if they could get the game over by four o'clock in the afternoon. I can remember Harold Larwood really slipping himself. I went in towards the end of the innings, and one had to guess where the ball was going. I have never seen faster bowling in my life. The slips were standing somewhere near the railings. It was extraordinary. He got seven wickets, I think.

He really was, for a small man, astonishingly quick. Lovely action. I always said one of the most exciting things was the start of a Test match with Harold Larwood bowling the first ball. It was such a marvellous sight.

> At Cambridge, Maurice Allom had played with Maurice Turn-bull, and the pair were to become close friends, collaborating on *The Book of the Two Maurices* and *The Two Maurices Again*.

I wrote two books with Maurice Turnbull. We went together on the New Zealand and South African tours, and ultimately he was my best man when I got married. He was such a nice chap, a good cricketer and a very intelligent man who did an enormous amount for Glamorgan cricket. He really put it on the map. He was a Test selector, and then he was killed in Normandy. He was a lovely man.

He was a Roman Catholic, and I remember going out to South

[109]

Africa and when we were about two days out on the boat he got a telegram to say his father had died, and he wanted to get off at Madeira and come home. We all talked to him and said, 'Now, look, what can you do?' And he agreed to stay.

He had quite a successful tour. He didn't have a very good tour in New Zealand, funnily enough.

We did everything together on those two tours, and we wrote the two books. The first one, about New Zealand, happened purely because just before we left a New Zealander said, 'You ought to write a book about the tour '

This gave us the idea, and as we were coming home through the Panama Canal we were going to be on the sea for five weeks, and we had a go at writing the book because it helped to pass the time enormously.

The second book came when we finished the South African tour. A very great friend of ours called Bonham Carter was Flag Captain in Simonstown. We'd first met him when we were playing cricket against the Navy in Portsmouth. He'd gone out to South Africa in a light cruiser, the *Calcutta*, and taken a lot of good cricketers with him, including people like 'Monkey' Sellar who was not only a jolly good cricketer but a fine rugby player. Shortly before the end of the tour Bonham Carter said to us, 'Look, you two, I'm paying off a week after the tour's finished and the side's gone home. Would you like to come back as my guests in the *Calcutta*?'

And so we spent five weeks with the Navy at sea, which was a wonderful experience, and it gave us a great opportunity to write the second book.

Maurice might easily have captained England. He was a pretty good cricketer, and a good enough player to captain an England side and make a useful contribution to it. He got quite a lot of runs in South Africa.

First-class cricket in England in the late nineteen-twenties and in the nineteen-thirties was dominated first by Lancashire and then, until the outbreak of the Second World War, by

[110]

Yorkshire. The two northern counties took the Championship sixteen times in eighteen seasons between 1922 and 1939.

The outstanding county side of that time was, of course, Yorkshire. I first ran into them at Cambridge, for they were always down at Fenner's for one of the early matches. They were tremendous. I suppose the Yorkshire side of that period was as strong as there's ever been – look at the number of times they won the Championship.

Lancashire, too, were a very good side. I met them at the end of the McDonald era. Peter Eckersley to whose widow I am now married led a good side very successfully. He was an MP, had his own aeroplane and went into the Fleet Air Arm at the time of Munich. Then he was killed in an unnecessary accident at Eastleigh Airfield in 1940.

Another one who had his own aeroplane was Geoffrey Legge. He went on the New Zealand tour with us, played for Kent and was a very good cricketer. He was killed down in Cornwall somewhere about the same time as Peter Eckersley, but I suppose Hedley Verity is the one whom people think of most. He was a very, very good left-arm bowler, but when I started Wilfred Rhodes was still playing. He was a remarkable chap. He went on for ever and ever.

He went out to West Indies at the same time that I went out to New Zealand. In one of the Tests, West Indies had a chance of winning, but there was a slightly worn patch just outside the off-stump on a good length, and old Wilfred bowled into this bit of rough all day at the age of fifty-two. It was a remarkable performance, and it saved the match. He must have been one of the greatest of bowlers, and he was also a very good batsman.

I suppose if Hedley Verity hadn't been killed, he would have done a lot after the war. The war interfered with a lot of very good cricketers at the prime of life – Wally Hammond, Hutton and Compton, who'd just started – were all deprived of those years. What Denis Compton might have done during that period! He was

[111]

a tremendous cricketer and loved the game. He is one of the most unspoilt men that one could meet. He always greets you as though you're an old friend.

There were an awful lot of good players in the thirties. When you think of how little Andy Sandham played for England, and 'Dodge' Whysall who went in first for Notts was a frightfully good player. People like that played once or twice for England, but that's all. I think it's always been the way. It's very difficult to get into the England side, but once you're established it's very difficult to get out of it. I think the arch-example was Maurice Tate. They went on playing Maurice long after he'd really been a striking bowler. It does happen. There are very many other cases, I'm sure. Today one thinks they should be bringing in some of the young blood instead of sticking to the old ones. We're rather bad at it in this country.

You don't really know if a person is a Test player until you play him in a Test match. It's an extraordinary thing. There is this subtle difference all the way up the scale. There is the difference between school cricket and club cricket; and then between club cricket and second-eleven county cricket; and the difference between county second-eleven and county first-eleven. It all goes up the scale. It's just a slight margin which makes all the difference.

There are many who score prolifically in second-eleven cricket who never make it in the first team. In my time there were the Pratt brothers who played for Surrey Second-Eleven for years and never got a cap. They were at the Oval the whole of their careers, made lots of runs and took a lot of wickets for the Second-Eleven, but hardly ever got a chance in the First-Eleven. In those days, it was jolly difficult to get into the Surrey side as a batsman.

In 1980, I had a letter from the President of the New Zealand Cricket Council reminding me that they hadn't forgotten that on 22 January fifty years ago, I had done the hat-trick at Christchurch. He said he thought that there were only four players who had played against me who were still alive. When I wrote back to thank him for his letter I had to say that I was sorry to tell him that I was the only living member of that MCC side. The last surviving one before me was Frank Woolley.

'Tich' Cornford was the wicket-keeper on that tour. He was a tremendous keeper. Maurice Tate said he couldn't bowl unless 'Tich' stood up to him, and Maurice came off the pitch pretty fast. 'Tich' stood up to me, I remember, in New Zealand, and he was standing up when he caught Ken James, who was the middle one of my hat-trick. An amateur, Ted Benson, was our second wicket-keeper on that tour.

Cornford never got a look in after that series. He was one of those unlucky ones who coincided with Leslie Ames and George Duckworth. George came on tour to South Africa with us as did the other Lancashire wicket-keeper Farrimond. Les Ames would have qualified to play for England as a batsman at any time, and he'd had tremendous practice against 'Tich' Freeman. As far as taking slow bowling was concerned, he was a great keeper. I am not so sure if he was as agile a keeper as you would see today, for he was always heavily built, but he was a fine batsman. It's funny that Kent have produced so many good wicket-keepers.

I played against 'Tich' Freeman. I can remember driving Freddie Brown down to Blackheath to play against Kent for Surrey, and Freddie said, 'I've never seen this chap bowl.' I said, 'Well, perhaps if we win the toss, you'll get a chance today.' And that was the day that Freddie played that astonishing innings − 168 in two hours ten minutes. I've never seen a bowler hit so far as he hit 'Tich' Freeman. It's a small ground, Blackheath, at least it was then − I don't think they use it now − but 'Tich' didn't know where to bowl to him.

Freddie was a very great cricketer at that time although he couldn't play much before the war. For a big man he was very agile, and a great fielder. The best of his career really came late when he captained England after the war.

There were some fine captains in my day. Freddie Calthorpe was captain of Warwickshire before Bob Wyatt who was a fine player and a great student of the game. He thought an immense amount about how to play, what technique to use, that was his great quality. He was never very lucky as England's captain, but he had a splendid record; not a bad bowler, rather like Graham Gooch.

And, of course, there was Brian Sellers. He was a lovely chap, an enormous character, a broad Yorkshireman. He didn't spare himself in any way. He told you what he thought of anything, and he always had a fund of stories, most of them very rude. He really was a tremendous influence on that Yorkshire side. He kept them in control after they'd had a rather free hand with old Major Lupton who was captain when I first played against them. I think old Wilfred did most of the captaincy then.

Bill Bowes was beginning to play when I first played, and there was George Macaulay. He was a fiery character. I suppose they were a better batting side than bowling side.

There were two or three good sides around as well as Yorkshire. Nottinghamshire under Arthur Carr had some good players – Larwood and Voce were just coming on the scene – and there was Fred Barratt and the Staples brothers, and George Gunn. There were always a few incidents between Percy Fender and Arthur Carr. They were rather aggressive characters.

I played against old Johnny Douglas, and there was the famous match between Surrey and Essex when the coach Surrey were coming by broke down, and, at 11.30, there were only three Surrey players on the ground, Fender, Jeacocke and 'Struddy'. Fender and Johnny Douglas had been having words about something or other. Johnny Douglas won the toss and said, 'I'm going to start play. My batsmen are going in.' And Fender led out Jeacocke and 'Struddy', and he bowled one end, and Jeacocke bowled the other for the first three or four overs. Of course, Percy Fender was not going to give in to Johnny Douglas. They were liable to have an explosion.

Fender was quite a volatile character, but pretty astute. Peter Eckersley used to say, 'When you're tossing with Percy Fender you've got to have your running shoes on.' Percy Fender was a very keen player, but he never took advantage. He was not everybody's cup of tea, but I shall always be grateful that I served him.

Maurice Allom continued to serve cricket long after he had ceased to play the game, and he found himself President of MCC, a great honour, at a particularly difficult time, 1969.

I've rather severed my connection with first-class cricket now, but I was President at the Oval for eight years. It's rather different now. They have a new president every year, and I think he feels he must be closely involved during his year in office, but I wouldn't have been able to spend the time for eight years that the president does these days.

I was also President of MCC, and the Lord's one has always been a demanding job. It was particularly so in my year because I got involved in the South Africa affair. The Club pays for the entertaining and that side of it, but it is expensive in time, and I was still working in those days. It meant that during the year I was hardly ever in the office.

We had a special sub-committee appointed for this South Africa problem, which was in permanent session, and Billy Griffith used to ring me up and say, 'Look, we've got to have a meeting. Can you be here in a quarter of an hour?' It was like that. It rather spoilt my year. There wasn't a touring side, which is the nicest part of the job when you're entertaining. We had the World side that played 'Test' matches, but it wasn't the same thing, and nobody turned up to see them. It was a pity, but it was an interesting year all the same.

The events to which Maurice Allom refers were those which led to the cancellation of the South African tour of England in 1970 at the request of the British Government. Allom took office as President of MCC on 1 October 1969, so that he had the unpleasant task of being in charge at a time when there was constant political pressure for the invitation to the South Africans to be withdrawn. It followed in the wake of the South African Government's refusal to accept Basil D'Oliveira as a member of the England side to tour South Africa in 1968–69, resulting in the cancellation of the tour. South Africa's match against Australia at Port Elizabeth in March 1970 was to be

[115]

their last Test for twenty-two years. They were excluded from international cricket until 1992 when they were readmitted and met West Indies for the first time.

Such problems were far in the future when Maurice Allom played against the South Africans at Durban in 1931, in the third Test of a series which South Africa won by one game to nil. South Africa had been in England in 1929 and had lost two of the five Test matches which were played, but this was a young side, and, in 1935, under H. F. Wade, they won a rubber in England for the first time.

An outstanding member of the 1929 side was H. G. Owen-Smith, an all-rounder, who was barely twenty years old. He played in all five Tests and hit 129 at Headingley. This was to be his only series, for he went up to Oxford, won his blue in all three years and played for Middlesex, when available, from 1935 to 1937. He also won blues for boxing and rugby, a sport at which he captained England.

Owen-Smith returned to South Africa after the Second World War and reflected upon the South African side of 1929.

'Nummy' Deane, H. G. Deane, was our captain in 1929. I used to like him very, very much. I was very keen. I used to love fielding, and Deane was a very strict captain indeed, and when he was on the field you had to keep an eye on him all the time. If you didn't, he'd kick up, because you had to move when he gave the slightest gesture. He didn't have to clap. He was experimental in many ways, but I thought he was a first-class captain who was always ready to take a chance. He was a good batsman, and a good fielder, too, and a grand chap to be with. His tactics were to try to win.

We were very much a young side. The side that came over before us, in 1924, didn't do at all well, and, being a young side, we were rather looked upon as if we didn't stand a chance at all against the English team. They had just come back from beating Australia, Percy Chapman's team, and we didn't meet any of this England team before the first Test match. I don't know how the tour was arranged, but Maurice Tate and all the England bowlers were absolutely new to us. First time we saw them bowl was in the first Test match at Edgbaston.

Herbie Taylor was our vice-captain, and I was told to be very careful of him at the beginning of the tour. He was turned forty on that tour, and I was nineteen, and I was told not to call him 'Herbie'. On the ship, I always referred to him as Mr Taylor. Then, on the train from Southampton to Waterloo, he asked me something, and I said, 'No, sir. No, Mr Taylor.' And he said, 'Don't call me Mr Taylor; call me Herbie.' And from then on I did. He was an amusing man, very fond of a story, but he was very serious as far as his cricket was concerned.

He was a beautiful cutter, and I don't think many people could bat as well as he did. He moved his feet. He made S. F. Barnes look like an ordinary bowler. Barnes was bowling, and Herbie used to move his right leg across behind the off-stump and touch him round the corner for four. It got to the stage when Barnes actually threw the ball on the ground and said he wasn't going to bowl any more.

He was a funny chap, old S. F. Barnes. I played against him when he played for Staffordshire. He had certainly made the Australians think a bit. He was picked by McLaren, and he did very well in Australia.

He was quite old when I played against him, but he bowled a beautiful length at quite a good pace. I suppose you'd call it slow medium then. They would turn and jump, and some would come straight through. He was a good bowler.

When we played against Worcestershire in the first game in 1929, Bruce Mitchell must have batted about six or seven. He was a beautifully fluent player, a lovely player, made his runs delightfully, square-cuts, late-cuts, drives, cover-drives. He really was a great player. His score was 83 not out against Worcestershire when we declared, and he'd made the runs in even time. Not like his Test match when he made 88 in eight hours, or something like that. He was put in to open the batting after that, and that, as far as I'm concerned, ruined him. I thought it was an awful shame. I think he opened for the whole of his Test career.

[117]

I played against him in 1935, against Herbie Wade's side. I played for Middlesex at that time. I also played against Bruce at Folkestone, spent many hours bowling to him into a bit of a breeze, and he had a smile on his face all the time. It was a good side that thirty-five side.

> The vice-captain of the 1935 side was Horace Cameron, an outstanding wicket-keeper and a batsman of great vigour. 'Jock' Cameron had been with the 1929 side, one of five Jeppe High School Old Boys, and led South Africa in Australia. Tragically, Cameron died of enteric fever shortly after the victorious side of 1935 had returned to South Africa. He was thirty years old, and the most popular of cricketers.

Jock Cameron was a very shy person, difficult to talk to. When I first met him I thought he was 'stuck up', but he was shy. Once you got to know Jock he was a very worthy chap. Not only that, he couldn't stand anybody talking about himself. He'd soon put him back in his place. He was a truly great personality, very nice to know, and what a cricketer he was. I never played under him as a captain.

As a wicket-keeper, he was outstanding, and as far as I'm concerned he was the best wicket-keeper I've ever seen. I think Bert Oldfield is the only one to approach him. The thing about Jock Cameron was he used to stand up to the fast bowlers very often, but not a finger on his hands was scarred. He had the most perfect hands, no bruises, nothing, not like others I've seen whose fingers were all twisted. His hands were perfect, and the way he stumped Walter Robins off Neville Quinn at Lord's, against Middlesex! Walter Robins got a 'pair' then, both times he went to Quinn.

We were very sad when Jock died so young. We couldn't believe it.

He was a magnificent batsman. He used to open the innings for Jeffe Old Boys, and you'd see Jeffe Old Boys 89 for 1, Cameron not out 75. He clobbered poor old Verity, and Wood made that remark.

I can remember in that exciting match in 1935 when I was playing for Middlesex, and we lost by 22 runs, we had George Newman playing for us. Jack Hearne was bowling his off-spinners round the wicket. He was bowling from the Pavilion End, and George Newman was wandering around in front of the Ladies Pavilion at Lord's which was on the left as you looked at the pavilion. Hearne bowled one, and Jock Cameron hit it like a bullet, and it went slightly wide of mid-on, straight to the Ladies Pavilion, not very high, not higher than a room. It was six all the way, but George ran round and put out his hand, and it stuck, and Jock was caught Newman, bowled Hearne for about 40. George Newman's hand was split, and he couldn't field any more.

In that particular match, Bob Crisp was bowling, and we got to the stage when Ian Peebles was the batsman, and we had 23 to get. Bob Crisp was bowling from the Nursery End quite fast, and Jock Cameron was standing up. Ian was batting, and he got a very good length ball, and this was the year of the leather-jackets, and the ball stood up, and he was falling on his wicket. Jock Cameron caught the ball in one hand and pushed Ian Peebles with his other to stop him falling on his wicket. The next ball, Ian Peebles had a crack at, a great swing and missed. Cameron had the bails off, and that was the end of the match. That was typical of Jock Cameron's sportsmanship. He was a very honest fellow.

> The *remark* made by Arthur Wood to his team-mate Hedley Verity came after the South Africans' famous victory over the mighty Yorkshire at Sheffield in 1935. Cameron hit an unbeaten 103. He took 30 off one over from Verity, three fours followed by three sixes, and Wood said, 'Well, Hedley, at least you had him in two minds.'
>
> 'How was that?' asked Verity.
>
> 'Well, he didn't know whether to hit you for four or six.'
>
> Bob Crisp, who was with the 1935 side, went on to play for Worcestershire. Quinn, Vincent and Morkel were the most successful bowlers of the 1929 side, and Vincent was successful again in 1935, as was Bell on his second tour.

Dennis Morkel was a very good-looking fellow, tall, and he was a very good medium-pacer. We didn't have any really quick bowlers. We had this chap Arthur Ochse, 'Ochse from the Bush' they called him, but he was not really very successful. Dennis Morkel was a good batsman, but he couldn't play slow bowling. 'Tich' Freeman used to worry him enormously, and Jack White also worried, but faster bowling he could play.

He used to swing the ball late and cut them in. He turned out to be a very good bowler with the new ball. He bowled 'Patsy' Hendren with a beautiful ball at Lord's, knocked the castle down, and Hendren just said, 'Cor blimey!' Dennis was a good slip-fielder, too.

Charlie Vincent was a very steady left-arm bowler. He could spin the ball, but he didn't vary his pace. He was very consistent. He was a very useful left-handed batsman. He got 60 in the third Test. He was a good chap and a good cricketer.

'Sandy' Bell bowled a very good length. He never bowled a bouncer. He used to bowl a very late in-swinger, and he couldn't make out why he couldn't get people l.b.w. every ball. Every time he turned round he'd find Frank Chester looking the other way. Every now and then, he'd make one go the other way, and he got 6 for 99 at Lord's when England made 302.

At Headingley, Neville Quinn took 6 for 92. He was medium-fast, left-hander, tallish fellow, and he made the ball swing away almost as it came off the pitch. He could swing the ball away very late. He was very consistent, and the only time I played against him was on a matting wicket in Kimberley when he was bowling ordinary off-spinners. He was a good bowler, and quite a bit of a lad.

One of his victims at Headingley was Morris Leyland. Compared to Frank Woolley, who was beautiful to watch, an artist at work, Leyland was like a workman with a tool in his hand. At Headingley, in the third Test, we had several injuries, and we brought in Duminy who was in England on business. He was fielding at point for Neville Quinn who bowled to Leyland. Leyland hit the ball hard, a beautiful cut, and Duminy threw himself across and caught the ball inches from the ground. Leyland just stood there, and said, 'Well I'm buggered. 'As ever seen owt like it?'

> Jack Christy was one of the players who was injured and unable to play in that third Test match at Headingley in which Owen-Smith himself hit a century, and Bob Catterall made 74.

Bob Catterall was a cheerful cuss. He wasn't a great friend of mine. I seemed to spend most of my time with Bruce Mitchell and Quintin McMillan, and one or two of the younger ones. We were almost put into the kindergarten. Bob was a fine player, and he ran very well, but he had a hell of a temper, and he used to be very careless in the way he got out every now and then. In fact, in the last Test match, at the Oval, Nobby Clark, that curious Northamptonshire player, a good bowler, but not much to keep his ears apart, got him out. He bowled Bob a slightly short ball, third ball of our innings, and Bob tried to hook it, of course, and got the ball on the maker's name. It just popped up to short-leg. So, three balls bowled, South Africa 0 for 1.

He could stick there. I wouldn't call him a flashy batsman at all. When I saw him really he'd had his day. He was plainly out of cricket, I should have said.

Jack Christy was tall, very nice back player, very strong through the covers, batted beautifully. He had a lot of success in many ways, but on the tour he was always out to a bit of bad luck. He played Larwood beautifully at Trent Bridge. He made 148, broke a couple of bats, but he didn't do as well as he was expected to do. He was a very good player, and a very, very nice chap. He was very quiet, and he was a very good Catholic. He used to go to church on Sunday wherever he was. I believe he ended up coaching in Australia. I'd never met him before that tour. The first time I met him was on the boat when we joined it at Cape Town. He was one of the five Jeffe Old Boys in the side.

> Owen-Smith speaks of the vulnerability of Morkel and others to the leg-breaks and googlies of 'Tich' Freeman who took 7 for

[121]

115 and 3 for 92 in the Headingley Test of 1929, and followed this with 7 for 71 and 5 for 100 in the Old Trafford Test. In 1928, Freeman had become the only bowler to take 300 wickets in a first-class season. In all matches, he took 304 wickets at 18.5 runs each in that season.

Freeman played only twelve times for England in spite of his phenomenal record in county cricket, but countries rarely went into a Test match in the early thirties without a leg-break bowler in their side. Indeed, Robins, Peebles and Richard Tyldesley all appeared in the series against Australia in 1930, and when Jardine took the side to Australia for the 'body-line' series of 1932–33, there were two leg-spinners in the party, Freddie Brown and Tommy Mitchell. Brown did not play in a Test in the series, but T. B. Mitchell of Derbyshire made his Test debut at Brisbane in the fourth Test when England won the Ashes.

Mitchell enjoyed a highly successful tour, and he was to play four more times for England, once against New Zealand at the end of the tour of Australia, twice against Australia in 1934, and against South Africa in 1935. In 1936, he played a vital part in Derbyshire's taking the County Championship, the only time in their history that they have won the title. He played for Derbyshire from 1928 until the outbreak of the Second World War.

Where we lived, about a hundred yards away, was a yard. My father used to play cricket a bit, and I used to play cricket in this yard and bowl with a tennis ball and a coconut-shy ball. When I was a kid about five years of age I used to go to the nets at the colliery, and they used to tell me to 'bugger off' because I used to bowl them out. I give up going, and I used to have two good hidings a week. My father used to pay five bob a week for the club and nets, and they'd tell me to bugger off, and I'd 'ave two good hidings a week for not going to practice.

During the General Strike of 1926 Tommy Mitchell practised his leg-breaks near the pit head of Creswell Colliery where he worked, and a veteran local cricketer was amazed at the way the twenty-three-year-old could turn the ball. He recommended him to Creswell Cricket Club who played in the Bassetlaw League, and Mitchell was soon established in the first team.

Derbyshire came to play at Creswell, and I were playing with the first team. I did all right, and they asked me if I'd go on the staff at three pounds a week. I said no I wouldn't. I could earn more than that down the pit, and I were earning more. Then they offered me four pound a week, and I took that.

I went to Derby. I had a green canvas bag with me cricket bat and everything in it. A fellow called Albert Widderson was the groundsman at Derby at that time, and a good groundsman. And I went and said to him, 'Are you Mr Cadman?' And he said, 'Bugger off up there and wait for him. He'll come to see you.'

Sam Cadman was coach at that time, and Jimmy Cresswell was on the staff. He was a good left-arm bowler, but if he were picked to play for the county, he were all gone. He was all nerves. Anyway, Sam Cadman came. I had a letter of introduction from Alf Rose. He'd played once for Derbyshire, and he was our captain. Cadman read the letter, and he said, 'There's no pub crawling.' I said, 'If I can't go pub crawling, I don't want to play cricket.' He caught me in the Tiger Bar the same night having a pint. I used to like a pint of beer. I was twenty-four or twenty-five, and I used to enjoy myself.

It was two years before they put me in the first team. My first wicket was against Essex – 'Jack' Russell. The second was Jack O'Connor, a good pair to start with. Essex had a leg-break bowler, Peter Smith, and I used to say to Tom Pearce, 'You've got a leg-break bowler.' But he'd say, 'Ay, but he's not as bloody good as you are.'

There wasn't much difference between club cricket and county cricket. I enjoyed it. I think if I'd have been more casual when I got picked for Test cricket, I would have done better. I played for England, and I was a bit too keen.

I bowled well in Australia, 1932–33, and I played in the fourth

[123]

Test at Brisbane, and got Woodfull out twice. They called him unbowlable, but I bowled him out in the first innings, and then Wally Hammond caught him at slip in the second. I got a fellow called Love, their wicket-keeper, out l.b.w.

Talking about Jardine, I were fielding cover-point, extra-cover, mid-off, and Harold Larwood was bowling to Bradman. Bradman was stepping back and cutting him for four past point. There were only Bob Wyatt and Tommy Mitchell on the off-side, and Bradman batting, and I moved round from cover-point to point, and I caught Bradman out. Jardine said to me, 'Well caught, Tommy, but I'll move you when you want moving.'

Jardine was a good captain. Played to win. They called him the 'Iron Duke'. I got on all right with him. Second Test match, at Melbourne, Harold and me went out and fell in with some people who played in a pantomime at the Prince's Theatre in Melbourne. And we went there, and we went out drinking in the afternoon. We come back, and this is true, by God, it's true, and as we walked back into the dining room for dinner after the afternoon out, Harold Larwood went cracking people on the back, saying, 'How are you, you old bastard?' and things like that.

Jardine sent for me next morning. He said, 'I want you in my room after breakfast.' I said, 'Right you are, sir.'

So I went up to his room, and he says, 'You were a naughty boy yesterday.' I said, 'I were a naughty boy?' He said, 'Yes, you took out Harold and got him drunk.' I said, 'You can take 'orse to water, but you can't make 'im drink.'

That night we went to the Prince's Theatre. George Duckworth were following us. Harold Larwood said to me, 'George Duckworth is following us.' I said, 'We'll stop, and we'll tell him where we're going.'

George Duckworth caught up with us and said, 'Where you going?' I said, 'We're going to park.' He said, 'I were going there.' So we said, 'Keep going, 'cos we're going back now.'

We went to the Prince's Theatre and said to the stage doorman, 'They'll be a fellow coming, following us. Don't let him in whatever you do.' He let George Duckworth in, though, and there was a phone call came to the dressing room where we were. 'Harold Larwood wanted on the phone.'

Duckworth had got in and phoned Jardine up. He were a yes-man for Jardine. And Jardine phoned the dressing room, and said he wanted Harold Larwood straight away in the hotel. Harold went, and he said, 'I'll be back again at half past ten.' No Harold Larwood came at half past ten, or eleven o'clock. That were the end of being a naughty boy.

After that we played an up-country match, and Jardine decided he would play twelve men on his side. Larwood had to play, and Jardine made him bowl.

Larwood was the best fast bowler I've seen in my life. He was just like a machine. He was a good cricketer. He got 98 in a Test match. The wickets were fast, made from Bulai soil, from the river bed, but they didn't help him.

I think Bradman used to go mad sometimes when he were facing Larwood. I can see him making a shot now off Larwood, going down on one knee and hitting the ball straight back. But he were a good batsman.

I bowled him out in a state match. I bowled him out for one. I took twenty pounds to two I'd bowl him out. Bradman didn't share out, but there was Paynter. He laid me ten to one I couldn't bowl Bradman out. I had two pounds on it, and I bowled him out second ball. That were on the Sydney Ground.

> Tommy Mitchell was, and still is, a great character, full of fun. He played 303 times for Derbyshire and took 100 wickets in a season ten times.

Hedley Verity, Yorkshire, was a left-arm spinner. He weren't slow. I called him medium-pace. He was a good bowler.

We stopped the Yorkshire success. We came third in 1934, second in 1935, and we won it in 1936. I think in 1935 we had a better side than we did the next year. I had 171 wickets in 1935, but I've forgotten the good things I did. We were a good side – the Popes, Len Townsend, Stan Worthington, Copson, Denis Smith, Tommy Mitchell – a real good side. Worthington went to Australia later. Denis Smith went to New Zealand.

We played in New Zealand after the tour of Australia, and then we went to Fiji, Hawaii, Vancouver, across Canada, back to Greenock. Good trip.

Wally Hammond got 336 not out in New Zealand with my bat. New bat, brand-new bat. It had never been used. He said, 'That bat you've got there, Tommy, can I take it in and bat with it?' It were smashed to smithereens – 336 runs. And he pinched me trilby. He was a good cricketer, and there were none better.

We played Gloucestershire at Cheltenham, and Len Townsend dropped Wally Hammond at mid-off. I said, 'That's eight years – it'll be another eight years before he gives us another chance.'

The first time I bowled against him was in the nets at Derby, and Sam Cadman, our coach, said, 'Come on, I want you to go and bowl at a fellow.' I didn't know it was Wally Hammond then, and I bowled him out, and I put the ball in me pocket. Wally Hammond said, 'Come on! I'd like you to bowl at me.' I said, 'I've bowled you out. That's enough for me.'

I got Jack Hobbs out twice in a match, stumped and bowled; and I got Herbert Sutcliffe out twice in one day. Hobbs was a great player, placed the ball well. Safety player. Waited for the bad ball to come, and scored off it.

I used to field at cover-point and kid 'em a bit. I was a bit of a joker. Life's very funny at times. Patsy Hendren was about the best batsman I bowled against. He knew everything I bowled – leg-breaks, googlies – it didn't matter what you bowled to him. We played Middlesex at Lord's, and Middlesex were batting. Harry Elliott, our wicket-keeper, said to Patsy Hendren about me, 'This fellow would be a good bowler if he could bowl a googly, wouldn't he?' Patsy said, 'Ay, he's bowled three at me this over.'

I didn't come up to expectations in Test cricket, though. As I said, you key yourself up too much.

There was really a big jump between playing a side like Somerset and playing Yorkshire. Somerset played about five or six amateurs. I think they were the worst-paid players, about fifty shillings. Warwickshire and Worcestershire were bad paid. We were bad paid – seven to ten pounds at home, eight to ten pounds away – against

[126]

Yorkshire's twelve pound home match, and fourteen pound away match. There was that class distinction as regards wages. But it was only a hard life if you made it a hard life.

We got two pounds a week in the winter, retaining fee. I went down the pit in the winter, and I earned more down the pit than I did at cricket. I sometimes earned twenty pound a week, and that was something in them days, if we were stone-heading. We made a winding engine house down the pit, twenty feet high, twenty to thirty feet wide. I put 'In Loving Memory' on it. I used to work down the pit in winter even when I was playing Test cricket.

I had no particular friends in that great Derbyshire side because I had no enemies, but Stan Worthington was one of my biggest friends. A. W. Richardson was captain of that side. He was a fair cricketer. His parents owned half of Derby. They made the leather for the cricket balls.

I remember when Guy Jackson was captain and we played Middlesex at Lord's. Middlesex had got 400 and something for six wickets down, and as we were leaving the field at six-thirty, Mr Jackson said, 'Come up to my room, Tommy.' I went up to his room, and he asked me what I'd like to drink. I thought 'I'll have a cocktail.' They were about three bob a time. I said, 'John Collins.' Jackson said, 'Will you have another?' I said, 'What about them people downstairs, the other professionals.' He said, 'They haven't earned one. You have. You've earned one.'

G. R. Jackson was a very keen fellow. If you couldn't play cricket, he made you play. We played Warwickshire at Derby. I'd been bowling, and I am walking back to fine-leg. Mr Jackson was clapping. I knew he were clapping me, but I took no notice. 'Mitchell,' he shouted, 'I'm clapping you.' I said, 'I'm sorry. I thought you were scaring the crows.'

I took all ten wickets against Leicestershire, 10 for 64, that were in 1935, and I had six wickets in thirteen balls against Middlesex, and eight in thirty-six against Worcestershire at Stourbridge, both in 1934. As I got closer to the all-ten, I never worried about it. Bill Copson were bowling to, I don't know, one of their left-arm bowlers, and I said, 'For Christ sake, bowl the bugger out, Billy.'

Old Tiger Smith was umpire, and he says, 'We'll have less of that, Tommy.' I got him caught at silly-mid-off. Stan Worthington caught him, and that gave me all ten, but I wasn't bothered a great deal. I did it once in league cricket and once in county cricket.

I played a one-day game against Lancashire at Chesterfield after the war, and I said, 'This is my last match.' I played Saturday-afternoon cricket, took 109 wickets in Saturday-afternoon cricket, that was here, in Thurnscoe.

George and Alf Pope went into the Bradford League – there was a bit of money there. I played for Lidget Green in Bradford League, but they asked me to come here, and I came. My wife went to stay with her mother in Doncaster. We left all the furniture and everything at Great Orme station where we lived in the station house. When we went back for the furniture somebody had pinched it all.

I still keep in touch with Derbyshire, but I haven't been for a couple of years. One-day cricket's spoilt it. It's been good for making money, but I think it's took the heart out of the game. There aren't any leg-spinners now. Essex had the last good one, Robin Hobbs. In my time, there were several good leg-spinners. 'Tich' Freeman, Ian Peebles, but he lost his leg-break bowling the googly too much. You lost your leg-break if you did that.

I lost mine once, but I never mentioned it to anybody. I knew I had to get this back, and I meant to. I tweaked it against a wall from about two yards away and made it bounce back. It showed me what I were doing.

Kent had two. 'Father' Marriott was a good bowler, an amateur, a schoolteacher. Then there was Doug Wright. He was fast, a fast leg-spinner. He bowled it quick. Freeman was a good length bowler, turned it a little bit. I used to be able to turn it on any wicket.

Indeed, Tommy Mitchell had more success in Australia than previous English leg-spinners, Freeman included. Having taken 304 wickets in 1928, Freeman was an automatic choice for the 1928–29 tour of Australia, but he did not play in a Test match.

When we were going out to Australia Harold Larwood said, 'Thy's got something on. There's been Dick Tyldesley. There's been 'Tich' Freeman. They never turned a ball out here. Thy's got something on to turn it.'

I bowled Fingleton round behind his backside, and he stood there and wouldn't believe it. Both umpires had to give him out. That was the same day I bowled Bradman. Fingleton stood there, wouldn't walk. He thought George Duckworth had knocked the bails off.

I enjoyed that tour. You couldn't do anything else but enjoy that tour. Cricket spoilt it. There were spectators who threatened to blind Jardine if he didn't give over his leg-theory.

We had a meeting at Adelaide. Sir Pelham Warner was one of the managers. He was the social side of it. Palairet was the financial side of it. Warner went to say something, and Jardine said, 'You sit down. You're nothing to do with it at all.'

We went to Canberra, and all the MPs said their party piece, and Jardine got up and said his party piece. He said, 'You, the Australian Government, believe the mother country this, the mother country that, and you borrow eighty million pounds off the British Government and spend it on American cars.' He talked like that. He were a hard man – Jardine. You couldn't do anything else but like him. He played to win.

He had an average of 39 before the fourth Test match in Brisbane, and he wanted dropping. He said to the selection committee, 'I'm not good enough.' There's some of them with an average of a lot less than that that's playing for England today. We couldn't have done without him.

Larwood was the instigator of leg-theory, not Jardine. He told me what he was going to do before we got there. Arthur Carr told Jardine what Larwood and Voce were like. He used to take Harold and Bill out and get 'em drunk then put them to bed after nearly every Notts match. He was a hard man, too. His father owned Golden Miller, the race horse.

We once backed Eddie Paynter to win a race. He was a very good cricketer. They were all good cricketers that went on that tour to Australia. We were sent out there as Empire builders, and we nearly broke it. 'Gubby' Allen wouldn't bowl leg-theory, but I never heard him and Jardine talk about it.

At Sydney, we came off the field at lunch, and Jardine said, 'Everyone who's not an England cricketer leave the dressing room.' And then he said, 'Are you aware there's been eighteen million bloody catches dropped this morning.' And first ball after lunch, he dropped one.

Bill Ponsford was a good player. At Chesterfield, he wanted one for his 100, and I gave him one. Then when I went in to bat he ran two hundred yards to catch me out for a 'duck'.

I never worried about batting. I only wanted to bowl. We were playing at Toowoomba, near Brisbane, and Jardine put Tommy Mitchell and 'Gubby' Allen to open. I had a bet I'd score more runs than him, but we got fourteen apiece and got out.

> In spite of his experiences in Australia of which there are constant reminders, including a gift from a grateful skipper and the ball with which he bowled Woodfull mounted and inscribed, Tommy Mitchell's most lasting memories come from his twelve seasons in county cricket.

I called Denis Compton a cheeky little bugger. He came dancing down the wicket to me. He was a good batsman. Bill Edrich was a good batsman, too, but Patsy Hendren was the best. I think so. He could drive me straight for one, and he could get 100 like that.

He asked me, 'You're a miner?' I said, 'Yes.' He said, 'You work down the pit?' I said, 'Yes.' He said, 'What do you do down the pit?' So I showed him.

We lay on our back and do what we call hauling. So I said, 'You do it.' Because we were taking the mickey out of each other. So he lay down, and I dropped a cricket ball on his head. And he said, 'What do you do that for?' 'To tell you to test your top before you go down the hole.'

There was just about room for your body to move down there, but I used to earn good money, and spend it. I lived a very fast life. Why not? You can only play once. Life's what you make it.

There were some good players in them days who never played for England. Frank Lee who played for Somerset, Jack Lee and Harry Lee of Middlesex. Jack Lee used to run up to the wicket looking too tired to bowl, and Stan Worthington used to look too tired to bat, and Jack Lee used to bowl him out.

Stan never did himself justice for England. He was a good cricketer. He could bowl, bat and he fielded at short-leg for me.

Hutton used to give me problems, but I got him out two or three times. He was a good player. They were happy days.

Brian Sellers was a hard man. Wilf Barber dropped a catch, and Brian Sellers said he wouldn't play in the next match. Because he dropped a catch! They used to say he was a good captain, but that Yorkshire side he had, there were people who didn't need a captain to look after them.

I once ran Brian Sellers out from cover point. I had been down at third-man, throwing in left-handed, and he hit the ball to me and said, 'Come two. He can't throw.' And I ran him out. He said, 'You'll never do that again.' I said, 'Once a year's enough for me.'

I used to save my bowling arm by throwing it back left-handed. I used to bowl a lot of overs, from twelve-fifteen to six-thirty. I bowled 57 overs against Middlesex at Lord's, for 106 runs, but I used to enjoy it. These days, if they bowl twenty overs, they're tired.

With Lidget Green in Bradford League, Arthur Barton and me bowled unchanged all one summer. Nobody else bowled. I didn't like batting, but I'd bowl all day. I even bowled with the new ball in Gentlemen v. Players at Lord's. Sutcliffe asked me. Robins said, 'You put the bloody hoodoo on me.' I used to enjoy my cricket.

They used to lay six to four at the sight-screen end that I'd take a wicket. I even bowled off-spinners once, and got seven wickets, but I only remember the good things I did.

I had my picture on cigarette cards, and they used to have my picture in shop windows – 'As Dressed by Montague Burton'. You didn't get paid for that in those days.

I think Percy Fender were the best captain I ever saw. I said to

Bob Wyatt, 'You couldn't captain a box of matches.' Wally Hammond said, 'He means it, Bob.' I got on all right with Wally Hammond, but he was a bit stand-offish. He was a big liver.

They were all good cricketers in them days.

5

THEY WERE GOOD DAYS

H. D. Read

N. S. Mitchell-Innes

W. H. V. Levett

Bill Andrews

R. H. Moore

Harold Larwood never played for England again after the Ashes series in which he had taken 33 wickets. Jardine led England against West Indies in 1933, and in India the following winter, but he declined to play against Australia in 1934 and left first-class cricket. The loss of these two men severely weakened England, and from 1934 until the outbreak of the Second World War, there was a search for the fast bowler who could take on Larwood's mantle.

One of those to be tried was H.D. 'Hopper' Read, an Essex amateur, whose career was short, but who bowled very quickly. He played in the last Test against South Africa in 1935 and toured Australia and New Zealand, 1935–36 with MCC. This was a tour that was arranged as a goodwill visit, an attempt to soothe relations after the body-line tour. It virtually marked the end of the career of a most promising fast bowler who took six wickets in his only Test match.

I got the nickname 'Hopper' because of my run-up, and it was when I was still at school that someone started it. My christian name is Holcombe, a family name, and when I got to school it was quite certain that I was going to get some sort of nickname because they are not going to call you that all the time. I was very happy to settle for 'Hopper' as quite a harmless name.

My father was a stockbroker, and our family had always lived in Essex, but he went to stay with a great friend of his from the City who lived in Englefield Green in Surrey. He was so enchanted with the golf courses at Sunningdale – Wentworth, I think, had not been completely built then – that he said we must move. I was aged four, but within a month the family had moved to Englefield Green, and I stayed in the same house for sixty-three years, before moving closer to my brother in Chichester, and then here to Somerset. That gave me a qualification for Surrey, but more than that really was that it allowed me to play club cricket there. If you can imagine, what you didn't want to do if you could help it, was to go to Essex, because you had to get right across London. If you ever played any sort of game in Essex, you had to go round or through London, and London is such a barrier.

When Surrey said to me, 'Would you have a trial?' I thought to myself 'Well, that's much easier', bearing in mind that I couldn't play the whole season. I could only play when I could get off from the office. I played against both universities as a trial, and unfortunately I broke down. I hurt my foot and really could hardly run up to the wicket. It would happen in a trial, wouldn't it!

Essex gave me a game after that. They had a brilliant secretary, Brian Castor, not everyone's cup of tea, but an extraordinarily nice chap. He'd heard I'd played for Surrey and that I had the Essex connection so he got in touch with Surrey and said, 'Look here, are you going to keep on with this fellow?' And they said, 'Oh, we don't think so.' So he said, 'May we?' And I played one match for Essex at the end of that year, 1933. Then the next year it so happened that I was extremely lucky. I took my intermediate accountants' exam, and the result took six to eight weeks to come through so I asked if I could go and play cricket while I was waiting for the result, and I was told I could.

Essex had probably five or six amateurs playing in every match, and they were often a trifle short because in May and June they couldn't rely on Denys Wilcox and the schoolmasters, and there were many of them that played so that they were very glad to have anyone. Had Leonard Crawley been able to play regularly, Essex would have had a good side. He was a great player.

In my third year, 1935, I got nearly 100 wickets – I know that I never got to 100 and I was just below Ken Farnes – and I played in the last Test against South Africa. I was very lucky again. Farnes couldn't play, and they had Nichols and Bowes playing, but they thought they'd try to have three fast bowlers. They were very much looking for a fast bowler to take over from Larwood. People said I was very fast, but you can't tell. You don't know yourself. I used to go in for speed rather than subtlety.

It was a huge jump from club cricket to county cricket, but it was not such a big jump from county cricket to Test cricket. What was a big jump was a match against, for instance, Somerset, and then a match against Yorkshire. A match against Yorkshire was always a terrific thing. It was much more like playing in a Test match.

One of my best ever days was against Yorkshire, but every dog has his day. We beat Yorkshire by an innings at Huddersfield. It was a very fast wicket, beautiful weather, and everything went right. There was a breeze coming just down the pitch slightly over my shoulder at mid-on. I took 6 for 11, and things went vastly well. I used to leap in the air as I bowled, and Frank Chester, the old umpire, always said, 'Mr Read, you've beaten me again. I couldn't get it out in time to no-ball you.'

There was a lovely story about that match at Huddersfield. A cousin of the famous Yorkshire player Rockley Wilson, Macro Wilson I think his name was, came across to watch the match – I think he watched every Yorkshire game – and he arrived a bit late on this day. When he got to the gate he saw a side coming off the field, and he said, 'Oh my God, why do we play these people? It is a waste of time!' And a man said to him, 'I'm afraid it's Yorkshire. They've bowled us out for 31.'

Nichols got seven wickets in the second innings, and he'd got four in the first, and he hit 146. He was a most charming fellow. Take for instance, here was an amateur coming in when it suited me, but Nichols played in every match he was told to. He had a very hard season, and took quite a long run, but if ever there was a wind at one end, he would say, 'Let Mr Read have that.' He probably thought that I needed more than he did. He would battle against the wind the other end. He was a most wonderful fellow. He never got the number of Test caps he should have done, but there were so many good players then. Nichols was a wonderful slip-fielder. He would bowl forty overs one end and field in the slips the other and take some amazing catches with his enormous hands. I never had any resentment from the professionals when I came in. They were frightfully helpful. It was a wonderful mentality.

Yorkshire were just beginning to find other people challenging them at that time. Derbyshire won the championship in 1936. They had Mitchell, a wonderful leg-break bowler, and the Popes and Copson. Their success was based on their bowling, but they had Dennis Smith, a very fast-scoring left-hander, very useful, and Worthington.

I always thought the most difficult batsman to bowl to was Sutcliffe because if you bowled him a loose one, it went, and he remained completely unruffled all the time. He was awfully nice to young amateurs, too.

Wally Hammond was a much more brilliant player, but I would have said he wasn't as difficult to get out as Herbert Sutcliffe.

I also played a match against Bradman, and I did not bowl a single ball against him although he made fifty in the first innings. It just happened that I'd done my first spell before he came in, and he made fifty very quickly before I came on again. I would have said that he was technically superb. He was always looking to score runs. You couldn't really bowl a length to him. I think that's where they found it so difficult. He used his feet so well. If you bowled to him just a tiny bit too short, he was on it like a panther, and all the time he was looking for runs. And, of course, he did keep it down. You didn't see him hit it in the air as people do these days. He didn't do risky shots. He was a frightfully good hooker, but you didn't find him balloon it up in the air. He did what it was safe to do.

Ken Farnes was very fast, but he didn't go in just for speed. People hated playing against him because they were always playing him on the splice. He was a tall fellow with a most beautiful high action, and he had a lot of bounce so that the batsman was always taking him on the thigh. On a nasty wicket, with his height, he was very awkward.

Brian Sellers was a terrific personality. He had the respect and, I think, the love of all the Yorkshire players, and he was just a marvellous captain in the days when a captain played as a captain. He had no axe to grind. He didn't depend for his place on having to make 100. He was there running the thing, and they all looked up to him. It was the same with Pearce and Wilcox. They were all something apart. They weren't just one of the boys promoted because they'd stayed there longer than anyone else. Being something apart made a tremendous difference. How you can captain a side and be one of the boys, I just don't know.

If I'd have appealed too loudly or shown bad manners when a

chap got out by shouting 'Hurrah! Hurrah!' or something, I should have been taken off, and the skipper would have told me afterwards that I must behave myself. Well, if you're one of the boys, I don't think you can do that. The press make it so difficult for everyone, too, because they say how splendidly enthusiastic people are. Well, enthusiasm to one person is just rank bad manners to another. I think the way they behave when a chap gets out is deplorable.

There was never a suggestion of verbal abuse or gamesmanship in my day. There was even encouragement from the other side. A man like Arthur Carr would never have stood for verbal abuse or bad manners or that sort of thing.

Inevitably, 'Hopper' Read's thoughts return to the outstanding players of his time, and, in particular, to the wealth of top-class spinners that decorated the county scene in the thirties.

I think Hedley Verity was the best spin bowler of my time, head and shoulders above the rest. He was almost unplayable on a wicket that helped him at all, and he was just a super bowler if it was a perfect wicket. He was very well supported in the field, of course, but in those days every single county had a good spin bowler. Yorkshire liked a left-hander. By tradition they didn't have leg-spinners, but most other counties did. We had our own Peter Smith. He was a good bowler, and Mitchell of Derbyshire whom I mentioned earlier, and there were a host of others like Ian Peebles and 'Tich' Freeman. If they needed him, Frank Woolley was a good left-hander, and Jack White down in Somerset was jolly good.

Each county had a top-class spinner, but, as I said, there was a terrific gap between playing against counties like Somerset and playing against Yorkshire. The atmosphere was so very different.

Playing against Somerset, for instance, and I only mention Somerset because it's where I now live, and I do not mean to belittle them as they were a fine side, had a club-cricket atmosphere, at Taunton or Frome, but if you went up to Bradford or Huddersfield or Headingley, there was a terrific atmosphere to start with. There would be a big crowd, and they were very knowledgeable, and they liked Yorkshire to win, too.

[139]

Lancashire weren't such a good side by that time. They had lost their great players, like McDonald, but they were still a force to be reckoned with as were Notts and several other counties. Surrey were good, but not super, and there was always an atmosphere at the Oval or Old Trafford that was different to the ordinary county ground like Taunton. The Oval was always a fast wicket, but it was absolute hell for a medium-pacer or a spinner.

Errol Holmes was captain of Surrey at that time, and he took us to Australia, 1935–36, with Charles Lyttleton as vice-captain. It was a minor tour, the first after the body-line business, and you couldn't have had better chaps than Errol Holmes and Charles Lyttleton to be part of it because they would make a wonderful impression wherever they went.

Lyttleton was a great fellow and a wonderful captain. He had complete control, and all the players looked up to him and went to him for advice. They treated him like a father figure. I can't imagine players these days going to some captains for family advice. The Lyttleton family, all good cricketers, had played such an important part in Worcestershire cricket.

Norman Mitchell-Innes was on that thirty-five, thirty-six tour. He was recognized as a brilliant player when he was at Sedbergh as a small boy, but he had such terrible hay-fever that it was just absolute misery for him to expose himself to the air. Joe Hardstaff was on the tour, too. I should think he was the most elegant player to have played, very handsome, beautifully elegant strokes. And there was Jim Parks, who, a couple of years later, took a hundred wickets and scored three thousand runs in a season.

The wicket-keepers were a fellow called A. G. Powell, who played for Cambridge University and Essex and was a great pal of mine, and, of course, Billy Griffith, who had just come down from Cambridge. He was a jolly good player and played for England just after the war.

It was sent out as a goodwill tour, and the next year they got 'Gubby' Allen to take the Test side to Australia. He didn't play all that much because he was a stockbroker, but he was a hell of a good player. He got all ten wickets against Lancashire at Lord's, a wonderful thing to have done.

Of course, when you're touring, especially in Australia, you are at a great disadvantage because conditions are so different; the wickets are different; the food is different; and the heat is probably colossal. Also, in those days, you went by sea so you really were a long way away. Travelling by ship was pleasant, but it made a long tour. If you add a month each end to a tour already probably three months, it's quite a long time for some people to be away from home. They might be worrying about this or that, and in those days you couldn't fly back if there was a crisis.

Travelling in the nineteen-thirties was very different from travelling today with its sponsored cars and motorway driving. There was, perhaps, a more leisurely atmosphere, and there was also the week-end country house cricket where wealthy philanthropists would arrange matches as part of week-end entertainment at their homes. Most noted among these was Sir Julian Cahn who ran his own cricket team with its home ground at Loughborough Road, West Bridgford, Nottingham-shire. He attracted some outstanding players to his side.

My great friend Ian Peebles played for Sir Julian Cahn's team for a season, and I played against them once or twice. Walter Robins did, too. Cahn had a frightfully good side, and they could have played any county. He was terribly keen, and he used to take people on tour, and he gave some of them jobs. He thoroughly enjoyed that type of cricket, and it was fun to play against. He owned a Midland furnishing company. He made a lot of money, and he put it into cricket.

Peebles was a super bowler. Many leg-spinners lose their leg-break and can only bowl the googly, but I don't think it happened to him. He played for Middlesex as long as he was able, but, again, he was in the City doing a job. Walter Robins was an outstanding captain, not everyone's cup of tea, but he ran an insurance business and couldn't always leave others to run it. The same thing happened to his sons. They would like to have played.

Tom Pearce could play regularly because he worked in the wine business, and Trayton Grinter ran it. He was terribly keen on cricket, and Essex in particular, and he made Tom available. Tom also used to go off playing rugger and refereeing rugger. He was a top-class referee, and one wonders how he worked it all!

Some counties had to have the captaincy shared. Essex was a good example. Wilcox obviously would have been captain all the time, but he could only play in the holidays. He was headmaster of his school, and he had this wonderful arrangement with Pearce whereby Wilcox would captain whenever he could play and Pearce would do the rest. Charles Bray used to come in occasionally, and you'd get several people who came in to fill gaps. There was a charming fellow who captained once or twice when I was playing – Nigel Wykes. He was a master at Eton so that he could only play in the school holidays.

There were several who might have played more for England if they hadn't had to work – Ian Peebles and 'Gubby' Allen, for example.

My father was very supportive to me in playing. He had been a player himself so he did know what it meant, but, obviously, he also realized that I'd got to earn a living in the City, and provided that I realized that, too, it was OK. It was quite unthinkable that I should turn professional in those days. I think the first chap who turned professional was Paul Gibb who came down to Essex from Yorkshire and had been at Cambridge. He eventually thought he'd like to play and so turned pro, and that was a big step in those days, and that was after the war.

What the pros earned then may not seem an awful lot, but they weren't too badly off, and they used to know where they were. They had a fixed amount of so much a match, and they used to get a bit of talent money and bonuses, but I think they get much more now. The pros then, though, seemed much happier and contented.

Shortly after my time, Northamptonshire went four years without winning a county match. They ended it when they beat Leicestershire in 1939, and a lot of people turned up to cheer them. They really weren't that much inferior to other counties. They could easily get you out for a very small score. They had a fellow called 'Nobby' Clark, a very fast left-hander. He really was quick, but he was easily discouraged and rather temperamental because they used to drop his catches one after the other. He played for England. Then they had a fellow called Bakewell who was a jolly good bat. He was injured in a car crash as Milburn was later.

There were surprisingly more cricketers injured in car crashes in the thirties than there are today when, of course, there is much more traffic about. You didn't have tests or anything like that. You could get straight into a car not knowing which way it went, and you could drive off. Dudley Pope, who was an Essex opening bat in my time, was killed in a crash. I think he'd hired a car and when he got it and he tried to put the brakes on, there weren't any.

We used to go long distances by train, but I mostly used to go by car and give someone a lift. The amateurs usually went by car, and the pros nearly always went by train. We stopped in different hotels entirely by choice. The pros didn't awfully want us to be there, and we both had different interests. They liked to follow their own amusements in the evening, and we had different ideas.

I very seldom go to watch these days, but perhaps that's because it's too easy to watch on television. In any case, I would always rather have played than watched. Fielding is much better than it was in my day, but the places that they are asked to stand are ridiculous. I had a short-leg, but they weren't as short as that. At least they were able to see the ball. It may be all part of trying to put the chap off. If you have someone standing where you can touch him with your bat, it's obviously off-putting.

I enjoyed my couple of years tremendously. I was so lucky. I was just playing it for fun. I never did it for anything else. This was the problem for the pro. His living depended upon his performance, and there was a lot of worry if he was having an off patch. He might be dropped, and that would mean a loss of pay. It could be a hard life for them.

My first-class career was short, but I continued to play club cricket for quite a time. I gave up my long run, of course, and bowled off a very short run which was much easier, but which I would have to have done because, playing club cricket, I played Saturday and Sunday only. It was no good trying to do a great long

run because I wasn't in training for it. I played mostly for But-
terflies, Gentlemen of Essex, Free Foresters and I Zingari. I never
had a yearning to go back. I felt I'd done it for a couple of years. I'd
played in a Test match, and, in my case, I was now on a short run,
and I'd never have got away with that in county cricket. I knew
pretty well that it was likely to be my last year when I played for
England.

After the tour to Australia the senior partner of the firm I was
with came along and said, 'Well played, Mr Read, now you have
got to make up your mind whether you're going to be a professional
cricketer or a professional accountant.' He was right. Amateurs had
to earn a living.

> This was indeed the case with Norman Mitchell-Innes, a bats-
> man of outstanding ability, who played for England when he
> was still at Oxford. He spent his life in the Sudan Civil Service
> and became lost to Somerset, and to England, for long periods.
> He first played for Somerset while still at school.

Jack White gave me my first match, but that was sheer luck that I
got a match at all. I played the usual school term of cricket, had a
few days at home, and then went off to play on a school tour up in
Castle Eden and York, against Yorkshire Gentlemen and that sort
of thing. Then I sent my cricket bag back to Somerset and went on
with my golf clubs to play in the Boys' Golf Championship where I
was captain of the Scottish team.

Eventually, on the Thursday, I got knocked out at the twenty-
sixth hole, having three-putted six times. I didn't know that
Somerset had approached my father and said, 'Where's Mandy? Is
he available to play the odd game?' He told them I was up in
Scotland playing golf so they said, 'Well, if he's knocked out, let us
know. We might be able to fit him in.'

They heard on the Thursday evening on the radio that I'd been
knocked out. So my father rang up John Daniell who said, 'Tell
him to get the train down tomorrow night, and we'll play him on
Saturday against Warwickshire.' So a thing that could never happen
now happened. I was out on the Friday watching the golf and

saying to myself, 'I should have beaten that so-and-so,' when suddenly a telegraph boy arrived in the middle of the golf course and said, 'I gather you're Mitchell-Innes. Here's a telegram for you.'

'Catch the evening train down. The gardener will bring your bag. You're playing against Warwickshire tomorrow.'

I went off to Renfrew, got my clothes and just caught the train. I was glad that Warwickshire batted the first day. I had a couple of nets before going out, and I got a bowl. Jack White was the captain, and he gave me a few overs. As the pros didn't know who the hell was bowling at them, I got a couple of wickets. I didn't bowl much after that, although I got one or two wickets, largely because they didn't know where I was bowling at compared to the old pro.

At Oxford, I again took on opening the bowling because I wasn't going to have a bowler who was a useless fielder and no bat, who could only bowl and might bowl a good ball, and might bowl a lot of bad ones. So I said, right I'll open and hand on to Sandy Singleton and the spinners either sooner or later depending on how it goes. So Randle Darwall-Smith and I opened, and the following year, Sandy's year, David Macindoe had come up, so he and Randle opened.

Randle Darwall-Smith had a prep school at Seaford, and he went straight into school-mastering and didn't continue with first-class cricket. I still see him occasionally, quite a good cricketer, but I don't think he would have got into a senior side. He was about medium-fast.

There were several fine players who couldn't play much because of work. 'Tuppy' Owen-Smith was a doctor, and he was a great player. Ian Peebles could only play patches of cricket. Freddie Brown couldn't play much until he was really too old. Cyril Walters, Alan Melville, Gerry Chalk, Hugh Bartlett – all good players who had to give time to business.

I played thirteen county matches for Somerset before I went up to Oxford, but Hugh Bartlett played one match each year for two years for Surrey, and three of the six days it rained. He wasn't given any further games so he then switched to Sussex where he became captain. He was a lovely player, a left-hander, great hitter of the ball. If you didn't get him out very quickly, you were in trouble. He got 175 for the Gentlemen against the Players.

At Oxford and Cambridge we were always short of really good players because you were always mucked about by exams, and it's a very short season. 'Derek' de Saram was a great cricketer. He got his 1,000 runs in 1934; I missed by two runs. 'Derek' had the remarkable capacity – the Nawab had it, too – of being able to say I'm going to do so and so tomorrow, and doing it.

Just before the Varsity match, we were at Reigate, and he got 200. David Townsend and David Walker had scored about 80, and 'Derek' and I were in. Somebody had walked past the dressing-room window and had said, 'You know, there's only been five people since the war who've made 1,000 runs in a university year.' And 'Derek' heard this and decided to be the sixth. So he went in and went on solidly piling up the runs.

When we got to the new ball, 200 it was in those days, I thought 'I want to keep this bat for the Varsity match,' got an old bat, swished around and holed out somewhere. Not so 'Derek'. He went on until he scored 208 and got his 1,000 runs. I finished up after the Varsity match two short.

He was a great player, but, on the other hand, second ball of the Varsity match, he was fast asleep at long-leg. Rickey Tindall bowled a long hop, and Allen or Parker, whichever it was, waved it away to leg. 'Derek' didn't have to move. He didn't have to go forwards, backwards or sideways. It hit him in the chest, and he never got a hand to it. It just went down on the ground. He was fast asleep. I suppose he was at long-leg because he wasn't a very good fielder.

He was a very good tennis player. His first two years at Oxford he played tennis, but he wasn't made captain of the tennis club, and so took up cricket and walked into the side straight away. He also played in a lot of golf matches. He was very quiet, very reserved, and, at Oxford, he was automatically into Benson's Club and any other club. There was no colour feeling, but whether he thought he wasn't made captain of tennis because of colour I don't know. Anyway, he came across to us, and thank God he did. We always got on well together, that's why we ran between the wickets as well as we did. I was very fond of him.

At Worcestershire, Gibbons and the Nawab of Pataudi ran each other out frequently. They didn't have the rapprochement. One would say 'no', and one would say 'yes', and there'd be an argument in the middle of the pitch. They were both good players.

Pataudi was another of these chaps like 'Derek'. He'd decided he was going to be the third to get 100 in his first Test match in Australia. The fact that he took too long, which wasn't what his side wanted, didn't matter.

'Mandy' Mitchell-Innes was to play in only one Test match, against South Africa at Trent Bridge, 1935, while still in his second year at Oxford. As he tells, he was also selected for the Lord's Test, and he went on the tour of Australia and New Zealand with the MCC side under Errol Holmes, the side of which 'Hopper' Read was a member.

There was a great difference, I think, between Varsity cricket, county cricket and Test cricket. The bowlers gave much less away, and the batsmen certainly gave nothing away. I got 150 against the South Africans at Oxford which gave me the match at Trent Bridge, but I only had one innings because Bob Wyatt, Herbert Sutcliffe and Wally made so many. I had my pads on from eleven a.m. until three-thirty when I went in to bat because we always padded up two down the line. Bob Wyatt was a good captain, knew his stuff, and I could never make out why he wasn't popular. I thought the world of him. I suppose I didn't play again, but there was a lot of good batting about in those days.

I can remember that Test match when Siedle and Mitchell were batting, and they put on Hedley Verity to bowl. There was Herbert Sutcliffe short-leg, and I was in at silly mid-on, and Siedle could have knocked my cap off with his bat. The first one on the leg-stump Siedle tried to drive me away, and he just hit it down to Sutcliffe at short-leg. The next one I rather wavered, I suppose. It felt like it. He hit it past my left leg, and it was picked up at mid-on, and the third one he missed and was castled. That's how good Hedley was.

When 'Jock' Cameron came in Bob came to me and said, 'You all right there?' I said 'yes', for it was far better for me to be there and be hit than for any of the pros. He said, 'Well, for this cob you can go back two or three yards.' And I did gratefully, as he'd just hit Hedley for three sixes and three fours in some previous match. That was when Arthur Wood made his famous remark about having him in two minds.

They were a wonderful lot those wicket-keepers, the remarks they came out with. In that season, Eric Rowan and Bruce Mitchell put on 330 for the first wicket against Surrey at the Oval, and, as they were batting, a lorry went down the Vauxhall Road and let off a terrific back-fire. Brooks, the Surrey keeper, turned to Errol Holmes and said, 'There you are, skipper, number three's gone and shot himself.' Just what was needed at that appalling moment with Errol Holmes wondering what to do next.

'Jock' Cameron was a very good wicket-keeper. He died just after that tour.

They chose me for the first two Tests, in fact, but, being June, came the hay-fever season so I rang up 'Plum' and said, 'I'm merely reporting that much as I'd love to play I could well understand it if you feel I'm not one hundred per cent fit and shouldn't play.' He said, 'You seem to be getting some runs.' I said, 'Yes, I'm all right at the moment, but it's up to you to say whether you feel I might miss a slip catch, and the chap might go on to make 100 or whatever.'

He said I shouldn't worry about it, but finally he said perhaps I was right. 'You should be one hundred per cent fit if you play for England. What are you going to do if you don't play?' I said, 'I shall go across to the Oval and play on the Oxford tour against Surrey.' He said, 'You'll probably get 100.' I said, 'Yes, quite likely. I like that wicket and the bowlers.'

Three of the Oxford side were staying with Errol Holmes that week-end, and Errol, instead of going to the Oval, went to Lord's, and I went to the Oval. Sure enough, when it came my turn to bat I was absolutely sneezing my head off, and Jake Seamer went in instead of me. Ten minutes later, when the next wicket went down, I'd got over the sneezes, and I went in, and I did get 100. Errol and the rest of them at Lord's were bamboozled by Balaskas and lost. He'd had to bowl in two or three sweaters at Oxford among the snow. I know. I'd batted in two or three sweaters.

I was one of eight amateurs who, with six pros, a sort of 'A' side, went to Australia the following winter. The idea was to give people experience. There was so little cricket played in those days. It gave us the experience of getting on with each other and seeing what cricket abroad was like. It was a wonderful trip.

Joe Hardstaff did very well. Everyone had their moments. Charles Lyttleton was a great character, and we were very lucky that he, Sandy Baxter and I were very low handicap golfers so that, at week-ends, the local golfing clubs organized games for us.

> Most of Mitchell-Innes' first-class cricket was played on the county circuit, with, and against, some of the finest players the game has known.

My hay-fever affected me to the extent that I felt I wasn't absolutely fit to play in Test cricket, but otherwise I went on, and I don't think I ever did sneeze as a catch was coming. There was always that possibility. It's a funny thing, hay-fever. If you're absolutely immersed in something, you don't actually sneeze. At Oxford, going down to take exams in June, I'd sneeze all the way down the High Street until I got into School. Immediately the invigilator said, 'Start writing!' I'd stop sneezing and write, and I wouldn't sneeze again until the end of the exam – except once when I didn't know enough to write all the time.

When Jake Seamer went in at the Oval instead of me I couldn't have gone in at that moment, but then I settled down and went and was perfectly all right until Jake was out. When I stood there waiting for the next batsman I suddenly began sneezing again, but when he arrived and had faced a few balls I was perfectly all right again.

There was never any resentment from the Somerset pros about being left out to accommodate the amateurs. In the early days, it was a case of their getting a team together at all. When I began, in 1931, I think we only had six pros anyway, and it wasn't long before that we only had four. And then we gradually got a few more.

I was absolutely astonished to read that Durham have taken on about twenty people straight away so that they can build up. I suppose they've got the money. They now want £1,500 for life membership, husband and wife. People haven't got that sort of money. It cost me £10 to become a life member of Durham some thirty years ago.

Arthur Wellard and Harold Gimblett were the only two of the Somerset pros of my time to make the England side. Harold, I think, wanted to be one of the new group, to be accepted in all places. He didn't accept so much the two doors to come out of. He'd been at school at West Buckland, or somewhere, one of those public schools. He was from a farming community. He felt a little bit of a chip on his shoulder. He was a wonderful player. We played in kids' cricket together, and then in county cricket together. He was not altogether a happy man. Wally Luckes always looked after him, and the others did, too.

Bill Andrews was a funny old stick. One needed to get to know him. Likeable person. Kindness personified, but he could also be stupid at times. Say the wrong thing. Arthur Wellard was a great heart. Wonderful chap. And Bertie Buse would never harm anybody.

If Harold Gimblett had been in Len Hutton's position, or in the Middlesex twins' position, having Herbert Sutcliffe or Patsy Hendren at the other end to take the dirty bowling on a dirty day, he would have been in the England team for years. He was a good enough cricketer, had a good enough eye, was a good enough player, but he had to do all the dirty work for us. If it was a dirty wicket, he had to take the bowling and see us through. Len Hutton was able to watch at twenty yards' range with Herbert at the other end, or the other two watched Patsy Hendren, how he coped, and then it naturally went into them, and they got away with it. The firm hand of those senior pros would take command at times and come down hard on a junior who was being idle. I can remember down at Taunton one day Denis Compton failing to back up, and we got two overthrows, and Patsy Hendren tore strips off him. I'm quite sure he never failed to back up again after that.

Wally Hammond was a wonderful player, wonderful. He had a marvellous physique, very strong, and a wonderful eye. He was very quick, superb slip-catcher, but he had all the shots, and he had the technique to make shots. In 1936, I was landed with the captaincy at Bristol, Reggie Ingle had split a finger. Wally took 150 off us in the first innings and 80-odd in the second. If I bowled Jack Lee with the leg-side field round the wicket, Wally just went back and hit it through the covers. If we then gave Jack the off-side field, and he bowled over the wicket, Wally went straight across and pushed him down past mid-on, no trouble at all.

As a bowler, he had a very good action. It must have been one of my very early games at Oxford when we were playing Gloucestershire that he opened the bowling. The third ball he pitched perfectly, a leg-spinner, which takes a bit of doing with the shiny new ball. I always remember somebody saying that he could have been as fast as Larwood or any of the rest of them, but he had enough to do in the other departments.

Apparently, in one match in the West Indies, I suppose Constantine and Martindale had been whipping them across their ears a bit, and the lads were getting fed up with this, so Wally said, 'Let me have the ball.' He pitched it all right, but it went over the wicket-keeper's head first bounce against the sight screen. If he really wanted to, and he could do that, he could have been as fast as any of them.

Hammond, Verity and all those boys always played against the universities. That Yorkshire side was a very tough side to deal with. Brian Sellers would have got into any side as a batsman. He was a good player as well as a great captain. You had Hedley Verity bowling at you, and 'Ticker' Mitchell sitting at the end of

[151]

your bat. You were absolutely snookered, as it were, and they were unrelenting.

I can remember Len Hutton coming down on the southern tour, which meant the two universities and the MCC, I suppose, and he took 50 off us. It took him a long time, but every shot was a gem whether it was a defensive shot or not. They blooded him on that tour. He saw how others did it.

That Yorkshire side needed somebody firm to deal with them, and Sellers did that. He knew his stuff. They had Bill Bowes, Emmott Robinson, Macaulay, Smailes . . .

I can remember watching a freshers match at Oxford with Emmott Robinson because we had him to help us at the beginning of the season after he'd retired, and I said to him, 'What do you think of this off-spinner?' 'Just that decimal. Just that decimal.' I can hear him saying it now. 'Just that decimal slower.'

We youngsters had no idea, but he knew, he could see, that the chap needed to bowl just that little bit slower. He was a great help in his way, as was Denis Hendren, Patsy's brother. He was a great person, used to umpire quite a lot and was such a kind person.

Bradman played against us at Oxford in 1934 when 'Derek' took 100 off them. The next time I played against Bradman was on the thirty-five–thirty-six tour at Adelaide. He hadn't gone on the Australian tour to South Africa because he'd had his appendix out. Errol put most of us on the boundary, and he hit about four fours in his fifty. All the players just wrote him off, said he was a has-been. So did I. He was to prove us all wrong. He was so quick, like Wally. They could pick it out. So could Herbert Sutcliffe.

I suppose the first time I really saw Herbert was in 1932. I was still at school, and we played Yorkshire at Sheffield. Three of us, Wally Luckes, Bill Andrews and myself, were out leg-before to Fisher, which was the first of these leg-before hat-tricks. There are about five now, I see. Herbert got 136. He skied one from Arthur Wellard off the top of his bat and I caught it at slip. I couldn't make out how this chap was *the* England bat. Arthur would be bowling just outside the off-stump, and Herbert would try to hook him, and he'd miss time and again, not out. By the time he'd got to 100, I knew why he was so marvellous. He knew to within a fraction as to whether the ball would be liable to hit the stumps or his legs covering the stumps and as to whether he would be out or not. He knew he wasn't going to be about leg-before because he knew to within a fraction where the ball was. He'd miss a shot and smooth his hair down and go on as if nothing had happened. The slips and the bowler would be tearing their hair out. He had absolute control. I saw Hobbs make his record 100 at Taunton, but I was a boy then.

There was always a great friendliness between the counties in matches in the thirties although possibly not when Arthur Carr was playing. He believed in playing it tough when it suited him, and if he didn't want to come in early in the morning, he didn't come. He told his batsmen to meet him at one o'clock. I believe he was behind body-line. He had Larwood and Voce with the ability to bowl adeptly on the line and not to wander vaguely. He brought the fielders closer in and in. It was a useless form of cricket because there was no joy at all in playing it. It stifled the whole flow of the game. It's no fun just being knocked about anyway. Patsy was the only one who once in those days came out with a sort of skull cap on, a motor-cyclist's helmet, to make a point of objecting to this form of attack.

The changing of the laws hasn't helped. I was out of the game by then, but I could never understand why they made the front line the bowling line. I'd have done just the opposite. You've only got to say it's a twenty-two yard game, not a nineteen-yard game.

The period in which Mitchell-Innes played for Somerset was rich in bowlers of quality, yet many of them played no more than a handful of games for England. Others, like Ken Farnes, the Essex fast-bowler, were not always available because of business commitments.

Verity was very difficult to play, but I quite enjoyed playing against the Lancashire, Worcestershire and Surrey bowlers usually. Ken Farnes and Morris Nichols were good. Farnes was very quick,

[153]

and he was six feet six inches and right up top. He was absolutely vertical, and he pinged it at you like a tennis ball.

I can remember a match at Weston-super-Mare where the wicket is usually greenish and where you get the morning breeze from the sea. He'd got a bit of a temper, old Ken. The two Lees went in, and God knows how many thigh pads they had strung round them. I never had a thigh pad the whole time I was playing. I would have said I had enough adipose padding of my own. Number three was 'Tom' Young. He was a delightful person, and he said, 'Be ready padded up, sir.'

I said, 'What's the matter, Tom, you're in next?'

He said, 'No, I shan't last long.'

I said, 'Why not? You can deal with this more than most of us.'

He said, 'No, I shall go in and have a swing. You know I'm only functioning on one cylinder?'

I said I didn't, and he said, 'The other lung's collapsed, and I can't afford to be hit and be sick. If I go into hospital, my wife and daughter get no money. So I'm not going to take any risks.'

He went in, got about 24 quickly, and holed out at cover. I never realized that there was that danger for some of these old boys who weren't that fit, and they looked at it as 'Tom' did. And quite rightly. The Yorkshire boys may have got a thousand pounds, but certainly our boys got three hundred and fifty at the most, and a winter job. If you didn't play, you didn't get any money. And it wasn't a case of being brave, like an amateur could be. He had to think of it that way. 'Tom' was a good person.

Ken Farnes was a good bowler, accurate, and Nichols was, too. He was playing in the Test at Trent Bridge when I played. Nichols would have had a regular place today.

Mitchell-Innes became lost to English cricket for long periods when he joined the Sudan Civil Service in 1937, but he was to return and captain Somerset briefly after the Second World War. His friend and Somerset colleague, 'Jake' Seamer, also worked in the Sudan.

Mitchell-Innes hit 207 for Oxford University against

[154]

Levenson-Gower's XI at Reigate in 1936, and he scored freely for Somerset, yet he has surprising memories of his best innings.

One innings at school, perhaps, the final of a house match in 1931 when I made 302 not out in an afternoon. I was about sixteen. I got about 240 for the Authentics against Durham Pilgrims at Castle Eden, which was a lovely little ground, and I got quite a lot at Kidderminster on one occasion.

I went out to the Sudan at Christmas, 1937, and in 1938 I didn't get leave so I couldn't play. Luckily I got leave early in 1939 so I was able to play about a month's cricket then. Then the war came, and we were not home until forty-six.

In 1948, Jack Meyer had retired, and George Woodhouse, Edward Woodhouse, G.E.S., was at Cambridge, and he was going to take over. They were the Woodhouse brewery people, and I think his uncle said, 'You can't take over until you've passed your exams.'

Nobody had really thought of that. The exams were in June. So Somerset scratched their heads and thought that the only possibility was to ask Jake and me to organize our leaves, and they sent us cables and asked us to do that.

I agreed to come home in March which would take me up until June. I would do the build-up in April, and Jake would come home in May and take over at the end of May until July when George would be available. And that's what we did. We had a triumvirate of captains. It was great fun. I don't know if it was very good for the side.

I didn't find it hard to take up again in forty-eight. I don't say I was as good as I'd been in the thirties, but I was young enough to have kept fit. I think it's possibly easier to be captain when you're slightly far away than when you're just one of the boys. It's very difficult for one of the boys to be captain and really take the others to task when necessary.

Wally was always slightly separate. Len Hutton was probably a big enough character to do the job, and he was a very mature player by the time he got it.

We had some fine characters, Arthur Wellard, Wally Luckes, the

[155]

wicket-keeper, Bill Andrews, Bertie Buse, and, after Jack White left, Horace Hazell. We played the game to enjoy it thoroughly. We knew we weren't going to win the Championship, but we were just as likely to beat Yorkshire as we were to beat Glamorgan. We had some comic grounds – Frome, Yeovil – it was fun going round the county. I don't think the more serious counties appreciated it because it might start a bad patch for somebody who was just getting through a bad patch. He could be unlucky and start all over again because the wickets were very doubtful. They still seem to curse the wickets today just the same, but they were a bit naughty, some of them, in those days when you didn't have all this covering that they have today.

If they are fitter today, they have a hell of a lot more injuries than we did in spite of having PT all the time. The Yorkshire people turned out and were ready to go out to practise at ten-thirty. We were a bit more slack about it at Somerset. We got there at eleven, and if you wanted a net, you asked a couple of people to help you. But there was much more of a regime about it with Brian Sellers and the Yorkshire people, and probably with the Nottinghamshire people. I didn't know the Derbyshire people so well, but I know Copson was a good bowler. There was none of this running to the hotel, or jogging from the hotel to the ground nonsense.

I said to them down at Somerset a year or two ago, to one of the players, 'You're sponsored for your flannels?' He asked me why. I said, 'Well, your flannels are all green, and that sort of thing. You're always throwing yourself about as if you play soccer.'

'Oh no,' he said, 'we're not sponsored, but we do get our flannels cleaned.'

'You're bloody lucky,' I said, 'In our day we had to clean them ourselves, and it's an expensive item. Why the hell can't you clean your boots? You have all these attendants laid on nowadays. We used to have one attendant, but you never saw a team going out without clean boots.'

I played half a dozen games in 1949, and that was that. That was Wally Luckes's last year, and, I think, Arthur Wellard's.

'Hopper' Levett, who kept wicket for both Kent and England in the nineteen-thirties, confirms Mitchell-Innes's view on the different attitudes to pre-match training at that time.

You watch Kent before a match these days, and this Australian chap Foster has them doing all sorts of contortions. Frank Woolley, 'Tich' Freeman and 'Wally' Hardinge would have taken one look at what goes on today and gone back home.

I got in a bit of trouble when I started because I used to let the pros call me by my first name, or call me 'Hopper', and there were people who didn't think that was right, believed that they should call you 'sir' or 'mister'. That didn't suit me. I've always remembered the girls that used to come down from London to do the hop-picking in Kent before the war. If you could have cleaned them up and given them a decent dress, they would have been among the most beautiful women in the world, but they were poor.

In spite of his attitude to today's rigid programme of physical fitness, Levett himself practised hard and long when a boy.

I became obsessed by wicket-keeping when I was at prep school, and I used to go down to the boot room and practise taking the ball and catching. There was an old tip-up desk, and I had the gutta-percha inside of a golf ball. I'd throw the ball on to the wall so that it would bound back off the lid of the desk, and I'd try to catch it whatever angle it came off. Sometimes it would miss the desk, and this gave me a different problem, but I used to keep at it for hours. When I first started I'd never played in a match.

I remember that the first batsman I ever stumped was my father. I was eight years old and I kept wicket for the school against the Fathers' XI at Linden Park, Tunbridge Wells. We had a bowler named Maidwell who was quick for a boy, and I stood up to him. The second ball he bowled to my father beat him. My father lifted his heel, and I stumped him. I was eight years old, and it was the first stumping I can ever remember making. It still gives me pleasure today.

[157]

I wasn't so lucky my first game for Kent. That was against Worcestershire at Tunbridge Wells in 1930. I dropped Fox, the opener, off 'Tich' Freeman. He went forward and edged the ball, and it hit my gloves and I dropped it. I'd followed it instead of going with it, and it went down. At the end of the over, 'Tich' said to me, 'Young man, if you do that sort of thing, you won't stay long in the game.' But 'Tich' and I got on all right after that. I could always read his googly, but I never took it for granted. Les and I were always surprised that so many batsmen were so unable to read it.

I always treated every bowler with the greatest respect, and I insisted that they gave me difficulty. In that way, I kept my concentration. I loved it. I saw the best batsmen in the world – Sutcliffe, Hobbs, Hammond, Bradman – from a closer view than anybody else had, and it was a joy to see them get runs.

I had a lot of fun, and I had many catches and stumpings not given out, but I never argued, and I always tell youngsters, 'Never embarrass the umpire.'

> One of the professionals who played with Norman Mitchell-Innes was Bill Andrews, a most entertaining and lively character who lived and breathed Somerset cricket until the day he died. He began as a worshipper and came to play with and against those whose autographs he had once sought.

I came to Weston when I was about eleven, and at that age I started to do the score-board down at Clarence Park where Somerset played their annual nine-day festival, three matches. I started there about 1920, and it was a fascinating game. There weren't so many of us then, but it was good because you got to know the players. I used to go to Taunton, too, but not to work the score-board.

One of the greatest things was when I went down to Portsmouth to see Yorkshire play Hampshire. The great Herbert Sutcliffe came up to me, and I asked him to sign. He said, 'Did you write Yorkshire CCC at the top?' And I said yes, and he said, 'You're a very good hand-writer.' This rather pleased me coming from a chap like Sutcliffe.

[158]

I was brought up in the law, office boy at 7/6 a week to a firm of solicitors. I soon got on the engrossing side where you do the Old English and the German lettering. You had the vellum sheets, and you put the resin on it, and you had to push your pen through it, up strokes thin, down strokes thick, and I got to like the writing.

I always remember in the old days, when I used to do overtime, I got tuppence a folio, which was seventy-two words, and it took at least half an hour. I liked the shorthand, too, and got up a good speed.

When I was a boy I used to bowl a few balls at Sammy Woods before a match. Harry Saunders, my old teacher, played about four or five games for Somerset at that time.

I used to get the umpires' autographs as well, and there was a chap named Board who used to play for Gloucestershire, and I asked him, and he charged me a penny for it, which was rather a lot of money in those days. I suppose it went towards the drinking fund.

Of the players in those days, Lancashire were a great side, but they never used to speak to us. They felt we'd never ought to have been in the Championship at all.

Wally Hammond wrote a good hand. They took care in those days. They used to sign in the same order. When I was a player with Somerset we only had five or six pros in the side. We used to sign at the bottom. We daren't sign at the top. We had to leave that room for the amateurs. So they signed in order of priority, how long they'd been playing.

I always told my boys when I was coaching they must never refuse to sign autographs. You must never lose the common touch.

That there was a social distinction between the amateur: the gentleman, and the professional: the player, is undeniable, but the emphasis on this distinction has tended to obscure the benefits that the amateur brought to the game and, often, the sacrifices he made.

R. H. Moore played for Hampshire from 1931 until the outbreak of the Second World War, and he captained the county

[159]

in 1936 and 1937. After his first full season, 1934, *Wisden* described him as 'probably the most promising young amateur in English cricket. Possessing considerable confidence and combining sound defence with powerful strokes in front of the wicket, he became an ideal opening partner for the more careful Arnold. Higher honours may well await him.'

It was to transpire that the higher honours were to consist of a single appearance for the Gentlemen against the Players at Lord's in 1938, although he also played in the fixture at the Oval and at Folkestone, which were considered of lesser merit. It was probable that he never became a Test player because his main concern, in the Hampshire tradition established by Lionel Tennyson, the third Lord Tennyson, grandson of the poet, was to entertain. In later years, *Wisden* was to mourn that Moore took 'enterprise to the point of recklessness', but he can claim that he is one of barely just over 100 batsmen in the history of the game to have scored a triple century.

Richard Moore points out how much Hampshire owed to Tennyson.

I heard Gooch talking the other day about how different the game is now and how amateurs used to have first-class travel and stay in luxury hotels, and you know it wasn't like that. Take Lionel Tennyson. He looked after me when I was a young player, and if he was going to stay out late playing cards with Peter Eckersley at Old Trafford, he'd say, 'Well, I think the best thing you can do is go to the pictures.' When we were playing at Bournemouth he'd stay at Branksome Towers Hotel. The Hampshire secretary then was George Muir, and he'd come into the dressing-room and say, 'Now, my Lord, what are your expenses for this match?' And Tennyson would say, 'My hotel bill this morning was sixty-seven pounds (and we're talking about 1934–35) – give me a tenner, and we'll call it quits.' Now, that was the sort of thing he did. He knew Hampshire had no money, and he wouldn't charge them.

All my home games never cost them a penny. My father used to pay the expenses. I was very, very lucky, and I'm so pleased that I played in the thirties because I think that was the best time.

Tennyson was responsible for me opening the innings. In 1934, against the Australians, at Southampton. He came into the dressing-room and said, 'Well, I've won the toss, and we're batting. You're going in first, Dick.' I didn't have time to wet my trousers or anything, and from then on I went in first, but he wasn't responsible for me coming into the side.

I'd played a lot of Club and Ground matches, and I was the local boy from Bournemouth School, and I was picked to play in the last two matches of the Bournemouth Festival in 1931. Then I started playing at the beginning of the following season, 1932, and I didn't do so well so I suggested I should drop out.

The man really responsible for me being in the side as a regular was Philip Mead who had the most terrible varicose veins. Hampshire came down to Bournemouth to play the last match of the 1933 season, against Essex. I was at business. We were in the food trade. Out of the blue, the secretary came on the phone and said, 'Can you possibly come and help us out, Dick. Phil Mead's varicose veins have burst, and there is no way he can play.' So I had a word with my father who was Chairman of the Company, and he asked how long it would take me to get home and collect my clothes. Anyway, I got to Dean Park on time and made 159, and I think I was in the side from then on. So I always thanked Phil Mead for his burst varicose veins.

> R. H. Moore had a somewhat fiery baptism to first-class cricket, but within five years of his debut, although still a very young man, he was county captain.

When I came into the side in 1931 the first game was against Leicestershire, and George Geary got me out, and the second was against Larwood and Voce, which was something of a jump for a schoolboy. There was once at Trent Bridge when Arthur Carr caught me at first slip off Larwood, and I reckon he was half-way to the pavilion when he caught me. Of course, I'd never seen anything so quick. He didn't need to bounce the ball then. He just bowled so beautifully. He moved the ball about. He didn't often have to bounce it in this country. He was such a great bowler, and you were almost mesmerized by his run-up to the wicket for starters. It was such a lovely run-up, everything in proper proportion.

Hampshire were a good side. When I became captain in 1936 I was twenty-two-and-a-half. Well, I had people like Phil Mead, Alec Kennedy, Stuart Boyes, John Arnold – these were my senior professionals. They were all very good really. Alec Kennedy was the only one just a little inclined to be prickly, but they respected anything I suggested we did. If there were difficult decisions to be made, I always had a word with Alec Kennedy although he was then in his last season and played little, but he was the senior professional, and really they were very, very good.

The others, of course, were no trouble at all, but I'd still got some of the old people who obviously wondered who this young chap was who was taking over, and there was dear old Philip Mead. He kept the pub down the road at Bear Cross, and he had two sons, and, unfortunately, they did not look after things while he was playing cricket so eventually he couldn't pay for the beer at the pub, and the brewers kicked him out. But the day he knew they were in taking all the furniture out and so on, he was busy making 100 at Dean Park. He had that sort of concentration.

He was marvellous. He liked to reach his 50 or 100 with a single, and you had to be on the look out for it. Johnny Arnold used to say that as they crossed in the middle of a quick single Phil would say, 'Good luck!'

My father took me to Southampton when I was about sixteen. Phil Mead had a sports shop there with a man called Toomer, Mead and Toomer. Of course, Phil wasn't there very often. He just gave his name. But that particular day he was there, and so we selected a bat, and he got me to play a few shots. A few years later, I was captaining the side he was in. It was rather unique.

He was very good except that we had quite a lot of trouble with him getting on the train without paying for his ticket. The train would be standing at Southampton station, and everyone would be there but Philip. We had to buy our own tickets then. No one bought them all for us. Just before the train went out Phil would rush in and say, 'I'm a bit late. I'll have to get my ticket at the other end.' When we got to the other end we all trooped out, and the ticket-collector took the tickets, and there was one short all the time, but it was not noticed.

> Richard Moore maintains that the joyful cricket which Tennyson insisted upon has become a Hampshire tradition, and that it is still very much alive.

We always had the attitude that we would go for a win if possible, and Hampshire have carried on that attitude. Recently, against Worcestershire, they declared overnight some 130/150 behind in order to make a game of it, but, of course, it's all totally different now. I don't know whether I could cope at present with knowing how many runs we had to get to get so many points and how many wickets we had to get. You need to be a walking computer.

I always believed in entertaining the crowd. They are the people who provide the money, or were, and they were entitled to be entertained. It's totally different now. I don't know what proportion of gate receipts contribute towards finances. It's mainly sponsors now, but there'd be no sponsors without the crowds.

The one-day game has been a great boon. Many people like to see one-day cricket and find five days a bore, but it's a mixed blessing in my estimation. Some of the shots you see the batsmen playing these days are one-day shots, and they don't appear to have the sense to know when they're playing in a one-day game or three-day.

> On 28 July 1937, R. H. Moore hit the highest score ever made for Hampshire, and one of the dozen highest scores ever made in county cricket.

The day I got my 316 against Warwickshire, Eddie Paynter got 322 for Lancashire against Sussex just down the coast. That's still a record, two 300s on the same day. I hadn't had a very good season up to then. I'd had to struggle for my runs, and I'd always said to the chaps, 'If ever I get in, if ever I really get in, I've got to make sure I stay there.' So we came to this match, and by lunch time I'd got 100. At lunch, the pros all said, 'Now don't forget what you said, skipper. If you ever get in there, you're going to stay there. Get your head down after lunch.'

So, OK, after lunch, I got my head down. Between lunch and tea, I got 80-something. I didn't get 100. We came to tea, and they all told me to carry on and not to forget what I'd said. And all the time, they were coming in at the other end, having a swing and getting out. It suddenly dawned on me what was happening. Cecil Paris was the only one who dug himself in. He made 73 and stayed there. We got 509 in the day. I got 316, and Cecil got his 73, that's almost 400, so you can see what the rest did.

On the next day, the ball started to turn, and Bob Wyatt was quite certain we'd fixed the wicket overnight. He said, 'You've done something to this wicket, Dick.' I said, 'Don't be silly, Bob, that's a typical Bournemouth wicket. It's beautiful.'

The first half-hour, forty-five minutes in the morning, there's a bit of grass, a bit of dew, and there's movement. After that it's just lovely. But the second day against Warwickshire, the ball turned, and we had three good left-arm spin bowlers, and we got 'em twice in the day. No trouble, but if you were to ask Bob Wyatt now, he'd still say they did something about the wicket.

Like Mitchell-Innes and 'Hopper' Levett, R. H. Moore reviews today's pre-match training sessions with some scepticism.

It amuses me today when I see Mark Nicholas have the team out training before a match. One day, our President, Sir Russell Bencraft, said to me, 'Why aren't the pros sitting out getting used to the light, Dick?' I said, 'I'm not quite sure, Sir Russell.' He said, 'Well, go and find out. See why they aren't.'

Well, of course, I knew exactly what the situation was, and when I went in Phil Mead was sound asleep lying on the bench inside, and others were doing the same thing. I said, 'I'm sorry, Phil, but Sir Russell thinks that you ought to be getting used to the light.' You can imagine what he said, can't you. Anyway, that was how we got prepared in those days. But you know, by and large, we seemed to be fit, and we played six days. All right, we didn't have any of this one-day stuff, apart from the odd charity

[164]

match. I think I only had one pulled muscle, and I didn't suffer any broken fingers.

I think the fielding today is probably better. This is one of the things that has been said to be a result of one-day cricket. I suppose people try a bit more. When you see this lad Lewis in the England side he is a magnificent field, and he obviously saves a lot of runs. They do dive and stop the ball going for four, which you didn't see in my time, but I don't think the catching is any better now than it was. We had probably the best short-leg fielder in the country, Stuart Boyes, and he used to pick up brilliant catches.

The only time we were a bit bothered in the Hampshire side in one match, I said to Cecil Paris, 'We seem to be a bit short in the field, Cecil. Who do you think it is?' He said, 'Have you seen where Phil Mead is standing at first-slip?' I said, 'No, I'll have a look when I get down the other end.'

Well, he was standing right behind the wicket-keeper. He certainly wouldn't get in the way of the ball when it came to him. I said, 'OK, I'll have to alter it.' So it was a question of saying, 'Phil, I think it would be better if you fielded at mid-off. Mr Paris and I are going to turn ourselves into slip-fielders.'

That took a bit of doing, and we took an awful lot of stick from the crowd, but we did make ourselves into slip-fielders, and, of course, it's a wonderful place to field, particularly when you've got a lot of good slow bowlers in the side. After that we weren't bad at all, but that solved the problem of being one short in the field with dear old Philip Mead tucked behind McCorkell, the wicket-keeper.

> Like others, Richard Moore valued the great players of his time, and he gives another dimension in his assessment of such men as Hammond and Jardine.

Two of the bowlers of that time whom I rated very highly were the West Indian pair, Martindale and Constantine. They were very quick and very lively, and I believe they even gave Wally Hammond some trouble. Now there was a cricketer of all-round ability. He was no mean bowler, brilliant slip-fielder and, of course, as a batsman second to none, well against slow bowling. I said to him,

[165]

'You seem to have so much time to play the slow bowlers, Wally. What's the situation?'

He said, 'I can see the ball spinning in the air.' I said that I didn't believe him. He said, 'I can. I can see it spinning.' So he knew which was the legger, and which was the top spinner or googly. I certainly could not do that. He was a very great cricketer. I didn't know much about his personal life, but I rated him above the rest as a cricketer.

And then there was Bradman, of course. In 1938, the Australians were playing us when he got his 1,000 runs in May. Towards the end of the day the weather was bad, and we gave him one or two down the leg-side but he didn't say, 'Thank you very much, now you can have my wicket.' He went on to get nearly 150 the next day.

There were so many good cricketers playing then. You take Morris Nichols of Essex. Nearly 2,000 runs and nearly 200 wickets every season, and he wasn't good enough to go to Australia. When people say the game was different in those days I just don't cotton on to it.

There were others, of course, who were fortunate to go to Australia. It depended on the balance of the side; what they thought they required; what the wickets were going to be like; whether they'd changed them in the period since we'd last been there – which they did.

Of course, when Wally Hammond was captain of the side the party went by boat in those days. The Australians met the boat at Fremantle or wherever, and they had a huge motor car on the quayside, and they said to Wally, 'Well, I don't suppose you want to be travelling by train, Wally. You'd like to have this car, wouldn't you?' So he and Bill Edrich drove everywhere by car in Australia, and, of course, they were always tired out. That was their best way of getting Wally out.

But Wally wasn't a good captain. I don't think he had that star quality like Douglas Jardine. Jardine had got it. He was determined to win back the Ashes in 1932–33. From what people told me, the first night the team were on board he got them all together and said, 'Right, gentlemen, now we're off to Australia. We can have a wonderful trip and enjoy ourselves, or we can win the Ashes. I am determined we will win the Ashes. Good night. We'll meet again tomorrow.'

That was the first meeting. The next day the team met, and Jardine had a blackboard upon which he proceeded to map out the basis of 'leg theory'. He was determined to win. People didn't approve of how he did it, 'Gubby' Allen for one, but when you see those films of Larwood bowling there – the number of times that Australian batsmen ducked into balls that didn't get above stump high! Today's bowling would be outrageous by comparison.

Percy Fender was OK as a captain, but he seemed to me a very dour sort of chap, and, of course, there was Percy Chapman who was such a fine cricketer and captain in his prime. I remember one time at Lord's, one of the times we had a box. People were drifting away at the end, and at the top of the pavilion dear old Percy Chapman was sitting on his own looking down at Lord's, having had too much to drink, and I thought what a sad sight. Here's a man who has been a magnificent cricketer, idol of the crowd, and he's come to this situation now, and there he is, and nobody's caring about him at all. And it was so sad to see him. Very sad.

Brian Sellers of Yorkshire was a great captain, I always thought that, and the Surrey man, Surridge, but he had a great side. When you've got a good side you've still got to be a good captain, but you probably don't have to be quite so good. After all, it's easier to win with a good side.

We invariably played Yorkshire at Bournemouth in the last match of the season, and they wanted to win the match in order to win the championship, and they nearly always did. Sellers was not really quite good enough to be in that Yorkshire side as a player, almost, but not quite, but for his captaincy he *was*. They respected him – oh, hell they did! People like Morris Leyland, Herbert Sutcliffe and the rest. There was no messing about. He had a good tactical sense, and there was his enthusiasm and his ability to use his bowlers. But he had a fine side. They were far and away the best side of the thirties, far above anyone else. Of course, they had

[167]

Hedley Verity and Bill Bowes, and Leonard Hutton. Boycott, of course, came much later. Boycott's trouble was he couldn't play for the side, but he was a very fine cricketer. I think there would have been one or two nasty incidents if Sellers had been his captain.

In our side, Lionel Tennyson used to send out a note to people like Jim Bailey who was being bogged down at one end. Lionel would send out a note saying, 'Either hit out or get out. Don't stay around doing what you're doing.'

Lionel wasn't a great captain, but he was a great character. He was very popular. He was one of the last of the swashbuckling captains. Hampshire's later answer to him was Ingleby-Mackenzie. He was the next Lionel. Lionel had his moments in the Gregory— McDonald tour of 1921 when he batted one-handed in a Test. Geoffrey Lowndes succeeded him as captain.

Lionel used to take one or two sides abroad, paid for by other people, of course, and he used to ask so many people during the season if they'd like to come that when it came to getting the side together he found that he had about sixty people willing to go. Of course, it was then a case of writing to say, 'I'm sorry, but there's no room for you.' He allowed players to take their wives on one or two of those tours, but he said, 'Never again will I allow wives to come because I had more trouble from the wives than the men.' It was a question of Percy's not playing today. Why isn't he playing? Percy wasn't complaining, but the wife was wondering why her husband wasn't in the side. So Lionel would never take women again.

> Richard Moore succeeded Lowndes as captain in 1936 and led the side for two seasons. He remains proud of what he was able to achieve for the Hampshire professionals during his brief tenure of office.

There wasn't really any opposition to me taking over from Lowndes even though I was very young. W. K. Pearce, who was vice-chairman of the committee at Hampshire and who was very friendly with Cecil Paris, did try to talk me out of the captain role and let Cecil be captain before me. I don't know, for some reason or other, because I'm not usually a dogmatic sort of person, I said, 'Well, I think I really am a bit ahead of Cecil, and I'm going to carry on for a couple of years, and he'll be able to take over when I've left.'

So that was the only opposition. It wasn't serious. Cecil and I were the best of friends and still are, and he took over from me in 1938. By then, I felt I'd been so fortunate to play all those years, and I hadn't really done an awful lot of work. I felt I should give up, but I continued playing. In fact, I topped the batting averages in 1938.

The trouble is that people today believe that all the amateurs in the thirties had lots of money. That was not the case. It wasn't the case with me, but I was fortunate that I had a father who picked up the bills. In those days, a lot of people played because they worked for firms who were pleased to have somebody who was involved in first-class cricket and were prepared to let him have time off and to continue paying his salary. After a bit that went out of fashion, although I think it's coming back despite the fact that there are no amateurs playing.

A company employing Michael Atherton would be only too pleased they'd got him on the books. He's a good cricketer. He's got the temperament, and he really is correct. He's the model for young people to watch, and he'll carry on all day without getting tired.

George Brown was a cricketer who had that sort of temperament. He was quite a lovable character, and a very fine all-round cricketer for Hampshire. He kept wicket, bowled and was very good at mid-off. He could let the ball run past him, turn round, pick it up and run somebody out. He was tough. We went up to Trent Bridge to play Nottinghamshire. He was getting towards the end of his days then, and he was going in first, and he was all wrapped up with towels around his thighs. One didn't have the proper thigh pads in those days. Old George had all kinds of wrapping around him, and about the fifth ball of the first over Larwood hit him high up. He turned round towards the pavilion and smiled at us as if to say, 'I've got all the padding I want.' Then he turned back to take his stance and fell flat on his face because his leg had gone completely

[169]

numb. He was a rough diamond, but a very pleasant man – good value.

He had retired by the time I became captain, and there have always been criticisms of the way in which pros were treated at the end of their careers. I think they were treated badly. Kent sacked 'Tich' Freeman the year he *only* took 100 wickets.

People have asked me when Philip Mead was sacked in 1936 whether or not it was discussed with me if he should be taken on again, and quite honestly I can't remember anyone asking me if we should keep him on. The next year he just wasn't there.

With Hampshire, the pros were paid so much in the week while they were playing and had nothing in the winter. I take pride in the fact that I said to the committee, 'I don't think this is quite right. A lot of these boys don't have jobs in the winter. I think it would be better if we could pay them – I think it was something like five pounds a week all the year round – and then pay them extra in the summer when they are paying for hotel bills.'

In fact, this is what they did, and those who didn't have a job in the winter did have something coming in instead of being entirely on the dole.

The other thing I managed to alter was the talent money that we used to pay in those days. There used to be so much for 50, so much for 5 wickets, a very small sum, and again I said to the committee, 'You know, somebody coming in at five-thirty in the afternoon when the opposition are getting pretty tired and it's no trouble to get 50 is not really entitled to talent money above the man who's come in first and plays the new ball, and plays it well, but doesn't make 50. And the same with wickets. When the wicket suddenly goes bad and takes spin it's easier to get wickets. Wouldn't it be better if you told me how much money you're prepared to pay for talent money, and then let me decide when I think somebody's entitled to it. If the pros don't agree with it, they'll say so.' But it proved to be quite right.

I wasn't entitled to talent money, but in one match against Yorkshire in 1932, I stayed in over two hours against Verity and George Macaulay on a turning wicket and made 19. One of the

Yorkshire papers wrote, 'After tea Moore removed his sweater and quickly increased his score from 5 to 6.' But it was pretty devastating bowling, and Verity on a sticky wicket was very difficult indeed.

If I had been a pro, I would have been entitled to talent money then because I helped the side at a time of great difficulty whereas 50 on a fine day in late afternoon wouldn't mean so much.

They were good days.

6

A MOST ENJOYABLE
EXPERIENCE

Sir Donald Bradman

H. G. Owen-Smith

T. N. Pearce

W. B. Morris

H. Sharp

B. Brocklehurst

Stuart Surridge

The recollections of those who played cricket in the thirties invariably involve the name of Don Bradman who, in the eyes of the majority, remains one of the three greatest, if not the greatest batsman the game has seen.

He made his Test debut, against England, at Brisbane, in November 1928. He scored 18 and 1 and was dropped from the second Test. Recalled for the third Test, he hit 79 and 112, and another century followed in the last match of the series. The finest career that Test cricket has known had begun.

At Headingley in 1930 he hit 334, 309 of them on the opening day, and in five Tests in the series he scored a record 974 runs, average 139.14. He led Australia for the first time in the 1936–37 series, and he created another record by leading his side to victory in the rubber after they had been beaten in the first two of the five Tests. In 1934, he had again dominated the series in England and hit a second triple century at Headingley.

He captained one of the weaker Australian sides in England in 1938, but they drew the series in which he hit three centuries in the three games in which he batted. He also reached 1,000 runs in first-class cricket before the end of May, as R. H. Moore has recalled.

He returned to lead Australia after the war, and the side he brought to England in 1948 was, in the opinion of many, the best Test side in living memory. He played his last Test match at the Oval at the end of that 1948 series and was bowled second ball by Eric Hollies, the Warwickshire leg-break bowler. Had Bradman scored four in that match, it would have brought his Test aggregate to exactly 7,000 runs and his Test average to 100.

In all cricket, he hit 28,067 runs, average 95.14, with a highest score of 452 not out for New South Wales against Queensland. This was one of 117 first-class centuries. No other cricketer has approached his career average either for Test matches or for first-class games. From 1930 until 1948, he strode the cricket world like a Colossus.

Bradman played with and against some of the greatest bowlers the game has known – Larwood and Voce; Miller and Lindwall; Gregory and McDonald – and his assessment of them is a valuable one.

The best ball I ever received was from the big Englishman Alec Bedser in the Adelaide Test of 1946–47. That was the game in which our opener Arthur Morris, and the Englishman Denis Compton both hit hundreds in each innings. The ball swerved in towards the leg stump and upon pitching it cut away and hit the top of the off-stump.

Bedser was a marvellous bowler, great stamina, and he ranks alongside Maurice Tate, the man who trapped me l.b.w. for 18 in my first Test innings at the Exhibition Ground in Brisbane in 1928. Bedser and Tate were men whose stout hearts were only matched by their long-suffering bodies.

In all the great fast bowling combinations, there was always one of the pair who had to take on the task of bowling into the wind. McDonald, Voce and Miller were the men who took on that job. Each had the remarkable ability to swing the ball and each would have been a wonderful bowler on his own with the wind. They all possessed a superb physique. Ted McDonald with the wind and Maurice Tate into it would have satisfied me beyond doubt as an opening pair.

In spite of all these great pace bowlers, of all the bowlers I played with and against, I rate Bill O'Reilly number one. In my opinion, the hardest ball to play is the one which turns from the leg to the off and this was Bill's stock delivery. He persistently bowled at a right-hander's leg stump and, when perfectly pitched, that ball would take the off-bail. There is precious little answer to such a delivery. The batsman usually gets an outside edge or the ball clips the off-stump.

Bill also bowled a magnificent 'Bosey', the wrong 'un, which was hard to pick and which he aimed at the middle and leg-stumps. It was fractionally slower than his leg-break and usually dropped a little in flight and 'sat up' to entice a catch to one of his two short-leg fieldsmen.

[176]

These two deliveries, combined with great accuracy and unrelenting hostility, were enough to test the greatest of batsmen – particularly as his leg-break was bowled at medium pace, quicker than the normal run of slow bowlers, thereby making it extremely difficult for a batsman to use his feet as a counter measure. Bill will always remain, in my book, the greatest of all.

> O'Reilly's outstanding leg-spin partner was Clarrie Grimmett who toured England in 1926, 1930 and 1934 and had immense success in the Test series, capturing 29 wickets in 1930 and 25 in 1934. Although he had reached the veteran stage, Grimmett was seen as a certainty for the 1938 tour of England, but he was a surprising omission from the party.

Grimmett was the greatest slow leg-spinner I ever saw. He had remarkable accuracy for a bowler of his type, and I once saw Grimmett bowl five successive maidens with a wet ball.

I know that Tiger has never forgiven the selectors for not selecting Grimmett for the 1938 tour of England, but I don't think we made a mistake in taking Frank Ward instead of Grimmett. We had O'Reilly himself as our spearhead spinner. Fleetwood-Smith was the up and coming young spin bowler, and it was out of Frank Ward and Grimmett for the number three spot in the touring team. There was simply no room for a fourth spin bowler.

> While Bradman is adamant in his placing of 'Tiger' Bill O'Reilly as the greatest bowler he knew he is more reluctant to place any one batsman above another.

Hammond was a great player; a strong driver with good technique and temperament. And Bill Ponsford was among the very great. Bill was a run machine. Apart from the hook and the pull shots his style was similar to mine. His bat always seemed to be so much wider than anyone else's: of course, it wasn't, but it seemed that way to me, and must have seemed even more so to the bowlers. Clarrie Grimmett always maintained that Ponsford was the batsman he least liked bowling against.

The best innings I ever saw in Australia was Gary Sobers' 254 for the World XI against Australia in the second innings at Melbourne. That was the series we'd had to arrange when the South African tour was cancelled in 1971–72. He just cut loose and hammered our attack into submission.

The greatest innings I have ever seen and would ever hope to see was Stan McCabe's 232 for Australia against England at Nottingham in 1938. Stan had everything: he had grace in his shots; he had power in his shots; and he had certainty in his stroke play. For the last wicket he and Fleetwood-Smith put on 77 runs in twenty-eight minutes, of which McCabe got 72. And they had five fieldsmen round the boundary for most of the time.

It was one of three truly great Test match innings Stan played. The others were his 187 in Sydney, against England, in 1932–33, and his 149 against South Africa at Durban in 1935–36. I didn't go to South Africa, but the players who did and saw his innings at Nottingham believe Stan's 232 to be the best of those three great knocks.

When he came off the ground at Trent Bridge, caught by Compton off the spin of Verity, he was shaking and sweating like a thoroughbred racehorse.

I took his hand and shook it and said, 'Congratulations, Stan. I wish I could play an innings like the one you played today.' And I meant it.

I had a great admiration for Bill Brown, and I pushed for his inclusion in the 1934 side. I think my support of him was vindicated four years later when he hit a magnificent unbeaten 206 at Lord's.

At Trent Bridge, he and I had put on 170 for the second wicket and helped to save the match, and Bill got 133. Then, in the next Test, at Lord's, he carried his bat through the innings for a double century. It was an outstanding knock. He really showed his worth that day.

In the last Test of that series, Hutton hit his 364 at the Oval. It was proof of Yorkshire determination. It was the longest and most remarkable innings for concentration that I have ever seen. From memory I think he batted for something like 800 minutes. Hutton was a beautiful player; lovely technique.

[178]

I think that the four greatest cricket teams in Test history were Joe Darling's 1902 team, Warwick Armstrong's 1921 team, the West Indies teams under Clive Lloyd in the nineteen-seventies, and my 1948 side.

Armstrong, who was a member of the 1902 team and who led the 1921 side, once said that the 1902 eleven could have whipped twenty-two of the 1921 team, and that's high praise from one who was a member of both outfits. I played against most of the people who played in the 1921 side, and I also watched much of the nineteen-seventies West Indians; however, I do think my 1948 side was better balanced than Lloyd's teams.

The West Indians based their attack exclusively on pace bowling. We had a better balance in attack, I think, to cope with the varying pitch conditions. In batting, we had Sid Barnes, Neil Harvey, Lindsay Hassett, and Arthur Morris who, in 1948, was as good a left-hand batsman as there has been. Then in our bowling we had Lindwall and Miller, the gangling, but very talented Bill Johnston, and Ernie Toshack, who bowled left-arm medium aimed at the leg stump. We also had the flighty off-spin of Ian Johnson.

Men like Neil Harvey were fine fielders, and I would place Don Tallon as the top wicket-keeper, above Godfrey Evans, Alan Knott, Bob Taylor, Wally Grout and Bert Oldfield.

When Bradman retired from Test cricket in 1948 he was succeeded as captain of Australia by Lindsay Hassett who led the side to triumph in South Africa in 1949–50. H. G. 'Tuppy' Owen-Smith played for Western Province against the tourists.

I didn't come up against any Australian side until I came back to South Africa after the war. That was Lindsay Hassett's team although Hassett didn't play much. My friend Arthur Morris was captain most of the time. I played for Western Province. I was in medical practice in Cape Town so I had no time for net practice and had a couple of days off to play.

Jack Cheetham got 98 against the Australians and batted well, and got knocked about by Keith Miller. He ended up being caught by Neil Harvey off Keith Miller at point. Miller started bowling

[179]

bouncers at him one after the other. He was getting fed up, and showing it, and about the fourth bouncer Jack Cheetham came down the wicket at Miller and had a bash at it. It was a jolly good hit, and it looked a four all the way, but Neil Harvey jumped in the air and caught him.

Neil Harvey was a very lively cricketer. He'd settle down then he was down the wicket after them, and he hit the ball tremendously hard, beautiful timing, beautiful footwork. He was really a very great cricketer.

Jack Cheetham was a useful fielder, and he used to bowl leg-breaks and googlies, but he gave that up. He was a difficult batsman to dislodge. I wouldn't say he was a great batsman, and he wasn't an attractive batsman, but he had endless patience, and he could stay there all day. He had a very good knowledge of cricket and great determination. He was very determined to succeed when he led the side to Australia, and nobody gave South Africa a chance.

I came in when Harvey caught Cheetham out, and first ball Keith Miller bowled to me, he bowled on my leg stump, just short of a length. It got up, and I played back and tried to turn it round the corner or something, but it got me on the thigh, and we didn't wear thigh pads in those days.

Arthur Morris came up with a big smile and said, 'Poor old sod, never mind.' I've never forgotten that. It was interesting, and great fun.

Miller could bowl all sorts of things. He'd bowl one round arm: next one very fast: then an off-spinner. You never knew what was coming up next – shortish run, tallish fellow, hair flowing. Ray Lindwall bowled me out. I thought he yorked me, but Keith Miller said I was late on it. He varied his pace so much.

When they came back in 1957–58 I had to look after them. They had another good bowler, left-armer, Alan Davidson. There was always something wrong with him, biggest neurotic, always his shin bones or something. You'd see him run up to bowl, and there was nothing wrong with him, but he was always lying on the massage table.

I believe at the end of the tour they had a get-together and made a presentation to Davidson. It was a tiny little masseur's table, and it was presented to him by both sides.

> While Australia had the strength of Bradman and Hassett, and South Africa made a remarkable impact under the captaincy of Jack Cheetham, England searched for a leader as fewer and fewer amateurs could give their time to the game. Wally Hammond retired at the end of the tour of Australia and New Zealand, 1946–47. Norman Yardley succeeded him, but he was unable to take the team to West Indies, 1947–48, and 'Gubby' Allen, forty-five years old and an infrequent participator in county cricket, captained the side.
>
> This was a surprising choice, not least to Tom Pearce, the Essex captain for much of the time between 1933 and 1950, and later a Test selector.

I was very lucky because I was in the wine business and working for Trayton Grinter who was a great cricket enthusiast. He was wounded in the First World War, and he could hardly use his left arm, but he went on playing club cricket, and they reckon he scored about 200 centuries. He had played a few games for Essex, and he was very happy to make it possible for me to play.

We had a good side in the thirties, and I believe that if Leonard Crawley could have played regularly, we might well have won the Championship. Jack O'Connor was a very good batsman. He could always read people like 'Tich' Freeman. They gave him no problems at all. I never knew which way the ball was going to turn, but I used to try to play straight, and the ball would go off the edge for four, and poor old 'Tich' would be tearing his hair out, and I couldn't help laughing.

Morris Nichols was a very good player, fine bowler, but he had to do so much work. He always used to take his dancing pumps with him in his cricket bag when we were playing away. He was very well endowed for that sort of thing.

We came across some great characters. There was Tom Lowry who played for Somerset and then captained New Zealand. He was

[181]

Percy Chapman's brother-in-law, and, like Percy, he enjoyed life. The social side of things was very important then. I remember one evening at the old Palace Hotel in Southend, there was a group of us, and Tom carried down from the first floor a huge cigarette machine, and it took four porters to lift it and carry it back up the next morning. He was a very strong man. Sometimes kept wicket and used to talk to you all the time you were batting.

I was able to play a bit when I was in the army during the war, and Essex asked me to captain again in 1946 because Denys Wilcox wasn't available, and Stephenson had moved. I was forty, but I was happy to do it for a couple of years. MCC were sending the team to West Indies, 1947–48, and Norman Yardley couldn't go, and many of the chaps like Denis Compton had been away from home a long time during the war and didn't want to go. Plum Warner asked me if I would take the side. I made all the arrangements at work, and everyone was delighted. Then one evening I bought the *Evening News*, and I read that 'Gubby' Allen was to captain England in the West Indies. And neither Warner nor anyone else ever said a word to me about it.

> In that period immediately after the Second World War, there was a tremendous enthusiasm for county cricket and attendances were high. Many of the leading players – Hutton, Compton, Hardstaff, Edrich – had lost valuable years to the war; others – Verity, Farnes, Eckersley, Turnbull – had lost their lives.
>
> The England sides of 1946 and 1947 contained several veterans. Bowes and Gover played against India in 1946, and Voce went to Australia in 1946–47. Some newcomers appeared, like Alec Bedser and Godfrey Evans, while others struggled to establish themselves in county cricket. Among them was Bill Morris, an all-rounder who played forty-eight times for Essex between 1946 and 1950.

I learned the hard way. At Ilford, in 1946, I took 3 for 4 against Somerset, and we won an exciting match. It was our first win of the season, and I wasn't picked again for another six weeks.

[182]

I learned about how to behave, too. We were playing Lancashire at Blackpool, and I was given out leg-before to a half appeal when I had hit the ball. I stood there astonished for a moment, and when I got back to the dressing room the old pros said to me, 'You stayed there too long, son. He'll have you for it.'

I didn't know what they meant. We didn't come up against the same umpire for another month, and then he gave me out the first time the ball hit my pads. I understood then. Captains used to give reports on umpires, and Cyril Washbrook once told me that when he became captain of Lancashire he reckoned it was worth 300 runs a year.

I began to get fewer and fewer chances as more and more amateurs made themselves available and two or three of us had to stand down to accommodate them.

Bill Morris became a noted coach, helping greatly in the evolution of the outstanding Essex side of the nineteen-eighties, and playing an important part in Graham Gooch's development into a batsman of world class. One of those who coached with Morris at Ilford was Harry Sharp who later became the Middlesex scorer.

Sharp played for Middlesex from 1946 until 1955, but he did not establish a regular place in the eleven until 1948, 1949. In 1947, the memorable year in which through the great deeds of Compton and Edrich Middlesex won the Championship, Harry Sharp played in only three matches. The first of those appearances was at Cheltenham on 16 and 18 August, and although he was later to hit ten first-class centuries and reach 1,000 runs in a season on three occasions, he remembers that game as his most exciting and the one, probably, of which he is most proud.

With both sides having played 21 of their 26 matches, Gloucestershire led Middlesex by four points before the start of the vital game at Cheltenham where, at the time, there was a wicket noted for taking spin. Unfortunately, the match clashed with the fifth Test match between England and South Africa at

[183]

the Oval, and Middlesex were deprived of the services of Denis Compton and Jack Robertson, both of whom were in the England side. Bill Edrich, too, had been chosen for the Test, but he had informed the selectors that he would be unable to bowl and so was omitted. Middlesex played him just as a batsman, and they brought in Harry Sharp.

It was my first game of the season, and it was only the second championship game I had ever played in. Laurie Gray was our only quick bowler, but Jack Young had done most of the bowling all season anyway. I was in the side because Denis was playing at the Oval and the Cheltenham pitch always helped the spinners in those days. I could bat a bit and bowled off-breaks.

The ground was packed. There were coach-loads of supporters came down, and when we went out to look at the wicket there were long queues outside the ground. One look at the pitch told us it would be a good day for the spinners, and it was important who won the toss. Mr Robins won it, and we batted. As Jack Robertson was also in the England side, Bill Edrich opened with Syd Brown, and he got 50, but we were 112 for 7 when I went in.

The quicker bowlers had done nothing, but Tom Goddard and Sam Cook had got among our middle order. Jim Sims was batting when I went in, and he'd already hit Tom Goddard for a couple of fours. Jim always spoke out of the side of his mouth, and he came up to me and said, 'I'll do 'em, Harry. Don't let 'em get you out.' They didn't get me out, and Jim and Jack Young had a go at Tom Goddard.

He was a great bowler, but he used to get very upset because he thought he ought to have a wicket every ball, and he wasn't very happy when Jim and Jack clouted a few fours. We were all out by the middle afternoon, for 180, but they didn't do any better.

Laurie Gray only bowled a couple of overs, and then it was Jim Sims with his leg-breaks and Jack Young with his left-arm. They bowled them out for 153, and we were batting again before the end of the day.

We had only ten minutes before the close, but we lost Bill who was leg-before to Tom Goddard. Mr Robins had said to me, 'You were not out in the first innings, Harry, get your pads on. You're in if a wicket falls.' So I was in at number three, but I had only a couple of balls to face on the Saturday evening.

There was another big crowd on the Monday, and the pitch was getting no easier. Tom Goddard bowled Syd Brown, and Mr Mann was stumped, but then Mr Robins came in. The ball was turning so much that I'd worked out exactly what I would do with Tom Goddard's off-breaks. I knew that when he pitched in line with the stumps it would turn away down the leg-side so I went with the tide and helped the ball on its way. I managed a few fours, and Mr Robins was always one to hit the ball. We managed to put on 70, and he got 45 and I got 46, but nobody else after us reached double figures, and we were all out for 141.

It was still touch and go because they only needed 169 to win, but we knew they'd have a hard job getting them because we could bowl well, and we fielded well. Laurie Gray was injured and couldn't bowl, but I don't think that he would have been used anyway.

Jack Young and Jim Sims opened the bowling, and they got rid of Mr Allen and Charlie Barnett. We were very pleased to see the back of Charlie, because he could hit a ball when he got going. Then Jack Crapp dug in with Bill Neale, who was a very experienced pro, and we were getting a bit worried.

Mr Robins came up to me and said, 'You're bowling. Just keep it tight.' He was right because you didn't have to rub the skin off your fingers to spin the ball on that pitch. It turned itself most of the time. I just tried to drop it on a length. It worked. I had Bill Neale taken at short-leg, and then I had George Emmett and Arthur Wilson, who was a left-hander, caught behind by Leslie Compton. All three went down for a couple of runs. As soon as they got after me, Jim Sims came back on, and it was all over very soon.

I played in the next match against Derbyshire which we won, and then I played against Northants at Lord's a couple of weeks later, and we won that and made sure of the Championship. I played quite a lot in the seasons after that, but I'll never forget that game at Cheltenham.

> By the time that Harry Sharp retired from first-class cricket at the end of the 1955 season much had begun to change in the game. Gloucestershire, Leicestershire, Northamptonshire and Warwickshire had professional captains, since amateurs found it increasingly difficult to give their time to the game and as social attitudes were changing in the post-war climate.
>
> One who gave his time to captain a first-class county was Ben Brocklehurst who led Somerset in 1953 and 1954.

Having played a season for Somerset 2nd XI in 1951, I played for half the 1952 season for the first team and then left to go back to the harvest on my farm.

The President of Somerset wrote to me at the end of the season to say the committee had invited me to captain the side in 1953. My priorities were to raise team morale, imbue a fighting spirit and get rid of the lackadaisical approach which had been allowed to creep in.

Having only played a handful of first-class matches, I accepted the challenge with some reservations and with the proviso that I would do it for one year. Despite a season's struggle, the committee asked me to lead the team again in 1954.

At the end of the 1953 season, my first as captain of Somerset, there was something of a rebellion in the county because the side was not doing well. It was led by Ron Roberts who was a good journalist and a friend and who made it quite clear that the rebellion was not directed at me and that they wanted me to captain the side once they had brought about changes.

The side needed strengthening, and I had heard that Bill Alley, the Australian, wanted to play county cricket, so I went up to Lancashire to see him in his cottage in the middle of winter. He said he'd love to play for Somerset, but that he had a contract with Blackpool, so I said I would go and see the chairman. He was a very nice chap, and I told him we wouldn't interfere until Alley had finished his contract, but that when he'd finished we would like to take him on. I felt that it was only fair that we should put our cards on the table. He said, 'Well, that's all right, and it's very nice of you to put it like that, but you can't see Bill Alley.' So I said, 'Well, I'm awfully sorry, but I saw him last night.'

He hit the roof, but he calmed down when I said that we had no idea of trying to make him break his contract. We were just trying to look ahead two or three years and hoping that he would come – which indeed he did – four years later. But I got an awful rocket from members of the committee who said, 'What do you mean by trying to rope in an old man like Bill Alley?' Seven years later, he got more runs for Somerset than anybody's ever got, over 3,000. I was the first chap to see him and I did the ground work which brought him to Somerset. On the way back, I went to see Colin McCool and roped him in, too, but neither of them was playing when I played.

Then there was a rumpus, and the rebels forced a meeting which was held in Weston-super-Mare. All the members turned up. It was an enormous gathering, and the committee, much to my embarrassment, because I was the good boy of the club in those days, asked me to speak on their behalf. I had reservations because I didn't agree with a fact that a rebel committee should throw them out at a time when we were struggling. I took the view that it was their fault for electing them committee members in the first place, and if they didn't like them, they shouldn't vote for them next time round.

> As well as helping to recruit players like Alley and McCool for the future, Ben Brocklehurst made very great efforts to give the side immediate strength, but he was thwarted by both committees, who would not release players, and by wives.
>
> At the meeting in Weston-super-Mare, he made this point when he addressed the gathering.

We heard about Lee, a Yorkshire opening batsman, and the secretary immediately got in touch with him, but, as a schoolmaster, he had to give three months' notice and could not play for us last year. We offered him terms for next year. He delayed in answering and eventually I went up to see him and found that another county had offered him terms before us. Although our terms were better and that on top of that, thanks to the Supporters' Club, we were able to offer him a rent-free house, he said that he could not accept because he was unable to persuade his wife to leave Yorkshire; so it's not only the players you've got to deal with, it's the *Mrs* as well.

> Charles Lee, in fact, enjoyed a successful career with Derbyshire from 1954 onwards and captained that county for two seasons. Somerset, having won only two matches in 1953 and having finished bottom of the County Championship, continued to seek replacements for players who were growing older and retiring.

The reason for the rebellion, of course, was lack of team success, but there was no point in hitting at that particular committee. It was the committee four years previously that had gone to sleep. And, of course, Arthur Wellard left. Robinson left. All the old timers had gone. And there was Harold Gimblett who had a nervous breakdown, dear fellow.

He was still there as senior pro – very sad. Unpredictable, but a brilliant player. There was an absurd situation when he was out for 0 and 5 when Yorkshire were playing down at Taunton. He went into the dressing room, packed his bags and said, 'I'm never going to play for Somerset again.' And he walked out of the gate with his cricket bag. Somebody ran up and told me what was going on. By that time he was out of the ground so I rushed up to the press box, which one could do in those days, and I said, 'Look, fellows, we've got a problem, but if you make a thing of it in the press, which you are perfectly entitled to do, we will have more of a problem because we'll never get him back. The poor chap's ill, but we can get him back, and the secretary (the Air Vice Marshal, Malcolm Taylor) and I will see him tomorrow, Sunday. We don't want anyone else there, and we'll talk to him like Dutch uncles. We'll say, 'Look. Have a rest for two or three weeks. We'll say that you're not particularly well. Come back and you can play as long

[188]

as you want to.' And the extraordinary thing was that in those days the press would honour that sort of thing, and they never said a word – the national press, the local press, the regional press – all round. But some bloody member of the committee got hold of it and leaked it to the press, and Harold never played for Somerset again.

He was very introverted, and he ought to have played for England more than the three times he did. He had one game, was chosen again, but had a carbuncle, or something like that – a boil. Most people wouldn't have worried about it and played, but he made a fuss, and he wasn't asked to play again. Hammond used to say his slip-fielding wasn't up to scratch, but, in fact, he was very sharp. He was a brilliant player, and if everybody had been quiet, done nothing about it and forgotten it, everything would have gone on as usual. It was just one member of the committee who let it slip. People do things for the wrong reason. They like to feel important.

> Not only did Ben Brocklehurst contribute much to Somerset cricket and to the welfare of cricket as a whole, he also made a business venture for which those who follow the game will remain eternally grateful.

At one time I was a farmer, and then I was in publishing with Mercury House. They published magazines, mostly technical journals. I was Managing Director of twenty-three of them, and brought in the *Cricketer* because Jim Swanton asked me to. It wasn't going very well at the time that it was brought into the fold of this large publishing organization. The chairman was an American called Philip Zimmerman who was a nice enough chap, but he didn't understand cricket, and all he was concerned about was the bottom line of the accounts. He called me in one day and said, 'The *Cricketer* isn't making money. Close it down!' So I said, 'Over my dead body. It's been going since 1921, and it's the voice of cricket throughout the world.'

There weren't any other cricket magazines at the time apart from Gordon Ross's *Cricket Monthly Playfair*, which we later bought up. At that time, we were living here in Ashurst, and I was tearing up and down to London by car or train. It was ghastly, and I was then fifty so I said, 'OK. We'll pack it in, and I'll take the *Cricketer* with me.' I bought it for peanuts. There was just my wife Belinda and I and a secretary. Jim Swanton and John Haslewood stuck with it as directors, of course, and we had a part-time editor, and we brought it up from there.

The circulation at the time I bought it was 13,500. We hadn't got any money really, but we had the subscriptions, about 5,000 of them. We had their money in advance and with it we bought the *Playfair*, which sounds a rather naughty thing to do, but we had our house at risk and everything else as back-up. They had a circulation of about 12,000 so they weren't making any money either. The sum of the two, funnily enough, was greater than the individual parts. We suddenly found we had a circulation in excess of 27,000, and eventually we got it up to 44,000, although it has dropped slightly now during the depression, like all magazines.

> During the Bath Festival in June 1954, Ben Brocklehurst told the Committee of Somerset County Cricket Club that he would have to resign at the end of the season because he had to earn a living. They tried to persuade him to continue, but, like others, he had no option but to forfeit cricket for business. In his short career, he met some of the great players of the immediate post-war period.

In my playing days, Len Hutton was captain of England, but not of Yorkshire. We all had the greatest admiration for him. I shall always remember that the very first match I played for Somerset was against Yorkshire at Taunton, and I scratched around and got 31, which was the top score on our side. The Yorkshire team was staying at the Castle Hotel, and, because I was living in Berkshire at the time, I used to stay there. I went into the bar, and Len came up to me and said, 'Well done! You didn't do so badly.' And I thought how wonderful that was, coming from him, such a great player. And then he said, 'One bit of advice I've got for you. You ought to oil your bat.' I thought that's a bloody stupid thing to say by a great man – you ought to oil your bat. They usually threw their bats away. They didn't bother to oil them. Then he added, 'You ought to oil your bat, particularly the edges.' And he shuffled away down the bar chuckling.

We became very friendly later. The Huttons always used to come here for Christmas, and his son Richard married my daughter. His wife Dorothy is a wonderful lady, and she was most supportive of him. Len owed her much. He was a charming chap in his later years. He was kind and warm, and I'm sure that's how he'd like to be remembered.

I suppose Boycott was his natural successor, but Boycott had a one-track mind. That's why he scored so many runs. He was always batting for Boycott, and he'd be top of the averages when Yorkshire were bottom of the county championship table. We had the same problem in Somerset with Botham and Richards doing well and Somerset down the bottom. Of course, if you are a professional cricketer and your livelihood depends upon it, your performances are all-important.

As an also-ran amateur, which I was, completely at the other end of the scale, I batted everywhere from number one to number eight. In fact, I batted in places where nobody else wanted to bat. When I batted low down in the order I either had to stay there for a day and a half in order to stave off defeat or I had ten minutes in which I had to get 100 to win the game, and that was impossible. The only time I ever started making runs was when I went in number one, and I went in one because nobody else wanted to after Gimblett had gone. Then I started getting runs.

I think the best I ever did was 89 against the Pakistanis in 1954. I had twenty minutes in which to get the fastest 100 of the season when I holed out, caught and bowled by Maqsood Ahmed. They were a good side and had just drawn with England at Old Trafford and won the fourth Test at the Oval the day before they came to Taunton. I kick myself for getting out, for that was the first chance I had of getting my head down and scoring some runs.

I played against Tyson. I got 71 not out against him at Northampton, and then played against him down in Somerset and got 2 and 22. Playing him at Northampton, there was time to pick the bat up and put it down, but on the Taunton fast wicket, my God! He was very, very quick. Quite the fastest, faster than any current fast bowler. He was a nice man, and he did pitch it up, which helped, unlike Freddie Trueman when you never knew where it was going. He was a dangerous bowler to bat against for that reason. He had a beautiful action, was very fast, but he sprayed it a bit in his early days. His temperament and technique were ideal for a fast bowler.

Tyson was very, very good, but he didn't last long. They all break down, these fast bowlers. Trueman had the perfect action, really sideways on, for that reason he went on for quite a few years.

The wear and tear takes its toll of bowlers. The Middlesex pair, Laurie Gray and Jack Young, both had hip trouble in their later days. I remember hitting my wicket at Lord's playing against Jack Young. He was a left-arm spinner, a marvellous man, full of tales. I got a four square of the wicket and then got a four between slip and gully. He pitched the ball further up and I went back to try and hit him for four again and touched my off-stump, and off came the bail. I'd never done that before, nor since. He was a crafty old bowler.

Two years after I left Somerset I played in a charity game against Hampshire at Hartley Wintney. Desmond Eager, Hampshire's captain, said to his players in my hearing, 'Don't be hard on him — he's been out of the game for a bit!' Full of Pimm's after lunch, I got 202 not out in 113 minutes with 17 sixes and 13 fours.

I don't see much cricket now. I'm too busy. We spend a lot of time on the organization of Cricketer Holidays, tour operations for over 3,500 people, and there is the *Cricketer*, which I oversee, and the competitions run by the *Cricketer*. There are 1,250 schools in the schools' competition, and there are now 639 villages which enter the National Village Cricket Championship. We also run the *Cricketer* Cup for thirty-two old boys' sides, and now we have started to run the European *Cricketer* Cup. That involves ten countries, so we keep pretty busy and are totally involved with the game at all levels. Some 40,000 cricketers play in our competitions.

[192]

In the years when Somerset were languishing at the bottom of the County Championship, Surrey were in the middle of a most remarkable run when they took the title seven years in succession. For the first five of those years they were led by Stuart Surridge. He was appointed captain in 1952, with the backing of Michael Barton, whom he was replacing, and he was to lead Surrey to the Championship in each season that he was captain, an astonishing record.

I had the field to myself when they came to pick a captain after Michael Barton, the last of the gentlemen. There was no one else they could choose. I'd grown up with half the players.

I'd started as a wicket-keeper at Emmanuel School, and I only became a fast-bowler, or at least they thought I was fast, when the School were short of one. Before the war I played for Young Surrey with the Bedsers, and Bernie Constable and Arthur McIntyre and Geoff Whittaker, among others.

My grandfather started the sports goods business, and when I went into the firm my father made me start at the bottom. I had to chop down trees with an axe and a hand-saw, and I had to work on the factory floor. My father said that I had to know every job in the firm, and that I'd never be able to give orders unless I knew how to take them. He was right. The work helped to get you fit, too, and later, when I was playing, people like Frank Tyson and Alan Moss used to come and work for us in the winter to toughen themselves up.

When I took over I told the committee that we'd win the Championship for the next five years. I told them we should have won every year since the war, and I still believe we should have done. We had the players.

I'd learned my first lesson from Brian Sellers. We were playing Yorkshire, and we were on top for most of the match, and they beat us. I was naïve in those days and I said to Brian, 'We were winning. You turned it round on us.' And he looked at me and said, 'Remember one thing, lad. It's no bloody good being second.' And he was right. He was tough. He was hard. He stood no nonsense, and he led by example. He wouldn't ask anybody to field closer to the bat than he was prepared to field himself. I learned a lot from him.

I told the committee that I'd only take on the job if I had complete control of the team with no interference. Andy Sandham ran the second team, and he knew his business, and any time we needed a player I could rely on Andy to send me the right one. There were some old pros in the side who'd been playing longer than I had, but after a couple of matches I didn't have any problems.

I thought our fielding was awful, and I said so, and we had fielding practice before the season and all through the season when I was in charge. It made a big difference, and the lads enjoyed their cricket, and that's what you must do. We went out to win every game from start to finish, and we never believed we were beaten.

I knew from what I'd learned from my father at work that it was important to keep people happy, and I believed him, too, when he told me that the professionals needed to be encouraged. You must always give your bowlers a chance when the pitch is helping them or there are cheap wickets to be had. You need them happy when the going is hard. They've got a living to earn.

The thing that has always annoyed me a bit is when people say that our batting wasn't that strong. We had some good players. You don't need thousands of runs. If you get 200, the other side has to get 201. We didn't get a lot of runs. We didn't need to. We got enough. Besides, if we had got many more, I wouldn't have known when to declare.

People like Peter May and Ken Barrington, who came later, were great players, but we owed a lot to men like Bernie Constable. He was one of the unsung heroes of Surrey cricket, and Tom Clark. Then there were people like Dennis Cox. He was a good medium-pace bowler, a fine cricketer, but we were so strong he spent most of his time in the second eleven and grew old with the rest of the team.

There were great catchers in the side like Tony Lock, but what about Bernie Constable at cover. He knew exactly where to position himself. He had studied batsmen and knew their strokes so that he positioned himself at just the spot where he knew that they would hit the ball. He was a marvellous fielder.

Of course, our bowling was the best in the country – I don't think there's ever been better – Laker, Lock, Loader and Alec Bedser. And don't forget Eric. He didn't get a chance to bowl as much as the others, but he was a very good off-break bowler. If Eric Bedser was playing today, he'd walk into the England side. He's better than anyone around these days.

It was people like Eric who made it all possible. They were a wonderful bunch of boys. Take Laurie Fishlock and Jack Parker. My first year as captain was their last season, and it was a lovely way for them to end, winning the championship. They were wonderful pros – A1 men.

> Surridge's captaincy thrilled, delighted and astonished. Warwickshire were beaten in a day, and, in 1954, Worcestershire were bowled out for 25 only for Surridge to declare when Surrey were 92 for 3. He had heard that bad weather was on the way. His men thought he had gone mad, but Surrey won early on the second day just before the rain arrived. They began the following season with nine wins in succession in the championship, and when they went up to Headingley in June to play their nearest rivals, Yorkshire . . .

The place was absolutely packed on the Saturday and very, very full on the other two days. The atmosphere was like a Test match, and we lost. Kent beat us, too, but when we beat Sussex at the Oval we had won the championship. We lost our next match to Hampshire, and I think that that was the only time in my five years as captain that we weren't in the right frame of mind. We'd done well, and we had a little party and a few drinks before the Hampshire game. It showed.

We had some great players. There's never been a better spinner than Jim Laker. You see off-break bowlers today and all they do is roll the ball out of their hands. They never get calluses on their fingers. You never see them raw with spinning the ball like you did

[195]

with Jim's. He could turn the ball on anything. When I stood at short-leg to him I could hear the ball zipping through the air. He needed a little cajoling at times, but he always gave his best, and he could spin them out whatever the wicket.

I did leave him out once in his benefit year. He turned up to play Middlesex at Lord's, and he was worried about his finger. I felt that if he went into the match worried about himself, he wouldn't give one hundred per cent, which was probably wrong of me because he always did. It was a spur-of-the-moment decision, and I brought in Eric Bedser. Jim accepted it. He was a wonderful pro, and a great man.

We won the championship again in 1956, and then I stood down. Peter was captain of England, and it was right that he should be captain of Surrey. And there were so many good play-ers in the second eleven who weren't getting enough opportun-ities. They were all growing old together, and we had to make room for them.

When I gave up I said that Surrey would win the championship for the next three years, but I was a year out. They only won it twice more.

Peter May was a wonderful batsman. There haven't been many as good as he was, but he had his lean spells for us even when he was captain of England. I said to him, 'Look, Peter, there's a lot of good players in the second eleven. I can't go on ignoring them.' He said, 'Don't worry, skipper, I'll get 100 today.' And he did.

It was Peter as much as anybody who helped to lay all those ghosts of the great players of the past that we had at the Oval – Hobbs, Jardine, Fender and the rest. People were always saying what a great captain Fender was, but he didn't win anything, did he?

Old Jack Hobbs was lovely; a lovely man and very supportive. I remember one day we were playing Kent and we had to get 128 in the last hour. It all came down to the last over. Jack Hobbs was in the committee room, and he'd bet we wouldn't do it. I didn't see the first ball that Dovey bowled, but I got hold of the second, and we won.

All I wanted to do was to play for Surrey and enjoy it. Ronnie Aird, the MCC secretary, was at the Oval one day, and he said, 'Ah, Stuart, we must have you in the Gentlemen's side against the Players.' I told him he needn't bother. I thought the game was a waste of time and out of date. He didn't like that, and he didn't say another word.

I promised the committee we'd win the championship five years on the trot when I took over, and we did. It was a most enjoyable experience. They were great men.

7

I COUNT MYSELF
LUCKY

Frank Tyson

Alim-ud-din

Trevor Goddard

Peter van der Merwe

England were heavily defeated by Australia in 1948, wilting before the pace of Lindwall and Miller. In the Caribbean, they had been surprised by the strength of the West Indian batting, and, in 1950, England were equally bemused by the spin qualities of Ramadhin and Valentine, but, as Surrey began to emerge as the dominant force in county cricket, so a stronger and more successful England side began to take shape.

Alec Bedser and Godfrey Evans established themselves as players of world class. In 1949, Trevor Bailey, an all-rounder of exceptional talent and great character, made his Test debut, and within the next few years came Peter May, one of the finest batsmen the game has known; Colin Cowdrey, who was to play in 114 Test matches; and Freddie Trueman, the fast bowler for whom England had been searching for the best part of two decades. Denis Compton still held a place in the Test side, and he was strongly challenged by the elegant Tom Graveney.

The Lancastrian Brian Statham matured into a fast bowler of relentless accuracy and late movement, and, in 1952, the England selectors took a revolutionary step when they chose a professional, Len Hutton, to captain England. He was already something of a national hero as an opening batsman who was the natural successor to Jack Hobbs and who had established a Test record with his innings of 364 against Australia at the Oval in 1939. He became an even greater hero when he led England to victory over Australia in 1953, so reclaiming the Ashes for the first time in nearly nineteen years.

Hutton brought England back from 2–0 down in the Caribbean to draw the series with West Indies, and, in 1954–55, he retained the Ashes, leading England to their first series victory in Australia since the body-line series of 1932–33. The win in Australia owed much to Frank Tyson, the 'Typhoon', at that time the fastest bowler in the world, and still considered by many to be among the fastest of all time. Tyson had been born in Lancashire, read English at Durham University and qualified to play for Northamptonshire. His speed was soon noticed, but

[201]

he was a surprise choice ahead of Trueman for the tour of Australia in 1954–55. His first Test was against Pakistan at the Oval shortly before that tour. He took five wickets and opened the bowling with Statham, but England were beaten.

Tyson retains the keenest possible interest in the game and is a renowned coach. He makes a typically positive reaction when asked who was the best batsman to whom he bowled.

The Best! You might just as well ask me 'Who is the best musician you have heard?' Menuhin? The lead guitarist of Air Supply? Rubinstein? Benny Goodman? Or who is the best singer you have listened to? Pavarotti? Michael Jackson? Domingo? Phil Collins? Comparisons, as Mrs Malaprop remarked, are odorous, but if they are to be made, one should not compare chalk to cheese. Would you not baulk at making a judgement between the batting of Geoff Boycott and Ian Botham? The only things that their games have in common are their equipment and their lip-service to the laws of cricket.

Compare like with like. Don't be content with one *best*. Have a whole host of them: the best defensive batsman; the best attacking batsman; the most complete batsman; the fastest fast bowler; the most accurate fast bowler; the most versatile fast bowler; the best match-winning all-rounder; the most versatile all-rounder; the best wrist-spinner; the best finger-spinner; and the best wicket-keeper. Even within these categories there are sub-divisions: the best hard-wicket and soft-wicket finger spinners, the best keeper to fast bowling, the best keeper to slow bowling . . .

It is appropriate that cricket should have such a wealth of diverse specialist expertise, for, in Shakespearean terms, it is a game of infinite variety which age has been unable to wither or custom make stale.

What is a good defensive batsman? England's medium-pace maestro of the post-Second World War, Alec Bedser, gave me what I consider the authoritative definition. On a paceless Old Trafford pitch he was bowling against a strokeless South African batsman, during the Manchester Test of 1955. Alec should have been a

Yorkshireman, for he rarely found any source of amusement on the field. The Springbok batsman's lack of initiative put Alec more out of humour than usual and, as the overs passed without a run or a wicket, made him increasingly angry and frustrated. As he went back to bowl over after over to the South African Trevor Bailey, Alec repeated loudly to all within earshot: 'Piss-hole player, piss-hole player.' Two hours elapsed, and the immovable mass was still at the crease as Alec came back for another spell. Once again he reiterated: 'Piss-hole player' – then added – 'Bloody hard to get out, though!' Now, that South African was the ultimate in defensive batsmen!

On the evidence of figures, one has to accept the Indian opener Sunil Gavaskar's greatness as a defensive player. Any player who can go in first and score 10,122 Test runs and 34 centuries – 13 of them against the redoubtable West Indian fast-bowlers – must have a technique based on the immaculate conception. England and Yorkshire's Geoff Boycott would certainly have improved upon his Test tally of 8,114 runs and 22 hundreds if he had gained the selector's nod before his twenty-third birthday. He, too, deserves a grudging admiration as a pursuer of technical perfection.

> For Frank Tyson, Len Hutton remains the greatest defensive batsman of all, and, indeed, a batsman who holds one of the top places among the most accomplished batsmen in any category. Hutton began his first-class career in 1934 and retired in 1955. His Test career lasted from 1937 until 1955, and only once in that time was he not an automatic choice for the England side. He was captain of England in the first eight of the seventeen Test matches in which Tyson appeared.

From the first ball I sent down to Len in a practice game at Redcar, I realized with the certitude of death and taxes, that here was a batsman who knew his onions and the position of his off-stump to a whisker. But Len's genius went beyond the fact that he only played the moving ball when he had to; it surpassed mere correctness of style. The Yorkshire and England opener had the God-given gift of adjusting and adapting his style of play, either gradually with the development of an innings, or abruptly, in a split second and in the last stages of a delivery's flight. I have seen Len 'ride' a Lindwall swinger, his front foot following the movement of the ball until it took up the ideal position alongside its line and pitch. I have witnessed the reflex adjustment as an off-spinner jagged in suddenly from outside the off-stump. But not only was Len's talent for survival finely tuned, he also had the talent to seize the appropriate moment to move up a gear and carry the attack to the enemy. Once he'd steered his side through the tricky phases of the moving ball and the seaming wicket, there was no finer or more fluent driver and cutter of the ball. Above all, Len possessed the inner strength to be England's rock against fearsome bowlers like Lindwall, Miller, Johnston, Archer, Davidson, Meckiff and Rorke. From time to time, in the late forties and early fifties, he received support from partners like Cyril Washbrook and Bill Edrich, but by common consensus, Hutton alone embodied England's hopes for a solid beginning to a Test innings. It was inconceivable that England should go out to bat without his slim, sweatered figure leading the way. When he was dropped for Gloucestershire's George Emmett for the Old Trafford Test of 1948, there were howls of southern bias rattling the windows of the Long Room at Lord's.

If you compare a modern opening batsman with Hutton, it will show you what changes have occurred in technique over the past thirty years. Nowadays, openers go to the crease like a medieval knight into battle: head helmeted, legs protected by the modern equivalent of tasset, cuisse and greave, hands and arms by vambrace and gauntlet, and their chests by cuirass and plastron. It does not matter if their chest-on methods lead to their being hit by the faster bowlers, for there is no chink in their armour. Hutton and his contemporaries had only pads, batting gloves, box and thigh pads for protection, but they were seldom hurt by quick bowlers. They were side-on players, balanced and usually in position to defend, hook or take evasive action against the short-pitched ball. I rarely saw Hutton hit by a bouncer. This contrast between two generations of players raises the question as to whether batting armour encourages players to place less emphasis on technique and thus causes greater vulnerability in the execution of strokes.

[204]

Tyson also has the greatest admiration for many against whom as well as for those with whom he played.

One batsman who never underestimated the true worth of the side-on technique was Australian Colin McDonald, yet another good defensive player. He openly confesses that he went on the 1953 tour of England as an open-chested player. He returned a reformed, orthodox, side-on batsman, converted by the movement and spin which bowlers obtained under English conditions. Mac was never an exciting player. He had an obdurate back-foot defence based on a brief back-lift and was an adept dabber of the back-cut and pusher of the ball to mid-wicket. Under the Alec Bedser definition, he was 'bloody difficult to get out'. When Colin was first picked for Australia, against West Indies in 1951, he was paired with his fellow opener from Melbourne University, the equally unexciting George Thomas. The Sydney press were outraged by what they considered was a totally unimaginative selection, and one vituperative journalist described them as 'Stodge and Splodge, the two under-baked Undergraduates from Melbourne'.

South Africa's never-say-die opening batsman of the fifties was Jackie McGlew. Dangerous Dan, as we sarcastically dubbed him, got, on average, about one click on the scoreboard every ten minutes. In 1957–58, he took five minutes more than nine hours to score 100 against Australia in Durban. He was a competitor. For Jackie, winning was not the main thing, it was the only thing. I had him caught behind without scoring in the Manchester Test of 1955, but the umpire was not of my opinion. Without a flicker of emotion, Jackie repeated his characteristic mannerism of pulling the leading point of his shirt collar up defensively in front of his chin and went on to score a match-winning 104 not out.

During the game in 1956–57 between the MCC touring team and a South African Eleven, played on a crumbling pitch at Loftus Versfeld, the headquarters of Springbok Rugby in Pretoria, Jackie was fielding at forward short-leg to the bowling of a chap named Lawrence. The batsman was our vice captain Doug Insole, and he played forward to a ball which hit him on the front pad and rebounded to McGlew. He appealed confidently, but the umpire, inexperienced as he was, was able to say with a clear conscience that Insole had not edged the ball on to his pad. Though he knew that the appeal 'How's That?' covered every possible method of dismissal, McGlew decided to test the umpire's knowledge. 'How's that for l.b.w., then?' he demanded belligerently. Astonishingly, the umpire gave Insole out. Furious, the England vice captain temporarily refused to bow to McGlew's gamesmanship or the umpire's ignorance, and for a moment the tour was on the brink of a major incident. Finally, McGlew won his point, but his win-at-all-costs attitude was expensive in terms of goodwill.

> Tyson's career began after Don Bradman had retired, but he gives an interesting view of what Bradman's colleagues, though not always great supporters, thought of Australia's greatest batsman.

For more than forty years, the Australian duet of the peppery Bill O'Reilly and the caustic Jack Fingleton were the constant catalysts of conversation in press boxes from Sydney to London. As a Pommie broadcaster and writer in the sixties, I never seemed to agree with them. For instance, I maintained that if I had bowled against Bradman, I would have got him out. O'Reilly and Fingleton staunchly, if reluctantly, supported the view that my chances were as good as those of a celluloid cat chasing an asbestos mouse in hell. I was not being conceited. I merely adopted the attitude that all the statistical and anecdotal evidence pointed to the fact that I may not have got Bradman out, but if I presumed that I could not possibly dismiss him, then there would have been little point in my going out to bowl against him in the first place. One has to think positively.

The closest I came to Bradman in action was watching him play against Lancashire in 1948. As I recall, a young slow left-arm bowler from the Central Lancashire League, Malcolm Hilton, dismissed him cheaply on a rain-affected wicket. It was one of the few failures of a man who scored a century every third time he went to the wicket, averaged nearly 100 in Tests and scored over

300 on one day of a Test match. While I have always looked askance at the relevance of statistics as an authoritative interpreter of cricketing ability, this factual evidence can't be denied in Bradman's case. He must have been one of the finest, if not the finest attacking player the game has seen.

As an attacking bowler, I always preferred bowling to aggressive batsmen. It was an honest challenge. There could only be one outcome – a clear-cut victory for either you or them. Bowling against a defensive batsman is like charging a haystack: no reaction, just absorption of effort.

The most accomplished attacking batsman to give me problems was the left-handed Australian Neil Harvey. Nina always gave the faster bowlers a glimpse of a possible early triumph, particularly when he flashed his cut through the airy regions of gully, but if Harvey spent a day at the crease, the cost to the bowling side was certain to be high. Men like the West Indians Everton Weekes, Clyde Walcott and Gary Sobers, Australians Les Favell and Norman O'Neill, and the South African Roy McLean all displayed an equal degree of savage intent, but it just seemed to me that Harvey was surer in the choice and execution of his strokes. Moreover, Nina was a masterly player of spin. I remember Len Hutton describing Bradman as dancing to meet slow bowlers with the footwork of Fred Astaire. If Bradman was Fred Astaire, Harvey was Gene Kelly, scarcely inferior. He simply did not believe in letting the ball bounce. Christmas 1954 saw Nina score 92 not out in a losing total of 184 on a green Sydney wicket. It was the most accomplished and defiant innings I ever encountered on a cricket field, defensively tight when necessary and relentlessly harsh on the loose ball. When his side lost by 38 runs it reinforced the popularist concept that justice is blind.

A senior member of the party which brought back the Ashes from Australia in 1954–55 was Denis Compton who, in the years immediately after the Second World War, was the most exciting and entertaining batsman in world cricket. His deeds were legendary, and no player has drawn more people to watch the game. Frank Tyson remembers one of his early encounters with Denis.

I was bowling at Lord's against Middlesex in 1954. My confidence was high since I had just heard the news that I was generally regarded as being the fastest bowler in England. You can imagine my astonishment, therefore, when, as I was nearing the end of my run-up from the Nursery End, the newly arrived number five batsman began strolling down the wicket towards me. I stopped dead in my tracks and went back to start my run again. Again he advanced down the wicket so I jutted my jaw and launched a very fast bouncer. Denis Compton, for of course it was he, swayed slightly to the off side, swivelled on his back foot and hooked me for six into the Old Father Time Stand. Yorkshire Annie, the Lord's habitué who was regarded as the ground staff barracker of those times, could not contain her crowing delight for the next hour.

Compo was a throw-back to the golden age of aggressive batting. From what we've heard of Trumper and Jessop, he was like them, what the French call *un original*. His genius went beyond brute strength, supreme confidence and hitting the ball hard. In the whim of the moment he could fabricate different and impish ways of despatching it. People talk of Javed Miandad and Mike Gatting and such strokes as the reverse sweep. Pshaw! Flights of defiance provoked by frustration! What of Compo's draw shot between his legs to fine-leg? He could, and did, play the sweep shot so fine that he was caught by the wicket-keeper off the full face of the bat! His square-drive placed the ball through gaps in the field anywhere between extra-cover and deep-third-man. His moody impudence was not fettered by tight situations, ferocious fast bowling or nagging spinners. He simply stepped up to the batting crease and, like Botham after him, expressed himself with the bat. Denis's outlook on batting was expressed in the Latin motto, *carpe diem*, live for the moment. It was a philosophy understandable among post-war players, men who never knew from one day to another whether they would survive to enjoy another game of cricket.

[208]

Denis was far from elephantine when playing spin bowling, but, like the elephant, he never forgot and never liked being bettered. In 1960, in the twilight of his career, he led an international Cavaliers' side to South Africa. He was forty-one. His left knee was capless, his leg virtually stiff and his footwork but a slow-motion replay of his quicksilver movements of 1948, but in one hour of batting mayhem at the Wanderers' Ground in Johannesburg, he made the great off-spinner Hugh Tayfield look like a novice. He hit 70, splitting the field each time it was modified to counter his strokes and contemptuously hitting Tayfield over the top when there were no gaps to be found. The innings was Compton's revenge on the bowler who, thanks largely to Denis's knee injury, immobilized him during the South Africa–England series three years earlier. Thanks to Tayfield's 37-wicket haul, South Africa drew the rubber after losing the first two Tests.

Compton was never bested. His defiant attitude towards bowlers was perhaps best exemplified by his behaviour when it came to the crunch in the Adelaide Test of 1955. We needed 94 to win the Test and take the series three to one, but we lost Hutton, Edrich, May and Cowdrey for only 49. One senior England player voiced the pessimistic opinion 'The buggers have done us again!' Compo's reaction was immediate and positive, 'I'll show you who's done who!' He grabbed his bat and went out and steered us to victory. This was probably England's greatest achievement in cricket since the body-line series twenty-two years earlier; that was the last time an England side had won a series in Australia. Our skipper Len Hutton was off the planet at our success. He always maintained that for a touring side to win a series under the surveillance of foreign umpires on alien wickets, it had to be at least twenty-five per cent better than its opponents.

Since the time of Tyson and Compton, one-day cricket has come into fashion. Compton retired in 1958, Tyson two years later. The Gillette Cup, the sixty-over knock-out competition, arrived in 1963, the Sunday League in 1969. The first one-day international was played at Melbourne in January 1971. Tyson considers how some of his contemporaries would have fared in these competitions.

Denis Compton would have starred in limited-over cricket, and it is hard to see how opponents would have taken more than two runs an over off Lindwall or Statham. Lindwall was a quickie with the patient mentality and accuracy of a spinner. The best example of this is the story that is told about Bradman's side practising at Lord's before the 1948 series. The late 'Gubby' Allen, a former England captain, wandered down to the Nursery End nets determined to test the legendary Lindwall accuracy. He politely requested the great bowler to send down an outswinger which pitched in line with the leg-stump and hit the top of the off. Lindwall obliged. Gubby's next request was for an in-swinger, moving from off-stump to leg. The leg stump somersaulted out of the ground next ball, and 'Gubby' retired to the pavilion to pass on the gloomy results of his experiments to the selectors.

In the past thirty years, we have seen several fast bowlers – Hadlee, Botham, Lillee, Kapil Dev, Marshall and Imran Khan – who were more productive in terms of wickets than Lindwall, and they were, perhaps, more versatile in terms of swing, cut and variations of pace, but to make comparisons one must take into account many factors other than arithmetic – opportunity, the strength of the opposition, wickets, improvement in fielding, agility and fitness, and even scientific progress.

Take, for instance, the time when Brian Statham and I were measured for pace at the aeronautical college in Wellington, New Zealand. The calculations were done by means of a radio beam which was projected down the pitch. Brian and I bowled a ball with a small metal plate into the beam, and as it passed to the other end of the wicket it produced a whistling noise. The sound was recorded, its duration measured, and our speeds computed. The results showed that I bowled at 89 m.p.h., and Brian at 87 m.p.h. The validity of that calculation, however, must be open to question in view of the fact that the method did not measure our 'muzzle velocities', to say nothing of the fact that it was a bitterly cold day, and we contented ourselves with bowling in two thick sweaters and our street trousers.

In contrast with such almost prehistoric procedures, Jeff Thomson, the Australian pace-man, was assessed at 99.6 m.p.h., under ideal hot conditions and with the aid of a sophisticated radar speed gun. Scientific advances such as this lead me to place a greater degree of trust in subjective comparisons in cricket. When people now ask me whether I was faster than any other quickie, I simply say, 'Ask the batsmen who faced me.' The fallacy in this suggestion, however, is that no batsman has ever had the privilege, or misfortune, of facing all the fast bowlers down through the ages.

I believe, for instance, that Brian Statham, although more mechanical and less imaginative, was a better fast-bowling technician than Ian Botham or Bob Willis. Had limited-over cricket been as popular and as widely played in the Greyhound's day as it is now, he would have left an indelible mark on it. His accuracy was such that I find it hard to visualize where batsmen would have scored *multiples* off him. Godfrey Evans always used to say he could tell when Brian was about to have an off day, and his pessimistic assessment was based solely on the Lancashire bowler sending down one inaccurate delivery in his first over. If a batsman was on the receiving end of a Statham half-volley and despatched it, Godders always congratulated him on his good luck, adding that he would not get another that day.

Another of my viewpoints at which hands will be raised in horror is that the Australian, Keith Miller, was the best all-rounder I have ever seen. Sobers was undoubtedly the most versatile and complete cricketer the game has witnessed. What other batsman has scored so heavily at number six, and with such panache, bowled in three different styles and caught so unerringly around the corner at short-leg? No one. But all the same I just feel that nobody – except perhaps Ian Botham – could swing the fortunes of a game in the space of a few overs, with either bat or ball, like Miller. I agree that his figures cannot compare with those of Imran Khan, Richard Hadlee, Kapil Dev and Ian Botham, but my preference for Miller is coloured by my admiration of a superb athlete of my own time.

[211]

In the Melbourne Test, 1954–55, Miller, hampered by an injured back, sent down nine overs, eight of them maidens, to capture three English wickets for 5 runs in a spell of ninety minutes. At Adelaide, later in the same rubber, when we needed 94 for victory in the Test and the series, it was he who snatched the wickets of Hutton, Edrich and Cowdrey, and caught May in the covers to bring the issue of the match in doubt. Two years later, at Lord's, when I was not in the England side, he took 10 for 155 and avenged the defeats at Melbourne and Adelaide. That was the dynamic Miller at his best.

> Although one of the great Test fast-bowlers of all time, Frank Tyson has the greatest admiration for spinners. He ranges widely, and some of his choices among the best of their kind may surprise.

In my time, I've played against the master spin-bowlers – Australians Richie Benaud, Cecil Pepper, George Tribe, Bruce Dooland and Jack Walsh; the Indian leg-spinner Fergie Gupte, and Sonny Ramadhin, Hughie Tayfield, Laker, Lock and Wardle.

While he lacked infinite variety and acute turn, Benaud was a pin-point perfectionist who practised one type of delivery at the nets for hours and was never happy unless he landed each delivery on his chosen spot. He nagged and nagged until he worried batsmen out.

By contrast, Cecil Pepper was a volatile character. He was a wrist-spinner with plenty of spirit and zip. He bounced the ball off the pitch, and he was the master of a flipper which skidded off the wicket. His hostility towards batsmen and umpires was legendary. It was reported to have led to his ostracism from Australian Test circles. The story goes that once during a New South Wales versus South Australia game at the Adelaide Oval, he twice had the Don perilously close to l.b.w. with his flipper. Both of his raucous appeals were refused by umpire Jack Scott, and the reflections which he made on Scott's honesty in Bradman's presence effectively led to this great all-rounder being scratched from the selectors' short list. When one considers the calibre of spinners who have

[212]

been chosen for Australia before and since Pepper's time, the fact that he did not play a single official Test seems a very great injustice.

Bruce Dooland looped the ball tantalizingly, and it dropped slowly from the heavens. Parni Tribe, as he was known after unexpectedly serving tepid water to his Commonwealth XI team-mates during a drinks interval in torrid Bombay, was a wrist spinner with an ability to bowl an endless variety of deliveries, none of them visibly the same.

While he was unknown to Test cricket Jack Walsh was famous among his Leicestershire contemporaries as a left-handed, over-the-wrist spinner who was the biggest turner of the ball in English county cricket. The only problem with Jack's bowling was that neither his team-mates nor the batsmen knew whether he was going to bounce the ball once or twice.

India's Fergie Gupte was an amazing talent. His hands were small for a leg-spinner, but his wrists were like elasticated steel. And Sonny Ramadhin was the most mystifying bowler I ever encountered. When he was professional for Crompton in the Central Lancashire League he mesmerized batsmen with the windmill whirling of his arms and acute off-spin from the front of his hand. I think that I probably played twice for Middleton against him and faced, in all, two balls. Even though his opponents insisted that he kept his sleeves buttoned down to the wrist to give them a better appreciation of where his delivery arm was, it was horrendously difficult to pick up the flight of the ball. When I recall my batting nightmares against him my main impression is of batting in a snowstorm with the ball materializing just before it pitched and whipping back to rattle my castle.

The former Australian captain and off-spinner Ian Johnson believes that there are two main categories of finger-spin bowlers – hard-wicket spinners and those who are used to bowling on the softer and more responsive English surfaces. He maintains that pitches in Australia, South Africa, and sometimes India and Pakistan afford little turn after the ball pitches. Most of the slow bowler's deception occurs in the flight. Therefore hard-wicket spinners bowl into the air and try to beat the batsman by varied loop, drift and bounce. By contrast, turning wickets encourage orthodox spinners to fire the ball into the pitch to deny their opponents the chance to use their feet to reach the ball on the full and to get past the bat by differing degrees of spin.

In my time, Johnson himself, Hughie Tayfield of South Africa, and the West Indian Lance Gibbs all fell into the classification of hard-wicket bowlers, although one must confess that Gibbs was in a class of his own when it came to turning the ball on both hard and soft pitches. Many of Hugh Tayfield's Test wickets – 170 I believe he took – came from his arm ball which was the product of a full-body pivot over a braced front foot placed diametrically in front of the middle stump of the bowler's wicket. His swivelling front toe created a small circular pit on the spot where it landed, and as his bowling arm was over the top of the stumps at the moment of the ball's release, his accuracy was phenomenal. Overspin created loop which produced many driven catches to brilliant fieldsmen like Endean, who stood close in.

Gibbs was not blessed with a side-on action, but his long spinning fingers enabled him to make the ball turn on the hardest of pitches and to flop in the air just before reaching the batsman. I would say that Gibbs, the Indian spinners Prasanna and Bedi, and the latter-day Tony Lock of Western Australia were the finest flighters of the ball I have seen.

There were slow bowlers who excelled both in hot and temperate climes. The left-handed Yorkshireman Johnny Wardle was such a man. Playing for Yorkshire and England at home, Johnny seldom tried anything more ambitious than regulation finger spin. His Headingley directors frowned on anything more ambitious or imaginative. Wrist-spin they regarded as a 'bloody unnecessary luxury'. Why bowl over the wrist when you can turn the ball just as much and quicker following the example of Hedley Verity! They were not very fair to Wardle whom they thought inferior to his famous predecessors Rhodes and Verity because he had a 'dropped' wrist and could not spin the ball acutely. Moreover, their attitude handicapped Wardle's chances of selection for England at home since it placed him in head-to-head competition with Tony Lock who was a devastating exponent of medium-pace. However, Johnny had one thing which I think placed him ahead of his contemporaries Laker and Lock when it came to bowling on hard wickets – he had the ability to turn to bowling chinamen and googlies.

Northamptonshire's keeper, Keith Andrew, who was an outstanding and experienced keeper to wrist-spin, rated Wardle as more difficult to pick than Australian George Tribe and England's Freddie Brown – no faint praise. Wardle belonged to the Benaud school of thought which said that perfect practice makes practice. On the two overseas tours on which I accompanied Wardle, to Australia and to South Africa, the solidly built Tyke spent four hours a day practising wrist spin on the sports deck of the ships taking us out. The thump, thump, thump of cricket ball on the bulkhead was a regular feature of every day we spent on the RMS *Orsova* and *Stirling Castle*.

Len Hutton, Wardle's skipper on his first trip to Australia, always appreciated his fellow Yorkshireman, both as an astute bowler and as a swashbuckling lower-order batsman. And Len was a good judge.

> In his career as player, journalist and broadcaster, Frank Tyson has played with or seen all the leading wicket-keepers since the Second World War. He played with the highly esteemed Keith Andrew at Northants and with Godfrey Evans in Test cricket, and he gives his assessment.

Len Hutton thought the finest wicket-keeper he had ever played with or against was Don Tallon of Australia. That glowing opinion probably stemmed from the fact that Don caught him yards down the leg side off Lindwall when he had scored 30 in England's paltry first innings of 52 at the Oval in 1948. For me, Alan Knott's blameless hands and exceptional mobility place him at the top of the list. There are others who rate high in my esteem – Knott's permanent bridesmaid Bob Taylor, a brilliant technician and highly conscientious; and there was Rod Marsh, a great improver. Marsh's latter-day fitness, smooth gathering of the ball and amazing mobility was a tribute to his dedication to his task. Old Iron Gloves became Iron Will.

Subjective bias, however, leads me to favour over all of his rivals the man, or should I say character, who kept wicket for England when I played Tests. Godfrey Evans had the inspirational flair of a true showman. It was difficult to detect when he dropped a catch or made a gaffe, and even harder to condemn him for them. He did it with such style. His leg-side work was one of the seven wonders of the athletic world. Standing up to Alec Bedser, he stumped stumbling batsmen in the twinkling of his gloves.

On the final morning of the 1955 Melbourne Test, with Australia needing 165 to win with eight wickets in hand, he turned the tide of the game in England's favour by catching Neil Harvey yards down the leg side off the seventh ball of the morning. He literally plucked the ball out of the air at wide leg-slip, and less than an hour and a half and 34 runs later, England had won by 128 runs. His inspirational brilliance was one of his greatest assets. It lifted the spirits of his team-mates out of the deepest slough of despair. His dapper appearance and enthusiasm never flagged in the longest day in the field. And he used to shout 'Come on lads, let's attack' and 'Never mind boys, they can't stop the clock.' He could cheer even the most despondent of bowlers. It was typical of him that business reverses in his life after cricket never got him down. He was still the Max Miller of wicket-keeping, 'The Cheekie Chappie', that he had always been, advertising his own personality behind enormous mutton-chop whiskers.

I took 7 for 27 in that memorable second innings of the Melbourne Test in 1955. Since I've settled in Australia, I've often met people who saw my finest hour. They recall it with fierce passion. 'I remember you, Tyson, you bastard! I went to see that Melbourne game, taking my packed lunch and expecting to see Australia win that afternoon. Instead the game was over before lunch, and I had to eat my sandwiches in the Fitzroy Gardens!'

Of course, I sympathize, disclaiming any clear recollection of the event beyond the details that it was 5 January, a Wednesday, the temperature was 102 degrees, I took 6 for 16 in my last spell of 6 overs and 3 balls, and there were some 60,000 people watching!

[216]

Seriously, though, I don't regard my performance that day as the zenith of my cricket career. It won a crucial Test match, but I was extremely lucky. As I remember, in addition to the fact that I was indebted to Godfrey Evans for his brilliant catch to get rid of Neil Harvey, I was fortunate to have Benaud pull a long hop on to his stumps, lucky to see Len Maddocks skew a yorker around his pads on to his leg-stump, and I owed the wickets of Lindwall and Miller to the uneven bounce of the pitch. I think I bowled much better when I took 10 for 130 in the preceding Test at Sydney. Indeed, I often think that I bowled faster and better during my college days at Durham University.

For me, the underlying enjoyment of cricket stems from the intrinsic self-satisfaction which one gets from the game, not from public acclaim or media fame. I count myself lucky to have rubbed shoulders with great players and cricketing characters and to have shared sporting moments which have enriched my life. It's been a rewarding experience.

> Frank Tyson's first wicket in Test cricket came at the Oval in 1954 when, in his third over, after a somewhat erratic start, he bowled Alim-ud-din and Maqsood Ahmed with successive deliveries. This was the first Test series in which Alim-ud-din had played. He made his debut in the first game of the rubber at Lord's, and he was the opening partner of the great Hanif Mohammad. He scored 1,000 runs on the tour and hit centuries against Worcestershire in the first match of the tour, and against Cambridge University in the second. He maintains that it was chance that brought him a place in the Pakistan side.

We did not play Test cricket until 1952 so that the tour of England was only our second series. In the first series, against India, in India, Nazar Mohammad, the father of Mudassar Nazar, was Hanif's partner, and he scored Pakistan's first century in a Test match. Then, in 1953, he broke his arm in a domestic accident when he jumped out of a window, and he had to retire, and that's when I came in.

I had played cricket before partition. I was born in Ajmer, and we used to go to the local college and watch them practising in the nets. They were the princes who went to Oxford. We were sometimes given a chance to bowl and bat in the nets, even though we were not at the college. The selectors who chose the side for the Ranji Trophy matches used to watch, and one day they saw me and said, 'He is very correct, and he plays some shots. We should give him a chance.' And I played for Rajputana, which is now Rajasthan, against Delhi when I was twelve-and-a-half, the youngest player to appear in first-class cricket. Later I played for Gujarat, but the power in India was in Bombay, the Cricket Club of India, with Merchant and Mankad. After partition I played for Sind and then in Karachi and Bahawalpur.

I came to England in 1954, and this was very important to us because it was the first time we had played against England, and I played my first Test match at Lord's. I think we were paid a pound a day on the tour. Kardar was a very good captain, and he did a tremendous amount for Pakistan cricket. He knew the game, and he had played county cricket in England and at university. He was very much respected, and he knew his players.

Fazal Mahmood won us the game at the Oval with his bowling. He was a marvellous bowler, but a very poor captain after Kardar. We also had a good wicket-keeper in Imtiaz Ahmed. He and Fazal had practised a lot together, and they talked things over very much. And there was Hanif. He was such a great batsman because he was so patient. People don't know, but when he batted for over sixteen-and-a-half hours and scored 499 for Karachi against Bahawalpur he was run out not because he was tired, but because he was playing for the next day and trying to keep the bowling for the next morning. I have never seen anybody who was so patient in waiting for the right ball, and so much depended on him when we first played Test cricket.

England were a very good side when we came here in 1954 – Hutton, Compton, May, Graveney – they were lovely batsmen. Compton was majestic, and he made 278 against us at Nottingham. It was a wonderful innings. In the last Test, I met Tyson. He was very good and very fast, and I played against Trueman, Laker,

Lock and Wardle. And India had Mankad and Gupte, great spinners, and there was Ramadhin and Gibbs in the West Indies. Wes Hall was very quick and very good when he came to Pakistan, but the fastest of them all was Roy Gilchrist in the West Indies. He was very, very fast, and very dangerous.

In all batting, you need patience, and you need a little luck. There are days when you feel right, and all goes well. The days that gave me the most pleasure were those when I scored centuries for my country. My first was against India at Karachi in 1955, and then my greatest pleasure was getting 109 against England in 1962. That was particularly important to me. I was not in the Pakistan party, and I thought my days in Test cricket were over. A government minister asked me to captain Karachi Blues in the Quaid-e-Azam Trophy; there was great power in ministerial interest, and I scored three centuries, including one in the final, and we won the trophy. I scored more runs than anyone else, and they had to bring me back. I was picked for the tour of England, although I had not been in the original party of eighteen.

That was not a good tour. Javed Burki was not a good captain. He did not give enough encouragement to the younger players. There are always problems with Pakistan cricket, with the selectors. There are social classes. Javed Miandad understands the game better than Imran Khan, but Imran has the stamp of Oxford, and that is important. That is why Burki was captain although he was not the man for the job.

They were good days. Cricket taught me about life. You are on your own. You make one mistake, and you're out.

Alim-ud-din was Frank Tyson's first victim in Test cricket, but Tyson also talks about obdurate South African batsmen, men who were very hard to get out like Jackie McGlew and Trevor Goddard. Both men captained South Africa, and they formed a very sound opening partnership. They first came together in the first Test match against England at Trent Bridge. McGlew took over as captain in the third and fourth Tests when Cheetham was injured, and South Africa won

[219]

them both, but they lost the series when England won a low-scoring game at the Oval by 92 runs.

Trevor Goddard assesses his opening partner:

Jackie was a nugget. He was just there to stay, and they had to dig him out. They tried to knock him out many times. He was just a gutsy chap. He was a very good opening partner. I think the fact that he was short and right-handed, and I was gangly and left-handed was an advantage. The crazy thing was that he was a front-foot player, and I played it off the back foot preferably. He was a fine fielder, too.

I used to bowl a fair number of overs in those days. Jackie was more than often at mid-on, and the ground he covered saved me so many runs.

He was a very good captain. He was dynamic, and he led. He had success, and that's good captaincy. He was tactically very good. He had some tremendous sides under him, provincially and in Tests, and some very good attacks, but he handled them well.

One of the outstanding players in that first series against England was Johnny Waite. He is still to me the best wicket-keeper I've ever known. I can think of him catching Denis Compton, a brilliant catch, and he made no fuss at all. I think one of the best knocks I've ever seen was in the last Test we played against England, at the Oval, in fifty-five. He got about 60, and that still rates as the best innings I've seen.

Roy McLean was a wonderful chap. We were at school together. He never changed. He was a swashbuckler. He could annihilate an attack. He was a chap you always liked to have because he could put you right on top. He was a very powerful guy, hit the ball very hard. He helped me a lot when I first came into the side. He was very popular, very friendly. I appreciated it a lot.

Trevor Goddard had a good all-round series against England, 1956–57, when van Ryneveld led South Africa. The following season, Australia visited South Africa, and Jackie McGlew was reinstated as captain. In the first Test, Goddard and McGlew began the match with a partnership of 176.

Ian Meckiff played. He came out as a quickie, and I can remember feeling even then that he was a 'chucker'. I went down to Jackie and said 'There's something peculiar here!'

The wickets were strange, and the averages were very low. Like we've done many times, the Australians arrived not really on top, but it was Mackay, Benaud and chaps like that who really thrashed us. Alan Davidson, when he really wanted to motor, was one of the best I've ever seen. I can remember him bowling at 'Maritzburg, against Natal, and he took, I think it was, Roy McLean, Burger and Wesley, all South African players, all in one over. It was with the second new ball, and I stood at the other end. It was like a boomerang, it really was, quick, on target, moving like mad. I had a very healthy respect for him.

Neil Adcock was very good for us. I played against him many times when he played for Transvaal, and I played for Natal. He could bring it up off a length. He was very nasty. I was always glad when he was on my side. His partner was Heine. He was aggressive. They were a good pair. Quickies always seem to go together. They were like Tyson and Statham. Tyson and Trueman is a better comparison – one quick, one swinging it. They were different.

> Clive van Ryneveld returned to captain South Africa in the second Test of that 1957–58 series, and Australia won by an innings. It was in this series that Richie Benaud really made his mark. He hit a century in the first Test and played a leading role in Australia's victory in the second.

It was chaps like Burke and McDonald who were such a thorn in our flesh because they were so hard to get out, and then there was Mackay, and they gave such a basis.

> McDonald and Burke put on 190 for Australia's first wicket in the second Test at Newlands, and South Africa, having

[221]

followed-on 240 runs in arrears, were bowled out for 99 in their second innings. Trevor Goddard carried his bat for 56.

Richie Benaud bowled extremely well, but I don't think he was the one who got the success. Kline got the success, if my memory serves me right, including the hat-trick, but he didn't do a lot with the ball. I had enough of Richie in that innings to know that he bowled magnificently. I can remember getting down on the odd knee occasionally and sweeping, which I liked to do, and the ball going here or there and falling into a gap. And the critics were very severe on me for an irresponsible knock, which was pretty unfair as I got half the runs, and the side was bundled out.

Richie turned the ball very sharply, and he bowled much, much better than Kline, but Kline got the hat-trick, and he was the hero. That's how it goes sometimes.

Hughie Tayfield, of course, was our spinner. He could never believe that anyone could hit him. Whatever the pitch, he'd say, 'It's made for me.'

Goddard was appointed captain of South Africa for the tour of Australia, 1963–64, and, rather surprisingly, the series was drawn.

It was one of the most enjoyable tours, one of the best I've been on. They were a lovely crowd of chaps. I didn't have a tour where there were bad chaps, but that crowd were fantastic. Eddie Barlow frustrated every Australian bowler by slicing the ball over third slip's head. Before the tour, some people had said to me that he was no good, and he wouldn't make it. But you just couldn't get that guy down. He had an inner belief. He went from strength to strength. That tour matured him. He put the runs on the board. He was a joy.

At the end of the tour, I went to Sir Don. I had the greatest respect for him as a man and for his knowledge. All tour I had itched to go to him and say, 'Where are we going wrong? Can you give us any advice?' But I felt I couldn't do that because he was chairman of selectors, and I felt that would be imposing. So at the end of the tour I just went to him and asked if he could give me some advice, and what thoughts he could give me as to how to improve, and where I'd gone wrong.

And he was very generous and said that when we first came over he'd noticed the gaps in our field, and that was because I hadn't had that much experience. But he said at the end of the trip we'd strangled them. I thought that was fair comment from one so great. He was tremendous.

> One of those who made his international debut on that tour was Peter van der Merwe. He was one of six South Africans to make his Test debut in the first Test, in Brisbane. His first-class debut had come in 1957, and he was not surprised to be chosen for the 1963–64 tour of Australia.

It was not a complete surprise. I'd had a reasonably good season, and I was hoping, and expecting to be chosen. The side was captained by Trevor Goddard, and it was a very happy team. Quite a number of us had been to England before that on the Fezela tour, 1961, and that was the tour that created the nucleus of South African cricket teams for the next ten years, because Eddie Barlow went on it, Colin Bland, Denis Lindsay, Peter Pollock and myself. You can see that was the nucleus of the South African side for quite a while.

In that first Test, at the Gabba, six of us made our Test debuts. It was quite a gamble by the selectors, but we didn't really have much of an option because the other fellows who were chosen weren't that much more experienced.

I remember we played against Queensland before that. The Test wicket was right alongside, and it was covered the whole of the time. Queensland had just got a new curator, and his methods raised some eyebrows up in Queensland, and I think, in fact, that rain may have saved us on the last afternoon because the wicket was wearing pretty badly.

> The significant things about Peter van der Merwe's first Test match were centuries from Brian Booth and Eddie Barlow and

the no-balling of Australia's left-arm fast bowler Ian Meckiff. There was much concern at this time about the actions of certain bowlers, and Meckiff was one who had been under close scrutiny and criticism regarding the legality of his action. He was the most notorious of the 'chuckers'. In the Brisbane Test, he bowled one over and was no-balled four times by umpire Egar for throwing. Meckiff announced his retirement from all classes of cricket.

Brian Booth was a class player, and such a nice person. We enjoyed his company. We enjoyed his batting, and we probably enjoyed it more when he was out.

All I would say of Eddie Barlow's innings is that it was a typical Eddie Barlow innings – pugnacious, watchful, mostly off the back foot, and, of course, anything loose punished severely.

We had Colin Egar and Lou Rowan in all five Tests, and we knew that something was brewing, but we didn't really discuss much in our ranks. We said, 'It's an internal matter. Leave it to the umpires to decide.' The fact that it happened was sad, probably rightly so. I'd seen Ian Meckiff play in South Africa, and he certainly didn't seem side-on pure, but it was the umpire's decision.

We came down to Melbourne for the second Test. This was the biggest ground, the biggest crowd, made a lot of noise. We didn't have such a good preparation for that match. We'd been down to Tasmania and had a couple of games there. It was fairly easy, and we spent Christmas down there. Then we got back for the big game, and we really weren't quite in tune for it, but all credit to Australia. That was Bobby Simpson's first Test as captain, and he led the side pretty well.

Ian Redpath made his debut, and he and Bill Lawry put on 219 for the first wicket. Lawry got 157, but the biggest impression was one of those controversial things. He stood on his wickets, but the umpire ruled in favour of Bill. I was at gully and watched the whole thing, and let's just say it was the umpire's decision and that was it.

This was the only time I ever saw Colin Bland drop a catch, at silly mid-on. He never liked fielding close up. In the covers he was deadly. I could not imagine in my side anyone who could ever field better in the covers. He had an uncanny ability to know where the ball was going, and he'd position himself – how deep, how wide, how straight. The accuracy of his throw was phenomenal.

Wally Grout was their wicket-keeper, and he deserved his high reputation, but John Waite I rated very highly as a wicket-keeper, and then Denis Lindsay took over, and I can never remember him missing anything.

We were probably a little bit tentative in our attack. I loved that tour. Australia is just set up for cricket. We went on an enormous number of country matches, and so we saw a lot of Australia. I did feel that Trevor might have been a little more positive on occasions, but then that's his prerogative. He's the captain, and he's the man who decides. He didn't start the tour in the greatest of confidence, and this didn't help.

Graeme Pollock hit a couple of centuries in that series, and he wasn't twenty, but he had emerged a few seasons before that. He made his first century at the age of sixteen, and just before the side was chosen to go to Australia, he played in Port Elizabeth against Richie Benaud's Cavalier side. He made 209 not out, and I think that's when he came to the notice of the Australians.

I've a very soft spot for his brother Peter, fast-bowler, the villain of the piece as far as the crowd were concerned. He bowled for me in England a few years later, and he gave one hundred per cent. He was prepared to bowl right to the end of the day, and his last over was as quick as his first in the morning. A great trier.

My first Test was Richie Benaud's last as captain. I played against him twice in South Africa, and when he played for New South Wales. I enjoyed playing against him, a very positive player.

Peter van der Merwe succeeded Trevor Goddard as captain of South Africa. He led the side to England in 1965 and won the rubber, and, at home, he captained the side against Australia, 1966–67, and won the series by three matches to one. Few captains in Test cricket can rival his record of four wins and only one defeat in eight matches. He was captain of South Africa when they beat Australia in South Africa for the first time. The match was the first Test, at Johannesburg, in December 1966. Australia led by 126 on the first innings, and South Africa were 349 for 6 in their second innings when van der Merwe joined Denis Lindsay. The pair added a record 221. Lindsay hit 182, an innings which included five sixes, and van der Merwe made 76, his highest Test score. Lindsay had already taken six catches in Australia's first innings.

When I came to the wicket he played superbly. Denis was hitting everything in the middle of the bat, chancing his arm, hitting it to all parts of the field. He made 182. It was one of the most spectacular innings I've ever seen, and I was rather lucky.

As captain, I was very grateful to Denis for his batting in the series. When I saw the great Australian side come to South Africa in 1957–58 under Ian Craig, I then formed an opinion which I've never changed, and that is that numbers six, seven and eight were absolutely determined to use their batting ability in that series; Mackay, Benaud and Davidson. I was equally determined that, with Denis Lindsay and myself, we would get the equivalent six, seven and eight that Ian Craig had. Bobby Simpson was trying to win, and so were we. It was a most enjoyable series. The over rate was pretty good, and I think that there was a lot of good play, and a lot of spectacle, and fortunes seesawed.

South Africa made 620 in their second innings of that first Test at Johannesburg and went on to win by 233 runs. Trevor Goddard took 6 for 53.

He could bowl everything – spin, changes of pace, varied his delivery from close to the wicket to wide of the wicket, could bowl one from twenty-two yards – and this variety was too much for them. They also made one very bad error right at the start of the day. A mix-up between Simpson and Lawry ended in a run out, and that set us off on a good footing.

[226]

Keith Stackpole got 100 against us at Newlands, and Australia won, and that was the first time people began to take Keith Stackpole seriously and realize that he was a good player.

Mike Procter made his debut in the third Test at Kingsmead, in Durban. In those young days, he was very sharp. He looked as if he bowled off the wrong foot, and they had a lot of trouble with him. Bobby Simpson produced a trump card in Bob Cowper bowling some thirty overs of off-breaks on the trot, but Denis Lindsay batted well again, got 100, and saved us. Then Trevor Goddard and Eddie Barlow got a couple of wickets, and Mike Procter got some, and we were in a position to enforce the follow-on.

Denis Lindsay hit his third century of the series in the fourth Test, which was drawn. His 606 runs in the series was a record for a wicket-keeper in a Test rubber, and he also established another record with 24 catches in the five Tests.

We won the last Test by seven wickets. The wind was blowing from the south-east, and I won the toss and put them in. We got off to an excellent start. In the very first over, Bill Lawry was run out, and that's what started us on our way. Bobby Simpson hit a ball to fine-leg and set off. Eddie Barlow's throw was right over the stumps, and Bill Lawry had no chance.

Denis Lindsay was out for one in that last Test, he only batted once. The crowd cheered him all the way to the wicket, and he was so nervous of what the crowd expected of him.

8

TO DELIGHT IN THE PERFORMANCE OF OTHERS

E. R. Dexter

A. S. Brown

R. A. Hutton

While South Africa were being captained by Goddard and van der Merwe England were being led for much of the time by Ted Dexter. A sportsman of great natural ability, Dexter was recognized in his first year at Cambridge, 1956, as a batsman of outstanding merit. A year later, he played for Sussex, whom he captained from 1960 to 1965, and he was flown out to bolster the England side in Australia, 1958–59.

It was in 1958 that my Test career began. I had a good season with Cambridge, and I'd played a few games for Sussex when I was chosen to play for England against New Zealand at Old Trafford. Ray Illingworth and Raman Subba Row were also playing in a Test for the first time. It was a very unusual occasion for a Test debut because the selectors were to announce the party that was to tour Australia half-way through the match.

I'd done well for the Gentlemen against the Players, and as I'd made the eleven for this match, I felt I had a good chance of being in the seventeen to go to Australia. It rained for most of the first three days, and none of us had the chance to show our capabilities. When the party to tour Australia was announced I wasn't among the names listed. The following day, I scored 52, and the papers talked of a grave blunder that had been made in omitting me.

At the end of the season I went to work in Paris for a friend of my father's, although the life was more social than business.

Things in Australia didn't go well, and there was a lot of agitation for me to be sent out as a reinforcement. Watson, Subba Row, Milton and Trevor Bailey were all injured at one time or another, and then John Mortimore was flown out to ease the burden on Laker and Lock. Then, with the injuries to Willie Watson and Raman Subba Row more serious than originally imagined, I was asked to join the side.

I had become engaged to Susan, a London fashion model, and the journalists had a field day with the whole idea of a newly engaged Cambridge man socializing in Paris and being flown out to *save* his country.

I arrived in Australia suffering from a throat infection, and I didn't have much time to find form or fitness. After games in Tasmania and South Australia, I was twelfth man for the second Test in Melbourne.

Now I really had no idea of what a twelfth man was supposed to do. I thought that all I had to do was hang around when we were fielding and trot on if anyone had to leave the field, I'd never acted as twelfth man before, and I'd no idea about drinks and towels and drying clothes, and that sort of thing. I was totally ignorant and incompetent, and it was probably my incompetence that led to me being chosen for the third Test. They couldn't face the idea of having me as twelfth man again.

In the third Test, I made 1 and 11, and missed a catch. The next Test I played in was the last one, and I was out first ball in the first innings and made 6 in an hour in the second.

I was unhappy, and I had to think about the chasm that existed between the batsman new to the game, out of form and out of practice, and the established Test player.

I went into the nets, and I relied upon the comradeship that exists between those who play the first-class game. It was John Mortimore who spotted my failing. He told me that I was batting with the face of the bat open. I didn't believe him, but when I turned the bat a little in my hands, the timing was immediately right and I was hitting the ball properly again.

This handing on from one player to another, often in the middle, is one of the most important things in learning how to play Test cricket.

In New Zealand, I hit my first Test 100. I'd regained my confidence, but at the beginning of the innings I had to rely on others. Peter May talked me through the first half-hour, and later, Tony Lock nursed me, telling me to keep playing as I was, and he would stay with me. I felt that I'd come of age.

There is an enormous difference between Test cricket and county cricket. The county game is one of containment. You have periods of lull. Bowlers strike a length and keep the ball on the spot. In mid-afternoon, often, they are at half-pace.

Test cricket is very different. The match lasts for five days. It is altogether more open than the county game. The Test attack is more varied than the county attack, but it may surprise people to learn that it is often not so accurate, although it is much more aggressive. At a quarter to four or ten to five, often periods of calm in a county game, the Test bowler is still attacking the batsman. He is still trying to knock your block off or to fiddle you out. It's a very different game, and it takes time to adjust to it. You play on big grounds, and in front of large crowds. The whole game is surrounded by a great deal of ballyhoo.

What is certain is that at the end of a five-day Test match, one is mentally and physically drained. You return to your county side where people hope and expect you'll repeat what you've achieved at Test level. It's very hard to do so. The atmosphere is different, and your concentration wanders.

> Ted Dexter's career lasted little more than ten years, but it spanned a period of great change in English cricket. The distinction between amateur and professional was abolished, so ending the annual fixture between Gentlemen and Players, and limited-over cricket was introduced with the Gillette Cup, the knock-out competition.

There were, of course, certain high peaks in my career, like captaining England for the first time, but at county level, there was the great excitement of the first Gillette Cup Final in 1963. I'd been a bit sceptical of one-day cricket, but we soon saw it as another intellectual challenge, and we had theories and plans for the game and gave it much thought. They didn't all work out as we'd hoped, and things certainly did not go entirely according to plan, but we had a wonderful feeling of achievement that day at Lord's in 1963. People seem to forget that Sussex had never won anything before, and in winning that first Gillette Cup we felt we'd played a most important part in the history of a great county. The sense of pride at Lord's that day was one of tradition, but one of the first senses of personal achievement that I had was some years before that in a celebratory match at Old Trafford. It was played at the beginning of June 1957 and it was between Lancashire and MCC to celebrate the Old Trafford centenary.

[233]

My recollection of the game is one shot that I played. At that time, nobody had heard of Ted Dexter, and I didn't make the headlines with a first innings of 22, but, in the second innings, I hit one shot off the back foot through the covers, and it was perfect.

Cyril Washbrook, the best cover-fielder in the world at that time, reached down a hand to stop the ball and then realized that it was travelling at about 95 miles an hour and took his hand away quickly. I made 50, and Len Hutton, who was *the* great name in those days, came in and said to me, 'Keep it up, lad.' And I was out a couple of balls later.

It was a totally unimportant match, but I can still remember that shot off the back foot.

The most memorable moment of my cricketing life, however, was in a coach in Melbourne on 3 January 1963. It was the end of the final day of the second Test match. We'd drawn the first in Brisbane, and we took a lead of 15 runs on the first innings of this Melbourne Test. I got 93 – I'd scored 99 in the first Test – and Colin Cowdrey got 100.

Freddie Trueman was the main reason for us bowling the Australians out for 248 in their second knock, and this left us to make 234 to win, and we got them with an hour and a quarter to spare. I'm convinced that the Australians would never have got them if they'd been in our position.

Over the five days, nearly a quarter of a million watched the game. I was going well in the second innings. The ball was coming off the bat sweetly, and then the present Bishop of Liverpool ran me out. I said to him afterwards, 'They always say the fool of the family goes into the Church', and he proved me right by running himself out later, though he did score 100 first so we remained friends.

We won by seven wickets, and it was a marvellous feeling. It seemed to me that it was revenge for the defeat at Old Trafford two years earlier when Richie Benaud had skittled us out, and we lost a game we should have won. It was a personal triumph for me, too, because all through the previous season there had been a lot of debate as to who would lead the team to Australia. The selectors couldn't make up their minds between Colin Cowdrey, David Sheppard and myself, but in the end I got the job, and I felt that this victory justified the faith that people had had in me.

The strange thing is that the realization of that great victory at Melbourne did not come to me until we were sitting in the coach outside the ground after the match. Then it suddenly dawned on me that I was captain of England and that we had beaten Australia on their own ground.

It was the greatest sense of elation that I ever had in cricket, and nothing that happened later took away that moment of triumph for me.

Later that year I captained England in the drawn Test with West Indies at Lord's. That was the match when any of four results was possible off the last ball, and Colin Cowdrey was at the non-striker's end with a broken arm in plaster. In the midst of all the excitement, I was bitterly disappointed because I thought we should have won the game. But even that disappointment, and the disappointment of losing that series to the West Indies couldn't take away the joy of that moment in the coach outside the Melbourne Cricket Ground. Nothing will ever dampen that for me.

> Ted Dexter speaks of his debt to John Mortimore, the Gloucestershire off-spinner. Mortimore captained Gloucestershire from 1965 to 1967, and was succeeded, for one season, by Arthur Milton. Then, in 1969, Tony Brown became the county captain. He led the side with much distinction until 1976 when he handed over to Mike Procter. It was under Tony Brown that Gloucestershire won an honour, officially, for the first time, the Gillette Cup in 1973. Brown won the individual award in that match for his violent 77 not out, 1 for 33 in twelve overs, and his inspiring captaincy. That was an exciting Gloucestershire side with Pakistan Test players Zaheer Abbas and Sadiq Mohammad, David Shepherd, now an esteemed umpire, John Mortimore, and the great South African all-rounder Mike Procter.

Jack Crapp was captain when I first started in 1953, that's when I played my first match. I'd wanted to do one of two things, either

[235]

to go to agricultural college, and, of course, when we lived in Cirencester, with the Royal Agricultural College there, that was an ambition, or to play cricket. I passed the entrance exam for Cirencester Grammar School, but father was in the RAF. He was demobbed, and we all went back to Bristol.

I was too young to go to the grammar school there so I had to take the exam again, and I went to Fairfield Grammar School in Bristol. When I was in Cirencester I didn't want to be a cricketer because I didn't know whether I was any good or not, and it was only when I got back to Bristol in 1947 that I played cricket at school in various age group teams. Eventually, father sent me for private coaching to Reg Sinfield, the old Gloucestershire all-rounder, who was coach at Clifton College.

I played for the public grammar schools and for Gloucestershire Club and Ground, and eventually they offered me a contract for 1952. I was reputedly a batsman when I started, although I had bowled at school. I probably should have made more runs than I did. I bowled a bit during national service, and when I finished Gloucestershire were struggling when I came back, and they suggested I should bowl. I started in 1957, and that was it, so I finished up as a bowler who batted a bit as opposed to a batsman who bowled.

Jack Crapp was the first of the professional Gloucestershire captains in 1953. Sir Derrick Bailey was the captain before that. There were some lovely stories about him. For most of my early days after national service, George Emmett was captain. George was captain until 1959 when Tom Graveney took over. He lasted two years, and then they brought in Tom Pugh, an amateur. They obviously thought he was the answer.

Percy Fender told the Gloucestershire committee that Tom Pugh would be the next PBH May. I liked Tom Pugh. We got on well. He was a good bloke, but the only thing he had in common with Peter May was that they both batted right-handed. He had a wonderful eye. He was a tremendous rackets player, world champion, doubles. He could play. He made 1,000 runs. He was no sort of stylist, but very brave. He would have been a captain, but they only gave him two years, and then they fired him. I think it takes at least that for people to become decent captains. It doesn't matter how good you are at managing men or making decisions. Look how long it took Keith Fletcher.

There was a time at Essex when they weren't winning anything, and everyone wanted his head. And he didn't exactly cover himself in glory as captain of England. He got in a terrible state in India when he knocked his own stumps down. At that time, too, Boycott left the tour when he'd completed the record number of runs, and he joined Gooch, Lever and the others in the trip to South Africa which had been secretly arranged.

Tom Pugh did two years and was just beginning to get to know how to do it when they changed. Ken Graveney came back and did two years, '63 and '64. Then John Mortimore did three years. Arthur Milton, who was the one who should have done it in the first place, was captain in '68, but Arthur had always been one of these people who, behind the scenes, suggested what should happen, because he was very good. His knowledge of cricket was absolutely superb. And he did it for one year and then said, 'I can't stand all this bickering behind the scenes. I can't do it any more.'

They slipped me in in '69, and I did it for the next eight years. We won the Gillette in '73, and the Benson and Hedges in '77, that was Prockie's first year. We finished second in the championship twice when I was captain, and second when Prockie was captain. I think the Gillette was my best moment. All of those games were tremendous.

Glamorgan we beat first, I think. Prockie was not fit enough to play in that game. Next we had Surrey at Bristol. We didn't make many, about 170, having been struggling all the way through. They were going well. Younis was in fine form, and they looked as if they'd do it comfortably. Then he was run out, marvellous throw, Nicholls. Younis was just sort of strolling. I think they were 50-odd for 3, and they just collapsed.

The next was against Essex at Chelmsford. Zaheer got runs. That was a fairly close game. Essex got within 30 of us. The semi-final was at Worcester. Prockie made 101, dropped a couple of times, once before he'd scored, and then batted perfectly well. I was scared. It was a boiling hot day, and they needed six off the last ball, and they didn't get it.

The final was against Sussex, and this time Prockie got 94. When we were 27 for 3 I had my doubts, but Andy Stovold did quite well, and Prockie and I had a partnership, and we left them to make 249. I would have been disappointed if they'd have got these, with Prockie to bowl, and other good bowlers as well.

They were going quite well at one stage, but we had a couple of very good bowlers, Mortimore and Procter, and Jack Davey was useful. I was past my best by then, but Roger Knight was a very handy bowler, although you might not necessarily rely on him to bowl all his twelve. He was always likely to get a couple of people out, and it was nice to be able to use him for five or six overs if he wasn't having a very good day. Take what happened against Essex. He was slogged for three or four overs, and then came back and got a couple of wickets. Very handy cricketer. Good fielder.

We were a useful one-day side in that we had five bowlers. There was David Graveney, a bit of slow left-arm. So we had Prockie, Jack Davey, Roger Knight and myself who could bowl seam, and Mortimore and David Graveney who could bowl slow. So that made it six.

Those of us who played with John Mortimore and David Allen, the majority of us thought that John Mortimore was the better bowler. David played thirty-nine times for England, and Mortie eight or nine.

Mortimore could bowl on anything. He had more variation. David could bowl on anything, too. He was not just a bad wicket-bowler, but Mortie was a greater flighter, didn't spin it as much, but spun it enough. Wonderful control. You'd never see him really get clouted. Except on one occasion, at Old Trafford, 24 in one over. I'd never have believed it.

The occasion of which Brown speaks was the semi-final of the Gillette Cup between Lancashire and Gloucestershire at Old Trafford, 28 July 1971. It was one of the most famous of one-day matches, and it did not end until ten to nine in the evening.

We know what happened, with five overs to go, and 25 runs needed, and Mortie had to bowl one over. I would still have no hesitation in saying 'Come and bowl!' I just wouldn't expect him to be hit for 24. He'd been our best bowler, apart from Prockie, who'd bowled well. I'd bowled my spell. Jack had one over. Prockie had two. Mortie had one. I'd finished, so we were going to have to find one over from somewhere, if I remember rightly.

The light was running out. We finished at ten to nine. They had three wickets in hand. Mortie had bowled well. He'd got Clive Lloyd out. He'd got Farokh Engineer out. He got somebody else out. He bowled really well.

I suppose Hughes just said, 'OK, we'll have a whack at him.' Jack Bond was captain of Lancashire at that time, and he was very magnanimous in victory, which is always nice, and something you don't get quite so often these days. When asked about the light, he said, 'Well, it was dark out there, but at least we knew where the ball was coming from whereas the fielders don't know where it's going.'

I can certainly vouch for that because when Mortie bowled that over to Hughes I was at long-off. I remember saying to John, 'Well, you've got one over to go, Mortie, just keep it tight so that they don't get more than 12. Then we'll be all right.' I didn't expect that he'd go for more than 12 because Mortie very rarely went for more than 6 or 7 in an over, anyway, even if they were slogging. He managed to bowl for ones and twos usually, especially on a biggish ground like Old Trafford. He never got hit out of the park. So I thought they might well get 12, but not more.

The only time you could actually see the ball was when it got hit up into the sky. When David Hughes hit the ball along the ground you couldn't see it. I remember he hit one out to extra-cover, and the fielders were Mike Bissex at cover, Roger Knight at extra-cover, and I was at long-off on the pavilion side. Mike Bissex shouted, 'Where is it? Where is it?' And Roger Knight said, 'It's all right. It's coming towards me.' That was the sort of thing. You couldn't see it. He hit one over the top of me, and I saw it as a black pea in the sky against this dark blue, and it just went straight over my head. Jack Bond was quite right. It was more difficult to field. But they were a good side, Lancashire, absolutely excellent.

Tony Brown played with, and against some of the greatest players the game has known since the Second World War, not least his team-mate, the South African all-rounder Mike Procter.

Sobers was, I think, the greatest all-rounder I ever came up against. Obviously, I rated Prockie as a marvellous all-rounder, but he wasn't as good a batsman as Sobers. He was not far off, though. Sobers was a wonderful bowler with the new ball. He was a better new-ball bowler than he was a slow bowler, and he was a great fielder. He was a truly great player. Roy Marshall was a fantastic player. He still holds the record for the number of runs scored by an overseas batsman in English cricket. He was a fantastic batsman, but Gary, as an all-round cricketer – bat, bowl, field – was supreme.

But the best batsman of my time without any shadow of doubt was Richards, not I.V.A., but Barry. Barry Richards was technically perfect. He could play any sort of game, three days, one day. He didn't have the chance to play Test cricket after 1970, but he could have just accumulated runs or, in a one-day game, he could just launch into somebody and make 100 in 30 overs. He made 300 in a day in Australia. It was almost too easy for him. He got bored.

When I first started, cricket was full of Englishmen who were tremendous players. Len Hutton was coming towards the end of his career, and so was Denis Compton whom, I think, I played against once, and with him in one match, and Bill Edrich. They were obviously past their best. But Peter May, of course, Tom Graveney, and Colin Cowdrey were terrific players. So was Basil D'Oliveira. He was a very difficult chap to bowl at. He was such a good back-foot player that he just stood there, and if the ball did anything, he was very good at just letting it go. Great judge of length, and so strong. He had very strong forearms, hit the ball with a very short back lift. He was a wonderful player. But the best was Peter May. He made 85 first-class hundreds and retired when he was thirty-one. Don Kenyon was a tremendous opener, nothing bothered him. They rated him above all the rest at Worcester.

Tony Brown was a dedicated cricketer with a great joy for the game. His attitude to cricket meant that he got the most from it.

I just enjoyed fielding, and my dad said that above all else you've got to be able to field. When I played football and rugby you had to be able to kick with both feet, and when you were playing cricket you couldn't just be a batsman and a bowler, you had to field because it doesn't matter what you are, everybody's got to be a fielder. You can't hide away. You've got to be out there somewhere, doing something, so why not enjoy it. I used to enjoy fielding, and Gloucestershire had a wonderful fielding side anyway, and they'd always been very good. Arthur Milton and Tom Graveney were tremendous out-fielders when I started, and they both came in and were equally good in-fielders. I've never seen a better fielder than Arthur Milton anywhere. He could just field anywhere, slip, gully, cover-point and on the leg-side. Bobby Simpson and Phil Sharpe were wonderful slip-fielders, but they didn't field anywhere else. Tony Lock was a wonderful short-leg, but he didn't field anywhere else, but Arthur could go anywhere.

Tom was a great catcher in the out-field, as was Arthur, but George Emmett and Jack Crapp were both wonderful close-fielders so Gloucestershire always had a good fielding side, and we, the younger ones, when we started, had to be able to run and throw, although there was no limited-over cricket then, and do all the things you should do.

I was lucky enough to play in all four competitions. People talk about playing too much cricket. I'm not so sure it's the actual playing is the problem, but I think it's the travelling and packing you have to do. You'd finish a championship game at Leeds on the

Tuesday, and you'd have to play in a Benson and Hedges Quarter Final at Southampton the next day. There were some fairly difficult journeys, and to get to the next match and be all psyched up in order to play an important one-day game was probably not all that easy. Motorway travelling helps, but although the travelling has always been there, there were only championship matches.

The Gillette started in '63, the John Player in '69, the Benson and Hedges in '72, so from '72 we've had four competitions, and from '69 we had three. And travelling from Chesterfield to Bristol on a Saturday night, and then you pack your bag again and travel back to Chesterfield . . . They've managed to sort these things out now, but, in any case, if you like playing, you'll get on and play.

I don't really subscribe to the idea today that they play too much cricket. It does seem to me that we've tended to give in to the whims and fancies of the cricketers. I don't think it really follows that if somebody says, 'I'm playing too much' or 'I'm not playing very well because I'm playing too much', then they're necessarily right. If they are, there are two things you can do. You can give them a rest – they don't have to play every match – or we have to look at it. If we are playing too much, then do something about it. I'm not convinced that four-day cricket would necessarily be the answer. The three-day game that I knew from my boyhood and the early days of my career was when we bowled 120 overs in a day. A three-day game was 360 overs. Now we're talking about a four-day game which will probably not be more than 360 overs, certainly not much more. So you're talking about four days for a game we used to play in three. Why should we have to do that?

The other argument that Roy Marshall puts forward is that when he was a young man playing in the Caribbean, because one didn't play very much cricket, you had to make your innings count. You had one innings a week. Over here, if you don't do very well in one innings, you think it doesn't matter, I've got another one on Tuesday or Wednesday. I don't think chaps think like that, not the majority of them, but the other thing is that it could rain on Tuesday or Wednesday, and you could go through a whole season with your seventeen four-day games, eight of which are at home, you could finish up batting only seventeen times. I don't think the majority of cricketers would be better for that. If you are at number six or seven, you've either got to learn how to bat and move up the order, like most young pros have done over the years. You earn your spurs and move up the order. If you are somebody who likes to hit the ball and bowls a bit, you might stay in the middle order or you may develop into a rather better batsman and move up. I don't think you can say this chap is definitely a number four batsman. It depends on the team and the conditions.

> Successful county cricketer as he was, Tony Brown never won international honours, although he came close to consideration. In the sixties, there were more quality all-rounders than there are today.

The closest I came to Test cricket was when the MCC side went to New Zealand in 1960–61, with Dennis Silk as captain. I was told that if I'd got 100 wickets as I had done in '59, I'd go. But I hurt my back half-way through the season, at Old Trafford. Someone hit the ball back, and I went to stop it, and I just felt a little thing go in my back. I wasn't right for the rest of the season, didn't play all that much and then didn't play half the next season. Then I got it fixed and was OK, but I was told if I'd done as well in '60 as I'd done in '59, I would probably have gone to New Zealand, but in those days, there were plenty of other all-rounders, and there were even more in the twenties and thirties.

There was Barry Knight, for instance. He and I might have vied for a place, but he was probably a better batsman than I was. Today, there is a dearth of all-rounders. If you compare the records of people today with people like Knight, Ken Palmer and myself, we got rather a lot more wickets than they do today.

> At Edgbaston, in July 1974, Gloucestershire fielded all day as Jameson and Kanhai of Warwickshire established a second wicket record of 465.

[243]

When Jameson and Kanhai got the record against us I caught the catch second ball of the morning – Abberley, caught Brown, bowled Dixon 0 – we didn't take another wicket all day. John Dixon is now captain of Bath. In that game, we had Prockie played as a batsman. I just played as captain – batsman. We couldn't bowl because both of us were injured, so our attack was John Dixon, Shackleton, Roger Knight, John Mortimore and a chap called Philip Thorn, who bowled slow left-arm, that's all we had. But although they put on more than 450, I think you'll see that no bowler, or only one, went for 100 in that game. They all bowled and shared it around and went for about 80 or 90 each.

The thing we really needed to turn us into a championship-winning side was to be able to get more runs at the right times, but Gloucestershire had had better sides pre-war and immediate post-war, but they didn't win anything as we did. I think we lacked a truly fast bowler. Jack Davey and I took 100 wickets each when we opened the bowling, but we were never going to frighten anybody out. Maybe, if we had had a Procter at the time, we'd have done better and won the championship. And then, when we were taking wickets, the batting wasn't probably quite as good as it might have been. You need runs to bowl at, but you also need wickets.

Tom Goddard was captain of the Second Eleven when I started. He was an amazing chap, a very hard man. He was always moaning at you. You didn't get much encouragement in those days. You had to do it, and if you didn't, you got a bollocking. Don't do as I do – do as I tell you. I didn't learn so much from him, though, as I did from George Emmett. George was a really tough captain. They wanted you to get all the things right, like you may not be a very good cricketer, but you could go out looking like one. You may not be a good cricketer, but you must behave like one. Those sort of things. If you hit the ball and you knew you were out, you had to walk, and if you didn't, you wouldn't play in the next game. If you gave so much as a second glance at the umpire when he gave you out, you'd get a rollicking from the captain, and you'd get one from the umpire as well when he came off. The things which we took for granted are the areas nowadays where you get problems.

[244]

Rubbing the ball in the dirt for the slow bowlers to bowl was something you were allowed to do and was common before the Second World War and in the days when we started, so that wasn't frowned on. Shining the ball was always allowed, and everybody was encouraged to shine the ball. John Mortimore was one of the best shiners of a ball there's ever been. Keeping the ball in good condition was a prerequisite for every bloke who reckoned he could bowl. A lot of them don't do that so well now, but picking the seam was done by a few who were well known on the circuit. They'd lift the seam about half an inch so they could get a grip on the ball, but if anybody did more than that, the umpires were fairly strict, and they'd bang it down again and warn them. Chaps knew that they really couldn't get away with it.

The thing that perhaps we've seen the greatest difference in is that winning wasn't the only thing that mattered to those who started playing thirty years ago. All the teams we ever played against or played with were jolly hard in that they wanted to win, but they didn't want to win at all costs. They played very, very hard within the laws of cricket, but if you played against Surrey or Yorkshire, you had some pretty uncouth language thrown at you. Umpires didn't hear it because it wasn't that bad, but you were subjected to some pretty hard verbals, but it just made you get stuck in and be more determined than ever. You just played as hard as you could within the laws.

Alec and Eric Bedser were two of the biggest moaners and groaners you would ever meet, and Peter Loader was a very aggressive player, as was Fred Trueman. They were nice enough blokes. Norman Gifford was a very aggressive bowler for a slow bowler. They could all make an awful lot of noise. What you didn't do, and they didn't do – you didn't cheat. You didn't claim catches you knew weren't out.

Mike Procter couldn't believe what he was seeing in one game. He was bowling to Peter Sainsbury of Hampshire, and Arthur Milton and a few of us were in an off-side cordon, slip to gully. Arthur was at gully, and Peter Sainsbury played the ball to gully, and Arthur caught it. Prockie did a dance, and Peter Sainsbury stood there. Arthur looked at him and said, 'I caught it, Saint.' And Peter said, 'I don't think you did, Arthur. I think it probably didn't quite reach you.' So Arthur said, 'Oh, all right.' And he threw the ball back to Prockie who said, 'What's going on?' Arthur said, 'Peter doesn't think I caught it so let's carry on.' And we carried on playing. Prockie couldn't believe this, that two chaps had decided it between them. Of course, it worked the other way. If a chap at short-leg said I caught that, you'd walk. I see nothing wrong with that, but if they decide that the umpire must make the decision, then they must accept it, not just stand there.

> In his career, Tony Brown scored 12,851 runs and took 1,230 wickets. He also held 493 catches, equalling the world record in 1966 when he took seven catches in an innings against Nottinghamshire at Trent Bridge. It was not until June 1965, at Bristol, that he hit his maiden first-class century.

Glamorgan made somewhere near 350, and they tried to win by an innings. They thought they'd bowl us out twice, and they didn't. It was a very flat wicket, and they buggered the game up. We were in our second innings, and Peter Walker was keeping wicket, and he said, 'You've never made a first-class 100, have you? Well, you'll never have a better chance. Get your head down, and make sure you'll get it.' I had about 80 at the time. And he said exactly the same thing to David Brown at the other end, and we both made hundreds. That was the first time I ever made a first-class 100. I managed to make three more after that.

I remember Butch White coming in number eleven for Hampshire, and I'm bowling from the pavilion end at Bristol. We were quite good chums – seam bowlers – and as he walked out, he said, 'Hey, Brownie, have you ever done the hat-trick?' I said, 'No, I haven't.' So he said, 'Bowl it straight, and you will today.' Like an idiot, I didn't bowl it straight. He missed it. The ball missed the wicket, and I didn't get a hat-trick. I remember saying to him some years later, 'Butch, if I'd bowled it straight, you didn't suggest to me that you'd miss it deliberately, did you?' And he didn't actually say yes or no, but he said, 'Well, I'm not sure, but you'd have had a better chance of getting me out, wouldn't you, if you'd bowled it straight.'

There was certainly a camaraderie about the cricket that appears to have been better in those days than it is now. I think one-day cricket has changed the attitudes of those who go to watch. There are three competitions in which you either win or lose, and they go to see their side win. The championship gives you the draw option, and I can see nothing wrong in that, and that's why I'm not that sold on four-day cricket. If one side isn't good enough to win the match by actually out-thinking or out-playing the other side, then I don't think they deserve to win it. I don't think they should win just on the basis that over four days there'll be a result. Three-day cricket is all about being able to outwit the opposition, out-bat them, out-bowl them, out-field them, do all those things. If you can't do that, if they can hang on by the skin of their teeth, then they deserve to gain the draw. The draw is the good, old-fashioned English compromise, and I don't see anything wrong with that. Both captains should set out with the firm intention of winning the game, not jockeying for position so that you hope to be set a target on the last afternoon.

I think that we were luckier when we played in that we played on uncovered wickets so that there was always this element of doubt as to what might happen over three days. With the pitches as they are now, they are very much flatter, and there's not a lot to help anybody. They take the grass off because they've got a lot of Surrey loam, so they don't take much spin anyway. There aren't very many good spin bowlers about, but anyone who can turn the ball is worth his weight in gold.

Charlie Parker, the old Gloucestershire slow left-arm bowler, took more than 3,000 wickets, and he played for England once. Tom Goddard took nearly 3,000, and he played about eight times. David Allen got just over 1,000, and he played thirty-nine times. It doesn't really make any sort of sense because Tom Goddard four times got more than 200 wickets in a season.

Some people would say that he was bound to do that playing for Gloucestershire because the pitches at Bristol had got sand on.

What they fail to say is that the first seven in the Gloucestershire batting order all made over 1,000 runs, and the first two, 2,000, so they couldn't have been that bad. Hammond would make 2,000, Barnett or somebody else would make 2,000, and the rest would make between 1,200 and 1,800.

Look at Les Jackson and Cliff Gladwin. People say, well, the pitches are green in Derbyshire, but you only play half your matches at home. John Langridge made 76 first-class hundreds and didn't play for England, and you've people playing for England now who've made 9 or 10. Gooch played after one century. One's glad they went back to him after a very inauspicious start because he's a very, very good batsman, but he forced himself back into the team because he made sufficient runs at county level. Gatting did the same. If you average 50 to 60 in county cricket, you've got something to offer, and you've got to be given a chance, but you've got to prove yourself in county cricket first. Far too many are given the opportunity without having proved themselves.

> Tony Brown reflects on captaincy and the varying attitudes that different cricketers have to the task. In 1982, Bob Willis was captaining England against Pakistan and bowled to Zaheer Abbas with seven men in an off-side cordon, from point to first slip. The ruse worked. Willis dismissed Zaheer cheaply. Brown also assesses the all-rounder for whom he had the greatest admiration as a colleague, Mike Procter.

Willis probably felt that Zed was susceptible to fast bowling. He was. Anybody is. Prockie was the same. If you could bowl really fast at Prockie, you probably had a chance of getting him out, but anything less than extreme pace, he just murdered it – medium pacers and slow bowlers. He was wonderful. He got 157 against Middlesex at Bristol, and Fred Titmus was playing. Fred was a very, very fine cricketer, wonderful bowler even if it wasn't a wicket that was helping him. If it was a very good batting wicket, he was always very difficult to score off. Procter just hit him as if he were a schoolboy spinner. Fred was bowling flat yorkers to make sure that he wasn't going to get hit. Procter just came inside

him and hit him over extra-cover for six. He did the same thing at
Lord's another time. He was a tremendous cricketer, a wonderful
hitter of slow bowling, but somebody a bit quick he might just
have a chance early on, but once he got his eye . . .

His problem was that he was so good. If he didn't bowl fast,
he'd like to bowl slow. He wasn't a very good off-spinner, but he
was as good as most. His greatest asset as an off-spinner was that
he could bowl a bouncer off two paces.

From time to time, if he wasn't bowling, if he wasn't participating,
he'd stand at slip, and he'd watch some of the younger bowlers bowl,
and he wouldn't always encourage them. Instead of just walking down
the other end and saying 'Bad luck that over, why don't you do this?
Why don't you do that?' he'd walk straight past John Childs or David
Graveney, and didn't say a word to them, particularly when he was
captain, so I heard. He didn't do it very much when I was captain, and
it didn't matter because there were plenty of other people to encourage
the bowlers, especially myself as captain. He was so good, that was the
point, and he couldn't really understand why others weren't scoring
runs, taking wickets or holding catches all the time like he was.

I think Wally Hammond was the same. Talk to people of the
nineteen-thirties, cricketers who were playing for Gloucestershire
just before and just after the war. He told Charlie Barnett he was
just a slogger. He didn't want him to open. He had a hell of a row
with the Gloucestershire secretary and chairman, saying that he
wasn't going to play Charlie Barnett. They said not to be silly, he
couldn't not play him, and Wally said, 'I don't think he's a very
good player.' They persuaded him, but he said, 'Well, if he plays,
he can't open.' Charlie Barnett said, 'If I don't open, I don't play.'

So there was this big row, but Charlie Barnett was a wonderful
bat, and what happened in the end, apparently, they persuaded
Wally that he had to play and he had to open. Very reluctantly,
Wally said 'OK'. Charlie Barnett made either 80 or 100, but Wally
went in and made 200, and when he came in he chucked his bat
down in the corner and sat down. Charlie Barnett was sitting down
in his place, and Wally looked across at him and said, 'That's the
way to play cricket. You're just a slogger.'

[249]

In the end, I enjoyed being captain. In the beginning, you think it's nice to be appointed, an honour, but then you realize there's an awful lot to it. Then you do it, and you think 'I like thinking in terms of the tactics and cajoling some and jollying along others.' Then you get to the stage when you think 'I could do without all this hassle.' I think it depends how resilient you are, but you don't want to go on for too long. The players with you get a bit bored with the same chap saying the same thing in the same situation. There is a limit.

If you're captain of a county side, when you go past six or seven years, that's long enough. They've heard you say all before, but the basics don't change, so even if what you say sounds boring, it's still vital – bowl straight, teaching a batsman to play straight etc. Some people are more capable of getting more out of other people than others are. It is an indefinable quality.

You can have people cajole you into doing well, and you can have others persuade you to do well, and you may do equally well with a fellow like Jack Crapp, who was a lovely, mild-mannered chap, encouraging you. You could do as well, maybe better, with a chap like George Emmett, who'd be telling you what to do. He'd be pushing you every minute of the day, not only on what you did on the field, but in your general demeanour about the place. You'd have to be absolutely the best twelfth man there'd ever been. You mustn't miss anything. He was looking to develop your ability in every respect.

When you went into the nets you'd have to play the correct shot, and he'd be watching you. You could be in the third net along, and he'd be in the first net with somebody else, and you'd play a shot that wasn't very good, and he'd spot it. He'd shout at you, 'I just told you not to do that.' You would react to that sort of thing, but equally you would react to Jack who, a couple of minutes after you'd played the horrible shot, would come behind the net and advise you gently. In the end of the day, it's how you react to what you've been told. You can teach somebody to play all the shots, but what you can't teach is how to distinguish between the half-volley, the long-hop or the bouncer when they don't know what's coming. You need the ability to spot that it's a half-volley the moment that it leaves the bowler's hand. Botham, both the Richards, Sobers, and all the great cricketers have been able to do that. Don Bradman made 100 every three innings because he instinctively knew what shot to play to that ball, whereas the average cricketer takes that much longer to decide that the ball coming down to him now is a half-volley or it's not a half-volley; he can or he can't drive; he's got to leave it alone, etc. You can't teach that.

> Tony Brown retired from first-class cricket in 1976, and from 1977 to 1982, he was secretary/manager of Gloucestershire. He moved to Somerset in 1983, lived through the turmoils over the departure of Ian Botham and Viv Richards, managed the England side in India and the Caribbean, and took up a senior position with the Test and County Cricket Board.

It took a couple of years to get used to not playing and to be able to look at a game dispassionately. I'd watch the cricket and get agitated about field placings and the rest. I'd want to do things like change the bowling. It took a couple of years to learn to be a good watcher, but then I enjoyed being on the administrative side. Anybody who has played and enjoyed cricket gets so much fun from it, and I am lucky to be still involved with the game. I get self-satisfaction, but hopefully you are still helping those who are involved in playing and helping them to enjoy, and to watch. We need the next generation of spectators, so that the more who are encouraged, the better.

People like Doug Insole have given their whole life to cricket; and Peter May – captain of Surrey, captain of England, chairman of selectors. 'Gubby' Allen did about everything to keep the game going, and there are lots of people in club cricket who do the same. County cricket is just the tip of the iceberg, and that is something we should never forget, and players and administrators need to be reminded of it.

When we talk about the next generation of cricketers we mean not only the Test and county players, but those of limited or no

[251]

ability who still love the game and support it. It is a game, and not a war, and events in the Gulf bring that into perspective. Being run out for 99 is unfortunate, but it's not a tragedy. The definition of a game is that it is a test of skill, a piece of recreation, an amusement. And that shouldn't be forgotten. You have fun while you're trying to outwit the opposition, and you should be seen to be enjoying it.

David Gower gets criticism because he seems to be enjoying the game, and he plays a shot and mistimes it and gets out, and everyone is up in arms. They forget the last thousand times he played the shot he hit the ball for four. Equally, they say, 'You never saw Bradman or Hammond do that.' But they were exceptions. Gower has his own particular way of playing. I know from my time as manager, when he was captain, he certainly never let me down. Everything he did was right for England. He never embarrassed me, the TCCB or the England cap he wore. He could be high spirited, but he never embarrassed anyone.

We played against each other. Prockie bowled him, as he did all newcomers, before he was ready. David Gower was still waiting for him to put a foot down. Prockie did the same with Ron Headley. When he was bowled Ron turned to Ron Nicholls who was fielding at short-leg and said, 'It takes longer to come than you think.' And Ron Nicholls said, 'Are you sure you got that the right way round?'

It was the same with David. He was wonderfully talented.

I first met with him at Worcester, when I was appointed manager and he was captain, and we talked about certain aspects of the game and behaviour. I said, 'Look, we're all going to India to enjoy ourselves. As long as we get one or two ground rules, we'll have no bother. If we can agree them now, that would be fine.' We said we'd have no dissent on the field, and certain off-field things were taboo.

We lost the first Test in Bombay, which immediately followed Sir Percy Norris being murdered. Mrs Gandhi was killed first, you will remember. He was killed the day after we'd been to a party at his house. It came as a great shock to the team, and we didn't play terribly well. We were also umpired quite poorly, and a lot of decisions went against us. One or two of the chaps who'd been on the previous tour when Fletch was captain said, 'Oh, here we go again. We're going to get stitched up.'

David, Norman Gifford and I went into my room, and I said, 'That negative attitude has got to go. Tell them, David, we'll deal with the umpiring problems off the field. They mustn't let it get to them. If they're worried about bat/pad catches, then the answer is hit with the bat and get caught at mid-off or mid-on, but don't play in such a way that you might get caught bat/pad. Don't give them the opportunity to put the pressure on you.'

After that, David talked to the team, and there were no problems. They were very good. Come to the last two Tests, and they were asking us which umpires we wanted. David was excellent, and when things didn't go well in the West Indies it wasn't because the boys gave up trying. The harder they tried, the worse it got. There was a fuss and misunderstanding about 'optional' nets. We could never assimilate the conditions in the nets that we were finding in the Tests, but it was an option to players as to whether they used these nets or not. When we found adequate nets, all practised.

It was while Tony Brown was secretary/manager at Gloucestershire that the Packer affair rocked cricket. Kerry Packer, an Australian businessman with strong media interests, set up his own World Series Cricket, which was shown on his own Channel Nine television company in Australia. He paid large sums of money to attract the top players, and he introduced floodlit cricket. His differences with the Australian Cricket Board over television rights were finally resolved, but his two-year revolution in the late seventies changed much in cricket. It brought sponsorship into the game on a much wider scale, and it raised the standard of living of the majority of players.

The Packer affair did a lot for the game, but also it affected many people in different ways. Both Zaheer and Mike Procter came back just waiting for everybody to bowl half-way down at them, so they just stood back, didn't get in line with it at all and looked either to

[253]

cut it over third man or maybe to hook it. The whole thing was based on the fast bowlers bowling half-way down. The batsmen wore helmets – it was the introduction of helmets – and it was a war.

It took Zed and Prockie a little while to readjust. Neither of them made any runs when they first came back. They couldn't understand why, and we all said, 'Well, you're just not getting into line with it all. You're just standing there waiting to whack it.' They obviously realized after a while that the pitches we played on were suited to back play, and they could go back and bat as they had done before, which was wonderful cricket.

At Somerset, Tony Brown was to have problems of a different kind.

I enjoyed my time as secretary of Somerset. It was an interesting and successful time. We won the Benson and Hedges in '83. I went there in '81. Rosie was captain, and there was a lot of intrigue, and he was followed by Botham, and there was still opposition. Brian Rose had done too long, and was popular, and jealousies develop. Somerset thought it best for Botham to be captain. It had nothing to do with England's needs or wishes. He was a wonderful cricketer, but no way that anyone in his right mind would have him as captain. The same applies to Allan Lamb. If they took the trouble to ask the people who know, they would realize these things. Lamb's a super cricketer, but he's not a captain.

At Somerset, there were a number who thought Ian Botham was not a captain, but you've got to have a majority to think that way. Rose stayed on as coach and captain of the Second Eleven, and then he became team manager, which was a mistake, because his best place to help Somerset cricket was as captain of the Second team. There, he could get all the youngsters under him and teach them how to play. There was no point in him being in the dressing-room. If you've decided you need another captain, what can be worse than having the previous captain sitting in the corner when you've got a new captain trying to do the job.

There have been significant changes in the game during the years in which Tony Brown has been involved as player and administrator. For a young professional today, life is very different from what it was for the young professional of thirty-five years ago.

Tom Graveney gave you bats he didn't like. I had a bag from him. We got £2–10s. a week when we started, and we were delighted to have it. All that you were interested in is that you were a pro cricketer. When you went to do national service, in fact, it went down to 18s. a week, and to have a contract for £350 a year was fantastic.

I was capped in 1957, and, in 1959, my contract was £750 a year. I can remember dear old Reg Sinfield, who was obviously still fairly sprightly, saying, 'I've played for England, and I only got £750 at the height of my career.' But we said, 'Hang on, Reg, that was in 1939.' But then there were no sponsored cars, and with your expenses, you were only reimbursed for what you'd actually spent.

Richard Hutton's first-class career began nearly ten years after Tony Brown's. Both men retired from first-class cricket in 1976. As the son of one of the greatest of cricketers, Sir Leonard Hutton, Richard grew up in an atmosphere pervaded by the traditions of the game and of Yorkshire cricket in particular. Educated at Repton, he won his blue all three years at Cambridge, 1962–64.

I started in the same year as Boycott, but we'd played together in the Yorkshire Second Eleven the previous year. We played at Bridlington, against Cumberland. We opened the innings, and the first wicket fell at 64, and I was out for 49, but he was still there on the second morning when we declared, 154 not out, in a two-day match. I got my runs within the first hour, but he went on and on and on, and that was the first time I'd ever played with him. I don't think we won the match because we had to bowl them out twice. Yes, he was a good player.

There wasn't much else that was ever thought about except

cricket as far as I was concerned. I don't think my father was really that overboard that I should become involved, but it was an obsession for me from a very early age. As soon as I was old enough to watch Yorkshire matches and see my father play, I would go and watch and score, score the match in my own book. I used to read all the books on cricket, and when I was about ten or eleven I started to take *Wisden* to bed. I would know all the players' names, so I was really steeped in cricket. There was little else to life. When I eventually came to play first-class cricket myself, against some of these people whom I'd actually read about in *Wisden*, I found it very difficult to come to terms with. They were revered figures who had appeared in this book, and I didn't feel that I could possibly be on the same terms as they were.

My first first-class match was against Essex at Fenner's when I was at the university, and I was down to go in at number three. I had to wait until the middle of the afternoon because Craig and Lewis got big scores. I was shaking when I went out to bat, and I was so nervous at playing against Trevor Bailey. I remember Brian Taylor was keeping wicket, and people like Bill Greensmith, legspinner – terrifying. I was so nervous that I didn't have the strength to hit the ball. It took an awful long time for me to overcome that, and I was always nervous.

I was so nervous before my first match for Yorkshire. They pitched me in against Lancashire at Old Trafford when there were still crowds at the Roses matches. I came up to Manchester and stayed in the Queen's Hotel. Yorkshire had been playing in Middlesbrough so I was on my own, waiting for them, and they were late coming. I went to bed, and I just couldn't sleep at all. I stayed awake all night waiting for this match, and the next day, Brian Statham did me for a low score.

I felt it was just more than I could handle, but I like to think that I came to terms with it in the end, although I was always very nervous.

I think being the son of a famous father added to my nervousness because I was a marked man from the outset. People would have expectations of you, and, I suppose, on occasions, opposition might try a bit harder against you, so, from the playing side, I think it was a handicap. In social terms, it was a great advantage. He had been much loved and respected, and some who knew him were very kind; others probably felt that I'd been born with a bit of a silver spoon.

> Richard Hutton went to Pakistan with the MCC side under Mike Brearley, 1966–67, and, in 1971, he played five Test matches for England with considerable success as batsman, bowler and fielder. The following winter, he played in Australia with the Rest of the World side, but he was not picked for England again.

The wickets in Pakistan turn, but there is nothing in it for the seam bowler. Somebody who has got a bit of pace can be effective. They are generally low and slow. The batsmen out there thrive, but I can't say I did, but I did get a hat-trick. Ask Keith Fletcher. He caught the first one of the three, a stinger. There were some good players on that tour. Mike Brearley got 300, and there was Alan Knott, Derek Underwood, Dennis Amiss.

I always felt that I could play, but I was never quite sure how well I could play. I had one season in the England side, but then they discovered that Tony Greig was a better proposition. We both did the same things. I felt that I had the bottle for the big occasion, but I might have lacked a bit in terms of class and quality.

I always hoped the game would be interesting when I was playing. That was something I was very conscious about. I believed I shouldn't really be playing for my own benefit, but for the benefit of those who were interested in watching. I think, at the time, I was not solely concerned with my own performance and my own record. I wanted to play as attractively as possible so that those watching would maintain interest. I wanted to play it for the benefit of the team, and I did feel my responsibilities.

I think that my father felt very strong responsibilities, but I think that he felt that the best way he could fulfil them was in getting as many runs as he could, and staying in and staying in. He

[257]

obviously realized you couldn't get any runs if you were sitting in the pavilion. People had the expectations of him getting big scores, and therefore he responded accordingly.

I was much more inclined to get on with it. I would like to have got more runs than I did, and I'm sure I could have done and should have done. I bowled, I know, but so did my father. He got over 60 wickets in 1939. He was a leg-spinner, which was very unusual for Yorkshire. I don't know what were the factors which prevented him from bowling much after the war. He bowled at the Test match in Headingley in 1948 and went for plenty, but he hadn't bowled for years.

I think he felt a weight of responsibility on him, and he took it very much to heart. He was playing at a time when the game was still very popular and was watched by a lot of people on the grounds, therefore the response and the reward he would get would be immediate.

When I first started the game was turning off, the early sixties. It was losing its public appeal. There were fewer people available to watch it and therefore the feeling was to try to do something to reverse that trend, to play as interestingly and as attractively as possible to get them to come back to watch, but when something is on the slide it really takes so much more than that. You can't do anything about it. Certainly my father had a sense of responsibility towards those who came to watch him play. He finished in 1954–55 when crowds were still very considerable.

A lot of those cricketers of the past at the centre of the game were great artists. I remember watching my father when he played, and I felt there was great artistry about the way that he played even when he was in a defensive mode. There was a delicacy, an artistry, and the same with Denis Compton. They were great artists at work, and a lot of the other cricketers were entertainers themselves in their own way.

Johnny Wardle was a wonderful entertainer. People would sit in anticipation all afternoon for the entrance of Wardle into the arena, and they were rewarded because he would likely hit a ball straight over the football stand whatever the situation of the match. People

[258]

had the freedom in those days to play in their own way, and I think this is the way cricket has to be. Regimentation is bad for cricket. The theory was that people of pure ability had got to be allowed to play to that pure ability.

Basil D'Oliveira is a case in point. I played with him in five Test matches, and several times our innings was at a crucial stage. We were on the ropes, having lost several wickets for not many runs against the tricky Indian spinners like Venkataraghavan. Basil might hit his third ball just straight out of the ground, and I would say to him afterwards, 'How on earth did you come to play that shot?' Knowing that, in the circumstances, I would have been far too intimidated to play it. But for him, it was sheer instinct.

Of course, sometimes it went wrong. Once he swept a ball off the middle of his bat on to his leg stump, but you've got to allow players to have that instinctiveness in the way that they play otherwise it just becomes boring. Everybody plays differently. Basil D'Oliveira was a very instinctive cricketer, and you couldn't stop him playing that way. He was his own man.

There was freedom in Yorkshire. I remember I once hit two of the last three balls of a day's play in a county championship match at Scarborough over long-on for six. In fact, I blocked the last one, and I ran off the field. They always thought I was a bit of an amateur, and Ted Lester, who was the scorer, after he closed his books down, came in for the day. He used to whack it a bit, and he was in favour of people hitting sixes. And I looked at him because I thought he would have approved. It was an off-spinner I hit, and they were good shots, but Ted said, 'The last ball was there to be hit as well, wasn't it?' He thought I should have hit all three for six.

During Richard Hutton's career with Yorkshire, the county won the championship five times, and he played in two winning Gillette Cup Final teams at Lord's.

I think the business of no fours before lunch was very much overplayed. Yorkshire cricketers were a pretty aggressive lot on the

[259]

whole, and I think they used to like to hit the ball. I think a lot of it could have been Neville Cardus's creation, which was probably built around two of the most dour men you could ever meet in any walk of life, like 'Ticker' Mitchell and Emmott Robinson. They were the absolute opposite of Neville Cardus because there was nothing dour about him.

I was with Yorkshire at a very successful time. I first played for Yorkshire in 1962 when I was at university, and we won the championship that year. Surrey had been the leading side, and Worcestershire were very strong. In 1963, we won the championship, and in '66, '67 and '68. We won five out of eight, and we had two Gillette Cup wins, '65 and '69, and we got to the final of the Benson and Hedges. In '68, we lost Trueman. Illingworth went to Leicestershire. Ken Taylor finished. Jimmy Binks retired. A lot of important players stopped playing for Yorkshire in '68, but we soldiered on with what was left, and we came fourth in '70 and won the Gillette Cup in '69.

Brian Close soldiered on with what was left, and I must say in his favour that he never looked back. He felt that he'd got an equally good lot, but we did miss Illingworth dreadfully. We lost him because when he played in Test matches in 1968 we made use of the services of Geoff Cope, and he took forty wickets in five matches and finished top of the national averages. This put the fear of God into Illingworth. He saw his position as being under threat, rightly or wrongly – I think wrongly.

Ray Illingworth was very keen about security, and he asked Yorkshire to give him a contract, which was something that was becoming prevalent in other counties. Yorkshire had never given anybody more than thirty days' notice so they said we don't give contracts. Brian Sellers summed up the situation, 'If he doesn't like it, he can lump it.'

I think Ray had prepared his ground pretty well. He obviously had an offer from Leicestershire in his pocket. I think he had been very dissatisfied with Yorkshire's man-management style for some time. He was amenable to what people from other counties said to him.

Sellers was still the power in the land at that time. He was a very strong, powerful person. He was a great character in the game. He had had a great side under him in the thirties, an amazingly good side. I can only go on hearsay because I wasn't there, but I think he was a good captain. He was strict with them. He was a wonderful fielder, and he was fearless, and he liked a good time. My father respected him, but I'm not sure he liked him all the time. He found him a bit hard. He was a very sensitive man. Brian Sellers and 'Ticker' Mitchell must have downed thousands of pints of ale between themselves. I think Brian Sellers was very good fun, but I didn't have to play under him.

That was another thing about Yorkshire I noticed when I first played, it was good fun. Although it was hard and tough and all the rest of it, we had a hell of a good time, but that changed, and I think it's changed throughout the game now, which is a shame because cricket is something which should be enjoyed. It changed while I was there. Boycott's influence was to change it. He was very much a product of the Thatcherite age – all must be personal profit. I don't think that life will ever again be about what people do. Everything is now geared towards winning, specific objectives and achievements. I think they've changed the complexion of a lot of things, and cricket is definitely one of them.

In most counties people took pleasure from watching cricketers play, and the winning or losing was probably incidental. Now, it's all down to winning, and that is the measure of the enjoyment that people seem to get from it, not the enjoyment the players' performances give them and their worthiness within the bigger context of the match, like an innings of 28 on a turning pitch with the ball going past the edge three times an over. Everything is so regimented, from the medium-pace bowler to the low bounce of the ball going through to the wicket-keeper. Everything is the same. There is no variety. Many attitudes have been changed by television.

Vic Wilson, the farmer, was captain of Yorkshire when I first played. He had taken over from Ronnie Burnet, who had been Second Eleven captain and under whom I never played, but I knew well. Burnet did a good job. He took over from Billy Sutcliffe who had a very difficult time. Ronnie immediately ran into the Wardle business. At that time, Yorkshire had three world-class bowlers just as Surrey had, and Yorkshire kept coming second.

Yorkshire's bowlers were competing against each other as much as against the opposition. Ronnie was the chap who brought back the cohesion in the team. There was no doubt that there was a great deal of talent in the side, but it lacked cohesion. He had to get rid of Wardle who was one of my favourite cricketers, a tremendous entertainer. Johnny suffered from competition with Tony Lock for the England spot, and he felt that Tony Lock was taking an unfair advantage of him because of his action.

By the time I joined the team in 1962, team spirit had been restored and some marvellous team performances had put them back on top. In 1959 they won the championship, making 215 in 105 minutes at Sussex to win the title, and they got them for the loss of very few wickets. There were a lot of matches round about that time they won through run chases, and they became a team feared chasing a target in the fourth innings, with the result that declarations got tougher and tougher. But they did knock over some quite big scores chasing in the fourth. They were a powerful side.

Brian Stott was a good cricketer as an opening batsman for a short time. He would cut and carve away and get you going, and Ken Taylor was a very good player, and Brian was very capable of whacking it. And then you'd got Fred lurking down the order, and he was always good for a quick however-many, but more importantly his sheer presence was a threat to the opposition.

Trueman was really the biggest personality I played with. His stature was huge. I rated him highly in every respect except for, sometimes, his reliability, but I thought he was a wonderful bowler, and he was fearless, or he appeared to be fearless. He played some amazing innings with the bat when none of us could get any.

At Middlesbrough, we were bowled out for 23 by Hampshire, and we lost. Against Shackleton, who was a very fine cricketer, Fred was top scorer in the first innings with 55 – I think I was second top scorer – and we couldn't get to 150. Fred dealt with Shackleton with a cross-bat whereas everybody else tried to play him straight up and down the line and got out. Fred just heaved him in the general direction of mid-wicket which, under the conditions, was really the only way to play him. He was top scorer again in the second innings.

The great thing about the Yorkshire cricketers at that time was their supportiveness of each other. If you were in a group of people talking about a Yorkshire player and anyone said a cross word about him, the other Yorkshire player would leap to his defence straight away. Fred did that. He was very supportive of the people that he played with, and Brian Close was very supportive of the people he had playing in his side, which is one of the reasons the Yorkshire committee eventually found him tiresome. He was very loath to let in fresh blood. He wanted to stick to those that he knew, tried and tested. He would fight hard and long to retain the people that he wanted.

> As an all-round cricketer who scored more than 7,500 runs and took over 600 wickets in his career, Richard Hutton faced all the leading players of the sixties and early seventies, and, like all cricketers, encountered some very difficult opponents.

I rated batsmen in terms of their difficulty to get out. I found Tom Graveney extremely difficult, and Colin Cowdrey extremely difficult, and Graeme Pollock was impossible to get out. To me, they were front-foot players, and their bats were very straight, and I really wanted batsmen to play back to me. Tom Graveney used to play forward to everything, as did Colin Cowdrey, and Clive Lloyd was another who was extremely difficult to bowl to because he got a long way forward. I hated bowling to the batsmen who got a long way forward, but you don't find so many of them today getting far forward.

I found John Mortimore of Gloucestershire very difficult to bat against. He made clever use of the air, and some of his balls would spin and some wouldn't. He used to bowl in tandem with David Allen when Gloucestershire had two off-spinners, and David was

[263]

the England bowler most of the time. They were both exceptionally good bowlers, but I found David Allen comparatively predictable. John Mortimore, I found unpredictable. As a batsman, I always liked to be able to feel in my mind what the next ball was likely to be, and any bowler who didn't help you to come to that conclusion caused confusion.

I thought Brian Statham was an outstanding bowler, but, strangely, I did quite well against him. I always knew that the ball was going to be pitched in my half and that he was going to compel me to make a stroke. I think, more importantly, I knew that he was going to make me play, which, in some ways, is very comforting. It's as the game should be.

I got 81 in my last Test, against India, at the Oval. I should have got 100, but I was running out of partners. I once had to play Lancashire with my gloves at Headingley on an uncovered pitch. I think I needed a crisis to feel extended to my fullest. To go into bat after somebody had got 150 and somebody else had got 100 and someone else 90 was rather unchallenging. To go in at 40 for 4 was a much more interesting proposition.

I much preferred that we should be successful in the three-day than in the one-day game. I found them very artificial, and the games lacked sufficient scope for the individual to develop his talents fully, unless occupying one of the prime sites in the team. I find the restrictions of bowlers very artificial in limited-over cricket. There's no artificial restriction on the batsman as to the number of overs he can bat, and I don't see why there should be any restriction on the bowlers. I see nothing wrong with the principle that two bowlers should each bowl thirty overs, and I think that it would prove to be a better game.

The limited-over game is very regimented, and it follows a predictable pattern. It really makes the game itself less interesting because you can predict what is likely to happen. Without the restrictions on the bowlers, it would throw up a lot more options and opportunities. Wherever you produce restrictions and artificialities on bowlers you take away half the entertainment of the game because you no longer have the bowler and the fielding side

[264]

actively trying to take wickets. The one-day game needs to have in it an element which is concerned with the taking of wickets, which it doesn't at the moment. If you've got a good bowler who is likely to bowl the other side out, you should be able to bowl him all the time.

Close lost his job because of his reputed antagonism to the one-day game, the Sunday League, not the Gillette Cup, we'd had that for six years. He wasn't on his own. We all thought it would last the one season and then go away like a short illness. We could not believe that we would be required to go on playing it.

It's been a prostitution of the game. It's been bad for the public, bad for the players and bad for the image of the game. It's badly conditioned the attitudes of the public. It has changed players' techniques in that they have to do things in the game that they wouldn't otherwise do. It's been thoroughly bad. I cannot think of a single favourable thing to say about the Sunday League. It's just generally lowered the game and its standards in the minds of everybody. I think it's been appalling. I hated every minute of it, and it was a contributory reason why I didn't want to go on playing. It took a lot of fun out of the game, continually packing your bag.

I was thirty-two, and there wasn't a lot to go for, and there were these things happening in the game that were making it more difficult. It was before the great wave of commercialism so we were still in poverty. Having been a Yorkshire cricketer, there were very many compensations, so I didn't mind being poor. I didn't really see much prospect of getting back in the England side, and I was very worried at the way Yorkshire was moving. We had gone three or four years since Brian Close had left, and there were major problems concerning the style with which Boycott was captaining the team, and also the influences that he was having within the club and which were being communicated to the public at large. I didn't like it, but I had no idea of the conflict that would occur later. It looked to me as if there were certain elements in the club who had things firmly in their grip, and they weren't going to be loosened easily. It was best just to let them get on with it and see what they could do. Now the disaster is there for everybody to see.

[265]

I didn't really miss it when I gave up. I went to work in a place where I could still play cricket at a good level and be properly extended. I missed the sixties. I missed being involved with cricketing people, but you can't recreate.

It was a very good time in Yorkshire cricket in spite of shortcomings and in spite of disturbing things beginning to happen. It was a happy time. We had a good team that more often than not were always challenging for a major trophy. We were well feted by people. We had a big band of followers and supporters. It was interesting, and we had a great deal of fun, and that was very important. They were days I shall never forget. There's no substitute for playing.

Those are the lucky people who can get out there and play, for it's a wonderful game in every respect. It's not only your own personal performance. That makes up a big part of it, but also you can contribute to the activities of others. And that's the most important part of cricket, to be able to delight in the performances of others. The game needs to offer more variety than it does. We don't want all the pitches to be the same so that when you go from Essex to Northants it's exactly the same type of pitch. You must have these differences, and you must encourage people to be different within the game. What you want is highly motivated players and a good captain who will play the game in a good spirit, in a way that the public will find entertaining. If they give a good account of themselves and lose, they are just as worthy as winners. These are the attitudes we must get back, otherwise the game is contaminated.

I thought Norman Yardley was the perfect example of an England captain. He played the game hard in a Yorkshire way, and he was generous towards his opponents. He wasn't captain of England at a particularly easy time because we had post-war reconstruction problems, and he was playing against a crack Australian side, but Norman Yardley will go down in the annals of the game and be remembered for ever and ever for that one moment of generosity towards Bradman in his last Test when he led England in three cheers. It was an unforgettable moment.

[266]

I think all players in the game can have a cynical approach. I know when I played there was a danger that it could creep in. It's a short life, and you want to do as well as you can as quickly as you can, and then you've got to start life again, which is very difficult. But I think that cricketers need to have a sense of responsibility in that they are handing on something to the next generation of cricketers, and they shouldn't try to take it all out for themselves in their particular period. Good education is so important.

My father came from a background where religion and education were important. He came from a Moravian settlement which consisted of a school and a chapel and a Sunday school. It was an enclosed village that existed within these confines. The community spirit was very important, and he always recognized, although he wasn't educated himself beyond the age of sixteen, the value of education, the fountain of all knowledge.

The family had a building business that was effectively ruined in World War One, and when he left school he began to learn carpentry, but there was really no doubt he would become a cricketer. He was receptive to knowledge and always curious.

Sometimes, he felt people went over the top about things, and there were times he wanted just to be left alone. The great Herbert Sutcliffe was different. He made sure that his name was known.

He was one of those great characters, like Arthur Wood whom I knew. They were individuals, all interesting to know – Jack van Geloven, Dicky Bird. You didn't have to be Colin Milburn or Fred Trueman to be a character. Jack van Geloven did the double for Leicestershire, and he was quietly comical in conversation.

The umpires were marvellous at Cambridge. In one match we had Les Todd who used to open the Kent innings with Arthur Fagg. We used to spend hours chatting with the umpires at Fenner's, and then in the Prince Regent afterwards. We would learn more from the umpires than we did from the visiting sides. Les Todd once asked me, 'Is there a particular score you get stuck on or becomes a bogey?' I said that one, eleven and thirteen always troubled me. He said, 'I could never get off 184.'

[267]

It was marvellous to talk to the old umpires – Syd Buller, Eddie Phillipson. Buller had previously no-balled Griffin, the South African bowler, out of the Lord's Test match. I remember asking Syd Buller about the idea which we had been brought up with as public schoolboys, that the batsman always gets the benefit of the doubt. After some consideration, he said, 'There's no such thing as doubt. You decide one of two things – out or not out!'

9

IT'S GOT TO BE
YOUR LIFE

Ashley Mallett

Dilip Doshi

Peter Kirsten

In contrast to Richard Hutton, most of Ashley Mallett's cricket was played at international level. He assisted South Australia from 1967–68 until 1980–81, and he appeared in thirty-eight Test matches. He first represented Australia at the Oval in August 1968, the first of his four tours to England, and his final Test was the Centenary Test at Lord's, 1980.

He did not join Packer's World Series Cricket although he was a member of Ian Chappell's fine Australian side of that period. He did leave cricket for a period, but returned to play in the Test as mentioned above. He played against India, South Africa and New Zealand, and he is considered to be the best off-spinner to have represented Australia since the end of the Second World War.

I was lucky to have played with and against some very fine cricketers, but I think there are five batsmen I would put above others. The first must be Graeme Pollock, easily the best of my era. He only played twenty-three Tests, but he averaged more than fifty, and had he lived in the 'sunny' part of the cricket world, away from the shadow of apartheid, I believe he would have established a record comparable to that of Don Bradman.

He stood legs apart, used little footwork, but he transferred his weight perfectly when playing off the front or back foot. As an off-spinner, I always thought I had a chance against this tall left-hander, but Pollock had quite the most remarkable temperament I've ever seen in any batsman quite apart from his exceptional talent, and the immense power in his wrists. He was never beaten. He'd play and miss, and then, to your consternation, he'd dismiss the next ball to the boundary rope with the speed of a tracer bullet.

In the first Test at Newlands, 1970, I bowled a ball of good length to Pollock. He pushed forward, met the ball with the full face of the bat, and this defensive push sent the ball back to my right. I could have fielded it easily, but I let it run through to Bill Lawry who was fairly straight at mid-off. To my horror, I turned to see the ball gathering momentum, and the ball beat Lawry and careered to the fence. That forward defensive stroke told me that here was a man out of the top drawer.

His timing was so precise. He selected the right stroke for the right ball to put away, and he had oodles of time, even against the quicker-pace bowler, and that's a good guide. Apartheid not only separated the races in South Africa, it denied a large portion of the cricket world all but a glimpse of Pollock's genius.

I saw Pollock again at close range during a series of Golden Oldie matches which coincided with South Africa's Test centenary in 1989. He was then forty-five and still a great batsman who, I think, was capable of getting into any Test team in the world.

Pollock was also good at mathematics, for he always seemed to manage to get a single off the last ball of the over.

Bill Lawry was another 'mathematician'. I had a great regard for him as a batsman, though not as a captain. He was intense and meticulous. He was never beaten, and he had a fabulous temperament. There was probably no greater challenge, or joy, for Bill Lawry than opening the batting and surviving against the meanest, fastest bowlers on God's earth. He revelled in a tough battle, and with the bat, he was a calm and calculated champion. It is strange how different he is as a commentator where he is so excitable.

He liked to get on the front foot, a technique which served him well on English wickets. He would claw to survive. He was never beaten, and he was always alert for a single off the sixth ball.

Bill was, in the main, a dour batsman, although I doubt whether he had the same morbid dread as Geoff Boycott. The England opener seemed to have a fear, close to paranoia, about losing his wicket. There were some who claimed Boycott didn't tour Australia in 1974–75 because he was afraid to face Lillee and Thomson at their height. Courage is something Boycott did not lack. He was very courageous, but he did, I believe, fear failure.

Lawry didn't like getting out, but he sometimes took risks. Pat Pocock was the best English off-spinner of my time, yet he played only one Test against Australia, at Old Trafford, in 1968. Pat got 6 wickets in one innings, but it was Lawry who turned the Pocock threat. He swung him for two sixes in the space of a few balls,

Pocock was taken from the attack, and it gave Australia the winning edge. He was an outstanding opener, and he could play pace or spin. He combatted the best in the world of all types. He was a magnificent batsman. So was Barry Richards.

Richards was quick on his feet and technically as sound as Boycott, but he had what Boycott lacked, a superb sense of flair and adventure. In 1970, like the rest of the South African batsmen, he had no idea which way Gleeson was turning the ball. He decided to attack. He went down the track and hammered Gleeson on the full or half-volley. It was a tactic which caught on, and Australia lost a four-match series, 4–0.

He could cut and hook and drive. I shall never forget his 356 for South Australia against Western Australia in Perth. The Western Australian attack included McKenzie, Lillee, Tony Lock, Tony Mann and Ian Brayshaw, and he flayed them. Tony Lock conceded 100 runs off 9 overs. We were 513 for 3 at the end of the first day, and Barry had got 325 not out. Sadly, too little was seen of Richards in Australia. English fans saw more of him, but he played in only four Tests because of South Africa's ban, but he averaged over 70.

Obviously, I saw much more of Greg Chappell who began and ended his Test career with a century. He was an intense competitor, so intense that he would often seemingly suffer from a sort of depression after the match. His concentration was everything, and he concentrated as well, if not better, than any other player I played with or against. He focused on the ball, usually met it with the full face of the bat and caressed it firmly.

Strangely enough, I always thought I had a real chance against Greg. He was ever after you, trying to gain the ascendancy, but I can't recall him ever getting the better of me. He certainly got runs against us, but I claimed his wicket on more than a few occasions. I regard him as among the best of my time, ahead of the likes of Viv Richards who was an exciting player against all but anything remotely coming in the realm of reasonable leg-spin. That was a type of bowling he didn't seem able to play.

When Greg began he was predominantly an on-side player. He

was immensely strong in that area. It took a visit to the South Australian dressing-room by Sir Don Bradman in 1967 to set Greg straight. Rarely, if ever, did the Don intervene, but he'd seen a slight *something* in Greg's grip on the bat which was calling out for a change. The Don played a few shadow drives, and that in itself was worth all the effort in training just to see Bradman bat, albeit in the style of a shadow stroke. Sir Don recommended a change in grip, and almost immediately Greg became more proficient in many of his off-side strokes. He was never a good cutter, and he dismissed it from his range, except when he was going well and generally past the ton. He also rarely hooked. He played the percentages, but he could also cut loose as well as anyone.

> The careers of Ashley Mallett and Allan Border barely over-lapped. They played just three Tests together, but Mallett was quick to recognize the future Australian captain's immense potential.

I saw him play at the Adelaide Oval against Colin Croft and the West Indian pace barrage. I was at the other end, and I know the number of blows he took, but I shall never forget his nuggetty resolve. He has had a fabulous Test career, particularly when one considers that he has spent the greater part of it in a losing side. He was the shining star of world batting, eclipsing the likes of Viv Richards, who was far more exciting but far less consistent, David Gower and others.

Border is tough, and he has a spirit which doesn't allow for compromise. Look at the 100 he got in England when he batted throughout with a broken hand.

> Mallett is one of that elite group of bowlers who have captured 100 wickets in Test cricket. He is quick to give praise to his compatriots, but he also despairs at the plight of the spinner today.

I bowled a fair bit in tandem with Dennis Lillee. He was, quite simply, the greatest fast bowler of my era. He had technical expertise, fitness, the physical build, stamina and determination to match with any fast bowler of any time. He was quick to find a batsman's weakness, and most batsmen seemed to dislike the ball which pitches leg and moves to hit the top of the off-stump. Few batsmen are able to counter such an attack. Dennis had a not unusually long run, and he used his run to build to the right tempo at release point. He was rhythmical.

It's interesting to note that my greatest ambition, to snare 100 Test wickets, came in twenty-three matches. Lillee took only one game less, but in the next fifteen games, Dennis took his tally to 200 while I notched a paltry 32 more. Perhaps the dominance of pace had just begun to make the big impact in that period. That's why I'm able to understand the frustration of spinners these days, especially when the quickies do the bulk of the work, and the spinner is left to grab the crumbs of an over here and an over there.

Lillee had a nice easy action, superbly side-on. He usually bowled close to the stumps and made full use of the late outswing. He also had a very good leg-cutter and an explosive attitude to batsmen. When his body struggled he used bluff.

It worked in Brisbane in November 1980, when the New Zealanders were trying to establish their second innings, and he was virtually on his knees with leg pains and a heavy chest cold. He stormed in and bounced one, and then he stood and glared at the batsman. It was a chilling sight, and shortly after the mesmerized Kiwi presented short-leg with a bat-and-pad catch off Lillee's off-cutter. He was a great bowler, the best of the seventies and the early eighties.

England's best answer to him was John Snow. He wasn't built like a great fast bowler, and he didn't look like a bully boy with the ball, but he had a quiet determination, was an aggressive cuss and was the sort of bloke who held a grudge. I know, for I once made the mistake of telling him that he didn't have the pace to bowl me a decent bouncer on any wicket, let alone the one on which South Australia were posting up a huge score and pasting him all over the place. Snow kept his cool, that is until the fourth Test at Sydney, 1970–71.

[275]

Australia were heading to almost certain defeat, and Snow was bowling at his belligerent best. He went through us like a scythe, smashed poor old Graham McKenzie in the face with a brute of a delivery which seemed to explode off that dry Sydney track. I arrived, and Snow bounced me. Ray Illingworth refused to place a short-leg, and I had a real softening up. After an hour of sheer agony I was so relieved to play against the slower and less demanding pace of Bob Willis that I tried to hook and gloved a catch to Alan Knott. It was Bob's first Test wicket, and it was the last time I ever showed any disdain for John Snow.

Snowie could slow his pace and bowl with his head, as he did at Leeds in '72 when he bowled with intelligence and guile. He could mix it with the best of them.

Andy Roberts was another good fast bowler. He was a mean customer, and I think he might have played a bit on his fearsome stare from those black, unblinking eyes. He was hostile. He could bowl a good outswinger, but I always thought his ability to cut the ball, either way, made him a difficult bowler to combat on any wicket. I think he learned much of his cutting ability when he was trying to be effective on the sluggish wickets at Southampton during his long stint with Hampshire.

He was a key figure in Clive Lloyd's side in the late seventies. He was the consistent launch pad, the ace strike bowler who gave non-stop hostility. You must remember that for the majority of his career he didn't have a barrage of pace men with him. He had spinner Lance Gibbs and a couple of medium pacers. Lloyd's plan of *Bodyline Revisited* did not begin to evolve until Roberts' career was on the wane, but he was almost in the Lillee class.

> The great English spin bowlers like Laker and Lock, and Wardle, were in action before Ashley Mallett came on the scene, but he would place another Surrey off-spinner, Pat Pocock, as the best of his time.

He was a bloke who oozed class. He only played one Test match against Australia, but, in one innings, he took 6 for 81. It was a performance which made those of us in the '68 Australian touring side sit up and take notice. He flighted the ball, and, unlike many spinners in England, spun the ball hard.

There have been those who've suggested that 'Percy' didn't play more Test cricket because he was too outspoken. I don't know. All I know is that he was a very fine exponent of the art of off-spin. He bowled with great guile and used variations of pace and spin to great effect. I believe, as do many others, that he would have been a real handful on the hard pitches of Australia. Sadly, we never found out about that aspect of Pocock's cricket, but, as a spinner, I class him above the likes of Derek Underwood, a clever bowler on a dicey track, but not a match winner on a hard and fast wicket, and the Indians Prasanna and Bedi, and the classy Ray Illingworth, and the much underrated New Zealand left-armer Hedley Howarth.

I greatly admired Derek Underwood, but I considered him as basically a medium-pace bowler. He cut the ball rather than spun it, but he was very effective on the flint-hard wickets of Australia. He tended to shore up one end. He did it to great effect on the 1970–71 tour when John Snow had the batsmen jumping the other end. He was nicknamed Deadly, but he was just that on dicey wickets.

On the uncovered wickets in England, I can imagine the problems he would present to batsmen. He was quite sharp through the air, and given the slightest hint of assistance from the track, he was Deadly! The ball would rear, and if you were good enough, you might get an edge or a glove. On unresponsive wickets he used to rely on subtle changes of pace.

He was very well served by Alan Knott, easily the best keeper I've seen. He could take a catch standing back, much in the way that Rod Marsh could, but he was also the master up to the stumps. Whether the ball skidded through low or reared above shoulder height, Knotty took it all in his stride. Bob Taylor was a very good keeper, too, but I'd have to go for Knotty.

Rod Marsh was good, but not in Knott or Taylor's class. He was their equal standing back to pace bowlers, but he struggled standing up to the stumps. I know. He had over 350 Test dismissals, and only twelve were stumpings, seven of them off my bowling.

He once proudly reminded me of those, and I reminded him that had he been on his mettle during those years, the figure could have been three times that.

> Ashley Mallett played under two captains who believed in attack and for whom he had a high regard, Les Favell and Ian Chappell, but he would give an Englishman pride of place as the best captain he encountered.

Ray Illingworth was a master tactician, the best captain I ever saw on the Test stage. He was the man who brought a tough unit to Australia in 1970–71 and took back the Ashes. John Snow was his spearhead, but it was Illie who brought the best out of Snow. Snow struggled before the first Test, but Illingworth settled him down with great diplomacy, the odd harsh word all wrapped up in a sort of warm and friendly fatherly manner. It won Snow over, and he reached his pitch just at the right time. He was given all the plaudits, but it was Illingworth who had much to do with the strategy and the psychology.

Ian Chappell was also a fine captain, but I would place him just below Illingworth. Chappell seemed to inherit the attacking attitude of Les Favell, and the determination and never-lose philosophy of Bill Lawry. He brought together these opposites, added a bit of flair of his own, and Australia had the best leader since the Benaud era.

He worked very hard at becoming popular with team mates. He became one of the boys, but he still commanded respect as the figure of authority. It wasn't easy for Ian, but, like Illingworth, he had a good understanding of how an attack must be balanced in order to fully utilize all the options open to him. The balance of pace and spin was always taken into account in his thinking, unlike some of the modern captains who seem to think spin is something akin to those machines which dry clothes.

> Like Ashley Mallett, Dilip Doshi came to despair of the treatment of spinners in first-class cricket, which became obsessed with seam bowling. He also became disenchanted by the politics

[278]

which he felt contaminated the game, both in India and England, and, having played thirty-two Test matches inside three and a half years, he left the game in 1983. He played for both Warwickshire and Nottinghamshire and topped the Test averages with his left-arm spin when India toured England in 1982.

You see the prejudices in cricket, and it is ridiculous. How can a player like Alan Jones never play in a Test match? He was one of the best batsmen I ever bowled to.

I met the prejudices early on in my career for I played for Bengal, and the strength and influence in Indian cricket is in Bombay and Delhi. It is far easier to win international honours if you are from one of these two associations, and from Karnataka. I spent some time in Bombay, and it made a great difference to my bowling.

I came to England in 1972, and I had a letter of introduction to Sussex. They were very welcoming and invited me to play for the Second Eleven for the rest of the season. I did well and took over fifty wickets, but, most important, I got on very well with the skipper Mike Griffith, and with Tony Greig, who was very helpful. I also became very friendly with the South African batsman Ken McEwan, who was just starting, and who went to Essex. I used to enjoy bowling in the nets to the senior players, and it helped me to develop my bowling.

The problem was that counties were limited to the number of overseas players they could have, which was why Ken McEwan went to Essex. I found the same when I went up to Lancashire. Keith Goodwin asked me to go up to Old Trafford and bowl in the nets there, but they had Farokh Engineer and Clive Lloyd. Jackie Bond was very helpful, and he told me that I should play county cricket. He recommended me to Meltham Cricket Club in the Huddersfield League, and I became their professional in 1973. I had not received any money when I was playing at Sussex, because I was not a contracted player.

I had a good time at Meltham, and I played for Nottinghamshire Second Eleven, again with success. Gary Sobers was the captain, and he saw me take wickets and was very complimentary. I played against Cambridge University and got some wickets, and then I played against the West Indian tourists. I got Rowe twice, and Lloyd and Julien, so I was very pleased.

I began to qualify for Nottinghamshire, ready to play cricket from 1975 onwards, but Sobers announced he would not be returning. Then Nottinghamshire signed Clive Rice as their overseas player, and I felt badly let down. I didn't come to England in 1975, and, in 1976, I played in the Bolton League. I also played for Hertfordshire.

I had one of my first great memories with Hertfordshire when we beat Essex in the Gillette Cup. I took four wickets and won the Man of the Match award. This seemed to be the start of a good period, for I got a call from Mike Smedley, who was then captain of Nottinghamshire, and the county offered me a contract for two years, 1977 and 1978.

Clive Rice and I were the main overseas players, and there was also Kenny Watson, another South African, a medium-pace bowler. Rice and I played in all the championship matches, and I did well. I took 82 wickets in all matches, and there weren't many people in the country who took as many as that. County cricket paid much better than the leagues, and we began to enjoy a comfortable life.

I didn't often play in the Sunday League because Clive Rice had persuaded people in Nottinghamshire that spinners were no good in the one-day game, and it would be a chance to give Kenny Watson a few games of county cricket. I did play in the game at Northampton, and we were 130 in our 40 overs. I opened the bowling and bowled my 8 overs on the trot. I had 7 maidens, and took 1 for 1, which is one of the best performances ever recorded in the Sunday League. The 1 run only came when a young Bruce French – he was sixteen and just in the side – dropped Wayne Larkins and they got a run.

Naturally, I was very pleased with myself, and we won easily. Our next Sunday game was against Kent at Canterbury, and I got changed ready for the two o'clock start when Pasty Harris, who was captain that day, told me that I wasn't playing. I couldn't believe it. I hardly played another Sunday League game that season.

Pasty Harris was an opening batsman who'd come from Middlesex, and they made him keep wicket a lot of the time. He wasn't a keeper, and this was very hard on a spinner who relies on his wicket-keeper so much. I don't think attitudes have changed in this respect. They still think anyone can put the gloves on, and the chances that are wasted!

Before the next season, there was all the Packer affair. Clive Rice was sacked, and then he was reinstated. He was sacked because he'd joined World Series Cricket, and, in the meantime, Notts signed Richard Hadlee. Clive became the permanent fixture as overseas player, and Richard and I shared the other spot. I didn't like this. I was trying to develop by bowling against the best batsmen. The pay did not worry me, and the fact that I was still getting paid well for not playing didn't satisfy me. I left Nottinghamshire at the end of the season, and I played for Northumberland in 1979.

Then I met Bob Willis, and Warwickshire offered me a two-year contract. I was now in the Indian side, and I was the number one overseas player at Warwickshire. I took 11 wickets in the last match of the season in 1980, and this took me past the 100 for the season. We won the John Player League, and I played in nearly every match. It was a very good year.

I went to Australia with the Indian team that winter, and we drew the series, and I bowled well, but when I got back to England there were problems again. Alvin Kallicharran was back with Warwickshire after being with the West Indian team the previous summer. This meant that Warwickshire now had three overseas players, and only two could play. On top of that, I broke three fingers on my right hand so I was back to sharing with Anton Ferreira. As India were touring England in 1982, and I was almost certain to be in the side, it was time to part happily with Warwickshire. They had been good friends.

We lost the series in England, and although I had a good series, I was not happy. Our captain, Sunil Gavaskar, was very negative, and there was a terrible lethargy in the side towards the end of the tour. Then the political intrigues began before the selection of the side to tour Pakistan. Bishen Bedi came on to the committee, and when the team was announced I found that I was one of three left-arm spin bowlers in the side as well as the leg-spinner Sivaramakrishnan.

Gavaskar had not liked the popularity I had enjoyed in Australia, and he even went on to say my days were numbered. Bedi even said that Gavaskar was quite happy with the two young left-arm spinners and did not mind doing away with me.

I'd got eight wickets in the inaugural Test against Sri Lanka so it was a bit difficult to drop me straight away, but I was not asked to play in the one-day internationals. Gavaskar's judgements were not questioned. He had a high status in Indian cricket due to his marvellous batting record, and people didn't offend him or disagree with him.

I played in the first four Tests, reached my 100 Test wickets and was dropped. It became pretty clear that I wouldn't be in the side to face West Indies. Sunny, too, lost the captaincy. Kapil took over. Indian captains are always sacked if they lose to Pakistan, and we'd been outplayed.

In fact, I did play once more, against Pakistan a year later, and I bowled Wasim Raja, but I'd had a good run, and I'd enjoyed it. I feel privileged to have played with bowlers like Bedi, Venkat, Prasanna and Chandrassekhar. I learned much from watching them over the years. I loved the game, and I loved bowling left-arm spin.

The one thing I found it hard to accept in county cricket was that so many players treated it as a nine-to-five job. They took it seriously, but they seemed without ambition. I could never understand that. I loved the game, and I always wanted to do better.

I think standards have dropped. Look at the England side. Look at the bowling. In my time, John Lever, who was a super bowler, couldn't hold a regular place in the side. Today, he'd be number one, and you'd be looking for someone else to open the bowling with him. The present Pakistani side is good, but it hasn't got the stability in batting that a great side should have, or any Test side should have.

You can't treat cricket as a living, as a means of earning a living. It's got to be your life. You've got to love it.

> Like Dilip Doshi, Peter Kirsten played county cricket in England as an overseas player. He played for Derbyshire from 1978 to 1982 and passed 1,000 runs in each of his five seasons with the club. Like Doshi, he began his career in England at Sussex.

For a young man coming into the game, Eddie Barlow was a great man, ideal, upstanding, what many youngsters need. He could bat, bowl and was a great slip-catcher. He was a great motivator for a young man, good adviser, helped you along the way, a good man to have around. Eddie Barlow was instrumental in getting me the contract at Derbyshire in 1977. Garth le Roux, Allan Lamb and myself came from Western Province. We started off and shopped around and played for county second elevens. In 1975, I played for Sussex Seconds with Kepler Wessels, and I played against the Australian tourists for the county side.

In the end, Garth le Roux went to Sussex under Tony Greig, Allan Lamb was contracted to Northamptonshire, and I went to Derby. In that respect, a lot of credit must go to Eddie Barlow.

At Essex, there was Ken McEwan, Scotty as we like to call him, to me an extreme gentleman, one of South Africa's cricket greats. I've known Ken since schooldays. Always had some very daft stories, some very funny ones, especially after the day's play and a pint or two.

One of the funniest stories involving Ken was in 1978, which was my first year in county cricket for Derbyshire. We were playing against Essex, and Ken named me as a pretty good fielder, that was in those days. He told all his team-mates they should be wary of running quick singles into the covers. Kenny came in to bat, and I think it was about the third ball he faced. He stroked the ball into the covers and called for a very quick single. As it was, he was run out by yards. I hit the stumps with a direct throw, and he was the laughing stock of the Essex team that night. Needless to say, we had a few pints that evening, and it was all forgotten.

He did get his own back in years to come, catching me out in the slips and things like that. Of course, there was great pleasure to be around when Ken was with Western Province. He is a good friend, and a very fine cricketer.

He told me it did him the world of good playing for Western Australia. The season before he was with Eastern Province, captained by Graeme Pollock. It was a star-studded side – with guys like Graeme and Chris Wilkins, all very fine cricketers in that era. It was a side that should have won the Currie Cup, and never did. And Ken went to Australia and found out exactly what the game was all about.

He relates a story regarding Dennis Lillee, and, when he was in the Western Australian squad, Ken reckons Dennis Lillee taught him a lot about batting, especially at practice. Kenny thought that nets were where he just went to improve his strokes, etc. to get himself ready for the game coming up. Then he saw Dennis Lillee come storming in just as he would in a match, and the ball would be whizzing past his ear-hole ten to the dozen, and Kenny thought 'hang on' this is not how I know it. And then he realized that he would actually have to knuckle down to it. This was tough cricket, and ever since that experience against Dennis Lillee in the nets in Western Australia, he really has become the great player that he is.

Peter Kirsten was not one of the South Africans associated with Kerry Packer's World Series Cricket, but Eddie Barlow, Mike Procter, Barry Richards, Clive Rice and Garth le Roux, his colleagues, did join the Packer organization. As South Africans deprived of Test cricket, they eagerly jumped at the opportunity to play at the highest level. Peter Kirsten talks of the impact it had on them.

Garth and I were students together in 1977. Dennis Lillee and Jeff Thomson were his idols. As a young South African, he had no chance of Test cricket, and he could only talk about them and have their figures on the wall. But there he was a year later in Australia doing it, making a name for himself, so you can imagine what a great experience it was for Garth.

[284]

He had a fantastic time in Australia. He still talks about it today. He says after the Packer episode it was such an anti-climax to come back to the Currie Cup with no prospect of international cricket that it was very difficult to get himself back on to the necessary high. To his credit, he did. He had guts. He has personal motivation, ambition, personal drive, and he did well against Australia here in South Africa. Most importantly, for Garth's sake, he has extreme pride in himself and his performance. I still think it stems back from those pre-Packer days when he really wanted to be on the international field.

His killer instincts came to the top in Australia. He was fired by the crowds, and I think he was the Man of the Series.

Clive Rice I first came across when I was still at school. He played for a team which toured the country and played against schools, and I came up against him. He didn't get me out that day, but he has done since. He's a very, very serious competitor, and had he had more appearances on the international stage, I think he would have been one of the world's leading achievers, very similar to what Imran Khan has done.

He thrived in Packer cricket, batting and bowling in pressure situations. I don't think he was an achiever before that. Then he showed it with Nottinghamshire and Transvaal, and, of course, he became captain of South Africa, did a good job. He knows what he wants. I found him to be a quiet, subtle motivator. They call him the 'mean machine'.

I think he has taken a leaf out of Mike Brearley's book. He actually studied the book Brearley wrote. I've heard Rice talk about it, and there are some very good points that come out of Brearley's book. There were occasions when Ricey took things out of it, but Ricey himself has his own quiet personality. He's serious, thoughtful, effective.

I played with Graeme Pollock in my first year in cricket. I used to idolize him. I still remember asking him for his autograph on the steps at Newlands when I was fourteen, and, thirteen years later, I was captaining him, so that's the way in which things turn over.

Batting with the man, in pure cricket terms, takes so much off

[285]

you because he's a genius. He's also able to play shots that other people are unable to play, so the batter at the other end doesn't have to look for the incredible shot to keep the score running, especially in the one-day cricket. He's incredible.

Interestingly enough, in all the 'Tests' that I've played with Graeme, he and I put on a really substantial partnership. Maybe it's because he took so much pressure off me, and one of my attributes was that I was able to stay at the crease for a length of time. He wasn't a great runner between the wickets with the other boys, but this was his style, and as long as you understood it, it was fine. I'm still trying to get my stance as wide as his.

> Great player as the left-handed Pollock was, he was denied the opportunity to play in World Series Cricket. He was one of the first cricketers to be signed by the Packer organization, but the West Indian contingent would not accept him. The West Indians were in a difficult position with the politicians in their own country regarding playing with or against South Africans, and a compromise was reached by which they agreed to play only with South Africans who had appeared for English counties. The reasoning was that, by playing outside South Africa, these cricketers had shown a rejection of apartheid. It was a tenuous argument, but it meant that Pollock and Hobson, having travelled to Australia for the series, returned to South Africa without playing a match.
>
> On the other hand, Barry Richards, who had played several years for Hampshire, and Mike Procter, who was a faithful and popular member of the Gloucestershire side, were eligible.

Barry Richards was the greatest. It was a pity that the world did not see more of him. I batted with him in the series against West Indies. You always had a sort of inferiority complex batting with, or watching these guys bat. You'd read about him all these years, and to bat with the man was fantastic.

In Bulawayo, in what was Rhodesia, I played against Mike Procter. He was fast. He was totally different to Clive Rice in that he was a player's player, very popular with the players, able to put himself on the other players' level to a certain extent. Very well liked. Good captain in that season.

The first time I ever faced him was as a schoolboy. The first ball thundered into my shoulder, and I thought, 'Oh dear, I'm no longer at SACS.' (My old school). Second ball was a bouncer, and I hooked it for four, and I'll never forget the glare Mike gave me. He was an outstanding fast bowler. I always respected him.

Lucky me, for a few games later he had an injury, and although he still bowled quick, he wasn't as quick as he had been, but certainly a magnificent swinger of the ball, a fearsome bowler.

> Peter Kirsten talks of playing in 'Tests' with Barry Richards. The games he refers to are what have become known as 'rebel' tours when parties from West Indies, England, Australia and Sri Lanka played matches in the Republic. The players from these countries who took part in the tours were banned from international cricket because of their participation. The sides were scarcely fully representative, but Gooch, Boycott, Gatting and Emburey were among those from England who went; Rowe, Clarke and Kallicharran were West Indians who jeopardized their futures; and among the Australians were bowlers Hogg, Rackemann and Alderman, and wicket-keeper Rixon. Kirsten was captain in one series.

Because South Africa had been isolated and the chances of playing international cricket were so minimal, when the chance did come, it was quite a big thing as far as I was concerned.

I found Rodney Hogg a marvellously skilful bowler. Personally, I couldn't read which way he was going to seam the ball. Clive Rice gave me a lot of advice, and that's what you can learn from people like Ricey.

Carl Rackemann would blow hot and cold. You could get on top of him, and he went. But he could bowl some great balls.

Terry Alderman bowled a very skilful away-swinger and had a good change of pace, but, like Carl Rackemann, you could get on top of him. He showed his emotion. His emotions gave him away, but he was a great Test bowler.

[287]

The wicket-keeper Steve Rixon was a great catcher. He spoke a lot, often annoyed you, but that's what you learn at international level.

Peter Kirsten believed he had no hope of playing Test cricket. He captained Border on their entry into the Castle (Currie) Cup in 1991–92, and, suddenly, with political changes in South Africa, the Republic was welcomed back into the international community of cricket. He went with Clive Rice's side to play in the one-day internationals in India in 1991, and he was second only to Martin Crowe of New Zealand in the World Cup averages in 1992.

In April of the same year, he went to the West Indies with the South African side under Kepler Wessels and played in the Test match at Bridgetown, scoring 52 in the second innings. He was just short of his thirty-seventh birthday, and, after a wait of nineteen years, he had at last played Test cricket.

10

FOR THE LOVE OF
THE GAME

Eddie Hemmings

John Childs

Born in Leamington Spa, Eddie Hemmings joined Warwickshire in 1965 at the age of sixteen, and he played for them until the end of the 1978 season when he left to join Nottinghamshire. His career at Trent Bridge coincided with the most successful period in the county's history, Nottinghamshire winning each of the four major competitions between 1981 and 1991. Eddie Hemmings was the main spin-bowler throughout this period, and he played sixteen times for England. Few cricketers have enjoyed so long a period in the game or have enjoyed the game so much.

I left Warwickshire because of lack of a contract, really. The contract they offered me wasn't what I thought would be right for the job. So I left. I'd got a contract there if I wanted to stay, but I didn't feel I wanted to stay any longer. I'd been left out of the side mid-season for no apparent reason as far as I was concerned. I was the best spinner in the club, and I was left out because they said I hadn't got many wickets, which was a futile reason as far as I was concerned. If you don't bowl, you don't get wickets, and I wasn't bowling very much.

They'd started relying on pace all the time. There was a little bit of an influx of 'Willisism'. It tended to be overall what the captain was thinking, and spinners went out the window. It was that period of time when all clubs went through the same thing. Possibly Middlesex used two spinners, but, other than that, spinners were a dying breed.

It was very noticeable throughout the whole cricketing world between the years of say '78–'79 and the mid-eighties. We're looking at a black period when you'd either got old boys like me around, or there was nobody.

Notts gave me a new lease of life, but I didn't really need a new lease of life. I'd got plenty of get-up-and-go, but I was guaranteed a first-team place, and, basically, enjoyed it. Clive Rice took over as captain from Mike Smedley half-way through the season, 1979, and things just went better for the club and for me.

He was one of the greatest things that happened to Notts and

English cricket. He was a tremendous skipper. He was skipper for about eight years, and I think he was probably better in his first six than he was in his last two, although he finished up with all sorts of trophies. I think he involved the rest of the side and the squad, everybody, more, a lot more, at the start. Because, when he'd taken over, he hadn't done a lot of captaincy, he involved everybody, and he had ideas coming from all sources, but, in my view, once he knew it, or thought he did, he tended to ignore the rest of us.

I think that anybody can go on too long as captain. You lose that sort of bite. Gooch's still got it, but he's one of the few that I think seems to be OK. But he didn't like it at first. He started, then gave it in, and then went back to it. I think he probably did it the right way round in the end when he was matured a little. You needn't necessarily have a younger man, but you need somebody who's going to involve everybody. What they do is involve everybody first, find out how to do it, then start doing it and say, 'That's it, I don't need anybody now.'

> In the nineteen-eighties, if one combined one-day and first-class cricket, one discovered that Eddie Hemmings bowled more overs in a season than any other bowler.

I liked bowling. I still do. I've always enjoyed bowling. I try to fit into a situation. Ricey would always bring me on fairly early, anyway. It's come from there a little bit, where I've been bowling quite a lot.

The one-day game gave me an opportunity to get into the Warwickshire side on a consistent basis as a bowler. For me, it taught you how to bowl in a tight manner. You couldn't just run up and lob it up, and it helped. But I still think the hardest part of cricket is the time when you're trying to bowl a side out. You've got four or five men round the bat. That's always difficult. You've got to tease them out at times, and that's the hardest part, especially on the wickets we've got at the moment which don't do anything. They're very slow and low, very miserable.

Eddie Hemmings has achieved more than the vast majority of cricketers in that he has played in two finals at Lord's, which his side has won, has played for England in Australia, and in a World Cup final.

I've done most things, but I've never been to India, apart from the World Cup, which was very good, and I've never been to Sri Lanka, which is the only cricket-playing country I've not been to. You can never go above playing for your country. If you're born and bred in England as I was, you can't beat going out there and playing for England. That's got to be the biggest thrill ever. That, for me, is the best. And second to that is your Lord's finals. They are tremendous days, and not forgetting the semi-finals, really, which are very exciting affairs.

I suppose, in order – playing for your country; playing in the World Cup; and, the biggest memory, playing in the semi-final against India in Bombay. I was smashed out of the game then, and it didn't really look as if I was really going to be able to do the job I'd been doing the rest of the tour. Got back into it, and ended up with three or four wickets. Nipped in at the death, though we didn't deserve to, or rather I didn't deserve to, which, after all, was down to a good bit of captaincy – Mike Gatting. He'd always had confidence in you. He was good, but I went from there and didn't play again for the rest of the tour. John Emburey kept me out of the side. The reason was that he was a better batter.

I've had that labelled on me so many times. 'Yes, you can bowl, and we think you're bowling just a bit better, but we reckon the other bloke can bat.'

This seems rather a hard judgement on a man who has scored over 9,000 runs in his career, averages nearly 20, and has a first-class 100 to his credit. Against Australia, at Sydney, in the final Test of the 1982–83 series, he came in as night-watchman and scored 95 before being adjudged caught-behind by Rodney Marsh off Bruce Yardley, a decision with which he still disagrees most vehemently.

[293]

I was nowhere near it. I was very disappointed because I thought it was my last Test. It was for a long time. That was January 1983, and I didn't play again until '87, which was really a surprise after all the cricket that had gone by, to get picked for the World Cup squad. It was brilliant, great.

> Another memorable batting achievement from Eddie Hemmings was when he hit the last ball of the Benson and Hedges Cup Final of 1989, bowled by John Lever, for four, to enable Nottinghamshire to beat Essex.

The way I remember it, we made a mess of getting that score anyway. We should have knocked 'em off easily. That's the way we bat, I suppose.

It was nearly the same two years before in the NatWest Final against Northants. It went over to the Monday because of rain. We were dead and buried on the Saturday night. I think what turned the game round was a very quick thirty-odd from Bruce French. He scored it very, very quickly. Then Richard Hadlee took over, got dropped, and the game gambolled on then. It was brilliant. We'd been well out of it.

> When Nottinghamshire won the County Championship in 1981 and 1987, they were criticized in some quarters for the pitches that were prepared at Trent Bridge. To the delight and entertainment of the crowd, the wickets produced results, unlike many that have become the norm since.

We tried to leave them with a bit of grass on because, obviously, we had one of the best seam attacks in the world, for a club side, anyway. We'd have been ridiculous if we'd taken all the grass off and played against ourselves. They were quick, quick wickets, a good bounce, and a lot of people couldn't bat on them. The good thing is that in the one year we won the championship in that 'problem' time, I took 90 wickets in the season, and I took 47 of them at home and the rest away on wickets so-called *not prepared* for our bowlers.

We prepared good, quick, bouncy wickets, and we found that if we left a little bit of grass, we'd get a lot more bounce. People want to see a result, and we got results because we played eleven games at home and had a result in every single game. We lost one. If people took edges, it went through to the slips to the keeper. We have things now on some wickets where a genuine nick drops five or six feet short of the keeper. That's not good for cricket. They're not good cricket wickets.

I've played against all the leading batsmen in the past twenty years, and I've found quite a few harder to get out than others, but, to be perfectly honest, I don't bowl at a particular batsman. I just bowl at a person. If he has a good day, it's well played him, and sometimes I get them out. It's just the way the game is. I think if you start worrying, oh, crikey, I'm playing against Goochie today, then you'll never bowl at him. You're wasting your time. Basically, you just bowl at a pair of pads and a bat. There's no person inside there. Everybody has their good days, and their bad days.

I've never really wanted to be anything else but a cricketer. Cricket and soccer, really. At the age of thirteen/fourteen, I'd played county games already – Warwickshire under-fifteens, Midland Schools, England Schools. I also played a bit of football at a reasonable level.

I started out bowling seamers. I came on the staff as an all-rounder, batter/bowler, bowler/batter. I wouldn't know which was best. At the time, I would've said that I was a slightly better batter than a bowler, but marginal. I was a genuine number six or seven who bowled seamers. In my very first year, I did quite well. I got about ninety wickets, I suppose, in the Second Eleven – well, Second Eleven and Minor Counties, we were playing in both. Warwickshire were one of the richer counties so we had a lot of cricket. I got 90-odd wickets and eight or nine hundred runs. If you combine the two together, it's quite a good impact for a sixteen-year-old.

There are spinners who lose their ability to spin the ball or lose their effectiveness in some way. One such bowler was Basil

Bridge, an off-spinner who preceded Hemmings at Warwick-shire. He took 100 wickets in 1961.

He got 100 wickets one year and he couldn't let the ball go the next. I know what happened to him. He altered his action, and the problem was, as you have throughout the years, coaching is about how you're doing that wrong. Now to me, when I coach, I don't say 'You're doing that wrong.' I try to find out the remedy, and say, 'Look, if you try that, it might go right.' Of course, in the old days, coaches weren't there to look and see why you were doing it wrong. I knew I was doing it wrong because I was only seventeen at the time.

It was a simple thing with Basil Bridge. He lost his stride pattern. He'd got a long delivery stride instead of the shorter one he'd had. Because he was doing that, everything else would go wrong. He'd lost his rhythm.

Eddie Hemmings made his Test debut against Pakistan in 1982, and the following winter he played in three Tests in Australia. His results would suggest that he did not find the transition from county cricket to Test cricket difficult.

I think Test cricket, if you're a spinner, is a bloomin' sight easier to play than county cricket. You're playing two-hour sessions. You've got a shorter day to start with. The people that run Test cricket reckon that quick bowlers are the people who are going to do all the damage anyway so you hardly get a bowl anyway. You have a little bit of a bowl before lunch, probably a little bit of a bowl mid-afternoon, perhaps a bit after tea, and you might end up closing the show at night. There's no way that you're ever going to do the amount of work you have to do in a county match because they just don't believe in spin bowling.

In the Test matches I've played in, which are not many, in the real spells I've had, I've always picked up wickets. I bowled more under Goochie than I did under anyone else. The 1990 combined series, India and New Zealand, that was good for me, and I had obviously my best spell during that time. Against New Zealand, at Edgbaston, my old home, I got six wickets in an innings, that was a big highlight for me.

After standing at mid-off and hearing bowlers say, 'I can't bowl with this bloody ball. It's no good at all,' I said, 'Give it to me, I'll bowl the bastards out.' That was something like the conversation at the time. It was good. I enjoyed it.

I enjoyed touring. I just wish I hadn't gone to Australia the second time because it was a waste of time. It was great to go, and it was good to have the money, I couldn't fault that, but to go there and not play when you're in your forties is awful. I actually said in my local paper before the last Test, 1990, that it wouldn't be a forward move, it would be a backward move if they took me. I'd had a good season, and they should say, 'Thanks very much. You've had a good season.' And then take a younger player. Goochie was captain. I played one Test match and two or three one-day internationals, and it really was a waste of time and money.

A lot of people go off to South Africa and New Zealand coaching. I don't want to do that. I was born and bred in England, and I want to help and coach this country.

In August 1992, Nottinghamshire County Cricket Club an-nounced that they would not be offering a new contract to Eddie Hemmings. They were releasing him in order to pro-vide more opportunities for their younger players. His passion for the game undiminished, Eddie Hemmings signed to play for Sussex in 1993, when he will be forty-four.

Another cricketer whose career underwent a considerable change when he transferred from one county to another was John Childs. He played Minor Counties cricket for Devon and entered first-class cricket later than most.

I was twenty-five when I first came into the game, but I was quite happy. I'd done my apprenticeship as a sign-writer and was quite set in that, and just playing a little bit of Minor Counties. Graham Wiltshire, the coach of Gloucestershire at the time, was, in fact, watching another player on the Cornish side where we were playing Devon v. Cornwall. He just happened to see me and asked if I'd like to come up for a couple of games, no strings attached. Luckily, I did reasonably well, and from there on Grahame Parker offered me a contract.

A slow left-arm bowler, John Childs joined Gloucestershire in 1975. The county already had an established left-arm spinner on their staff in David Graveney.

David was there, but we were lucky in the fact that we had Sadiq who bowled a bit of leg-spin, Prockie who bowled off-spin, and David and I were completely different types of bowlers, different styles. David will be the first to admit he works very hard at his action, and it doesn't come all that naturally, being such a big lad, whereas I've always been a slow left-armer. I've never had any hankerings to be a fast and nasty bowler.

It was very unusual to have two spinners in a side at that time. It helped having Procter as captain because we had enough balance in the side to be able to do that. When it broke down was when Brian Brain and Procter finished in the same year, and I think Zed and Sadiq went, too.

Prockie was captain, and as a leader by example, he was a very brilliant captain, whether it be with the bat or whether with the ball, seam, spin, or even in the field. Just a pure genius. A great pleasure to play with. As a captain, I found him a little bit hard because he did expect an awful lot from you. He sometimes couldn't understand why you couldn't come up to the expectations of what he was capable of doing. I suppose, in a way, that's not a bad thing for a captain, but having been with a couple of other captains, and certainly Keith, there was certainly a difference.

After nine years at Gloucestershire, John Childs moved to Essex, who were captained by Keith Fletcher and who were in the middle of what has been the greatest run of success in the club's history. Before 1979, they had won nothing. In the years since they have won every trophy the game has to offer.

[298]

It's an interesting thing being in the two camps. Now one looks back and says 'Why didn't Gloucestershire win more things?' We had some very talented players and quite a good side. To put a finger on it, really, it's that in one camp they say, 'I think we can do it', and in the other camp, 'I know we can do it', and there's no other way of putting it other than a habit of being successful at winning things. One just expects to win games. At Gloucestershire, we were tantalizingly close one year, 1977. We were, I think, top of the table with one game to go, and we couldn't quite sway it against Hampshire at home, whereas Middlesex ran in and pipped us on the post.

I very much thought my career was over when I left Gloucestershire. It was a sort of mutual agreement. The two years prior to me leaving Gloucestershire were very average years. I didn't play an awful lot, and the confidence had waned dramatically. So we agreed to put the name around to all the other counties, bar Yorkshire at that stage, and, really, there were no responses at all at the end of that '84 season. That was one of the very low points of my career.

And then suddenly, out of the blue, in the midst of winter, a phone call from Keith Fletcher saying, 'We'd like to have a chat about signing you on a year's contract.' The amazing thing was that, suddenly, from nowhere, the county champions wanted me. I was looking through, and I knew that Ray East was finished, and possibly David Acfield was coming to an end, but to have a phone call like that, and also then to come up and meet Doug Insole, Graham Gooch and Keith Fletcher at the Great Western Hotel one winter's evening was absolutely amazing. Looking back on it now, to think that I actually got Fletch up from Lindsell to see me speaks volumes.

My first year with Essex was an absolute nightmare. I tried very hard, but things really didn't go very well. I played about seven games, and I think I got about 7 wickets for 700 runs. One automatically thinks, 'It was worth the try. Good job I'd left the family back in Bristol because it hasn't worked.' I was once again more surprised that they not only said, 'Well, we still think you can bowl', but they offered me another contract and said, 'Let's try another avenue'. This led to the saga with Fred Titmus and Don Wilson helping me.

We had about three sessions just before Christmas. It was really a question of changing my run-up slightly and bowling more positively rather than just putting it there. At the end of the day, as Fred said, 'I can't go out on the field with you. You've got to do it yourself.'

I think confidence is almost seventy per cent of this game, if not more. It is an amazing fact that there are not many players who can go through the game without actually losing it at one stage or another. The fact that Essex still believed in me very much helped. We still had a very senior dressing-room at that stage – J.K., Ken McEwan, Brian Hardie, Fletch, Goochie, etc. It was great to play in that side.

The great thing was, probably about the second game of the '86 season, where everything turned round. There was a very slow wicket at Northampton where I managed to get quite a few overs in, and I think I bowled about 40 overs and took 5 for 97. The feeling I got from the rest of the boys coming off that field was absolutely tremendous. It just really took off from there. It was a super season. I played on a lot of turning wickets, got a lot of stumpings, and we won the championship. It was real fairy-tale stuff in a way.

That was my first big moment in cricket really, although there'd obviously been some high points with Gloucestershire, such as when I got 9 wickets in an innings against Somerset, but, as far as the team goes, it was very important. It was a super thing.

In 1988, at the age of thirty-seven, John Childs was picked to play for England against West Indies. He was also chosen for the tour of India the following winter, but the tour never took place because the Indian administration refused to accept members of the touring party who had had connections with South Africa.

It was a surprise bonus playing for England, but it came, as we all know, as luck would have it, because Nick Cook unfortunately took a tumble at one of the games, and I was drafted in. It was that rather dubious series of 1988 when, I think, we used twenty-three players and had four captains.

Test cricket is a lot different. One's become accustomed to playing within the arena, whether it be for the Minor Counties or whether it be for the Second Eleven or for the county first side, but when you move up to Test level, the media coverage, and everything the country expects, is so great. Certainly playing at home, I think. Of course, I only played in two Tests, and really didn't become accustomed to relaxing. It was a very big leap, I suppose. Looking back on it, I've been fairly pleased with the way I bowled in the two Test matches. Perhaps I could have bowled a little more positively, but I don't know how many games you'd have to play to become used to playing at the Test level. Quite a few, I would expect, because of the pressures that are expected of you. Then I was picked to go to India, and the tour was cancelled, and that was the other great low point of my career.

> Trained as a sign-writer, working in the winter as part of the Essex County Cricket Club administration, John Childs has tried to earn a living playing county cricket.

Only if you are one of the top half-dozen in the game can you earn a good living, perhaps the Grahams and the Bothams etc., who can give their name to a few things as well. Certainly as far as a county player is concerned or an average Test player, it's a six-month living. It isn't a twelve-month living.

I like to think, without sounding mercenary, I still play for the love of the game rather more so than for the financial reward, as long as I can look after my family. One would obviously like to have a little bit more money all the time, like everybody else, but, in general, the winning of things and being successful at the game, that's enough for me.

In 1992, John Childs was the first bowler in England to reach

50 first-class wickets for the season. Essex won the County Championship for the second year in succession, and for the third time since Childs had joined them in 1985.

DRAMATIS PERSONAE

CHAPTER 1

John NYREN (1764–1837)

A useful cricketer who played for Hambledon, and later for Homerton and an England XI. He is best remembered for his book *The Young Cricketer's Tutor*, which was edited by C. C. Clarke, and published in 1833. It contains an account of the Hambledon Club and its players, and was the first classic in cricket literature.

Revd John MITFORD

Wrote under the name of *Sylvanus Urban* and edited *The Gentleman's Magazine*. He reviewed Nyren's book, and, in his enthusiasm, plagiarized much of it.

Revd James PYCROFT

A West Country parson who loved cricket and wrote *The Cricket Field* (1851) and *Cricketana* (1865). John Arlott gave him credit for his fine historical sense.

Richard DAFT (1835–1900)

In and around 1870, he was regarded as the best professional batsman in England. He ranked second only to W. G. Grace and captained Nottinghamshire from 1871 to 1880. His writing reflected on the great cricketers with whom he had played.

William CAFFYN (1828–1919)

A Surrey cricketer and one of the best of his time, Caffyn remained in

Australia after the 1863–64 tour, and his coaching had much to do with the development of the Australian side. His memoirs give a fascinating account of the cricket in the mid-nineteenth century, and of the status of the professional.

Sir Herbert JENNER (later JENNER-FUST) (1806–1904)
One of the best wicket-keepers of his day, he was responsible for the instigation of the Varsity match, was a youthful president of MCC and played for Kent. He was interviewed by A. W. Pullin (Old Ebor) towards the end of his life.

John JACKSON (1833–1901)
He played for Nottinghamshire, went on two tours with Parr's sides and was regarded for many seasons as the fastest bowler in England. He was interviewed by Pullin long after his retirement.

Fred LILLYWHITE (1829–1866)
The third son of William, the great Sussex bowler, organized the tour to North America by Parr's side 1859. He was closely associated with cricketers, but he was primarily a chronicler.

CHAPTER 2

Vyell WALKER (1837–1906)
One of the seven famous Walker brothers of Southgate, Vyell was the finest amateur all-rounder of his day. He helped to bring Middlesex CCC into existence and captained them in their early days. At the turn of the century he was one of those interviewed by A. W. Pullin.

George ANDERSON (1826–1902)
The Yorkshire cricketer who was one of the most prominent professionals of his time. He played for the All England XI for nearly twenty years, and he was one of those involved in the long-running feud between Yorkshire and Surrey.

William Gilbert GRACE (1848–1915)
Grace strode the cricket world like a Colossus for thirty years, and he

[304]

became the yardstick by which all records were measured. He is still acknowledged as the greatest of all cricketers.

Edward POOLEY (1838–1907)

One of the truly great wicket-keepers, Ted Pooley played for Surrey for twenty years, but he missed his one chance of playing for England through one of those flaws in his character which brought him to end his days in the workhouse.

Charles Inglis THORNTON (1850–1929)

An amateur batsman who won the reputation of being one of the hardest hitters the game has seen, Thornton played for Cambridge, Kent and Middlesex and was, for many years, the leading figure in the Scarborough Festival.

C. W. ALCOCK

One of the game's greatest administrators, he was secretary of Surrey for many years. Ever inventive, he brought Test cricket to England and much else. He was also closely associated with soccer.

Hon. R. H. LYTTLETON (1854–1939)

A member of a great cricketing family, Robert Lyttleton was more a commentator on the game than a great player.

Lord HARRIS (1851–1932)

A man of great power, authority and influence, Lord Harris was a dominant force in Kent cricket from 1870 until his death, and an equally powerful force in the affairs of MCC and the administration of the game. He captained in England in all four Tests in which he appeared, and he was a batsman good enough to score nearly 10,000 runs in his career.

Albert Ernest KNIGHT (1872–1946)

A Leicestershire professional who was also a Methodist lay preacher, A. E. Knight toured Australia in 1903–4 and played in three Tests. He wrote one of the finest of cricket books, *The Complete Cricketer*.

Charles Burgess FRY (1872–1956)

The world has seen no greater all-round sportsman than C. B. Fry, a

[305]

triple blue at Oxford, a double international, and a world record holder in the long jump. He also appeared in an FA Cup Final and was an active politician. He published his own magazine for several years and wrote a memorable autobiography, *Life Worth Living*.

Lord HAWKE (1860–1938)

Lord Hawke ranks aside Lord Harris as one of the game's greatest administrators. He created a mighty Yorkshire side and he did an immense amount to raise the status and lot of the professional.

George GIFFEN (1859–1927)

A great all-rounder, Giffen was known as the W. G. Grace of Australia. His writings on his Australian contemporaries are perceptive and invaluable.

CHAPTER 3

K. S. RANJITSINHJI (1872–1933)

An Indian prince whose batting charmed the Golden Age at the close of the nineteenth century, Ranji played for Cambridge University, Sussex and England. He excelled with his back play and delighted crowds everywhere. He captained Sussex from 1899 to 1903, and he was the author, or part author, of *The Jubilee Book of Cricket*.

William WOOF (1858–1937)

A left-arm bowler who began as a pace man and changed to slow, Woof played for Gloucestershire from 1878 until 1902. He was later an umpire, and his break with Gloucestershire, and his concern for his future made him one whom Pullin was eager to interview.

H. W. LEE (1890–1981)

One of a cricketing brotherhood, Harry Lee played for Middlesex for twenty-three years and shared in their triumphs in the early nineteen-twenties. He was an opening batsman and an off-break bowler. His book, *Forty Years of English Cricket*, is a fascinating study of the life of the professional cricketer in the years either side of the First World War.

J. W. HEARNE (1891–1965)

'Young Jack' Hearne was one of the leading all-rounders of his day. He played for Middlesex from 1909 to 1936, and he won twenty-four Test caps. He was a great stylist, and his name was always linked with that of Hendren. They were the first Middlesex 'twins'. A famous member of a famous cricketing family, Jack Hearne's deeds have been chronicled by his son, also Jack.

Sir Jack HOBBS (1882–1963)

The Master, Hobbs opened the batting for Surrey and England for nearly thirty years. He hit more centuries than anyone else in the history of the game, and, in the opinion of many, he remains the greatest batsman the game has seen because he scored his runs in a stylish and attractive manner.

CHAPTER 4

Maurice J. C. ALLOM (Born 1906)

A fast bowler who played for Cambridge University, and for Surrey, for all too brief a period in the thirties, Maurice Allom took four wickets in five balls, including the hat-trick, on the occasion of his Test debut against New Zealand in 1930. He became president of both Surrey and MCC.

H. G. 'Tuppy' OWEN-SMITH (1909–1990)

An all-round sportsman of outstanding ability, Dr Owen-Smith played cricket for Middlesex, Oxford University and his native South Africa, and captained England at rugby. He was a joyous batsman and a leg-break bowler whose Test career was limited to the five matches on the 1929 tour after which he concentrated on his medical career.

T. B. MITCHELL (Born 1902)

An ex-miner who played for Derbyshire throughout their halcyon days in the nineteen-thirties, Tommy Mitchell bowled leg-breakers and googlies and fielded brilliantly. He played five times for England, and he was on the 'body-line' tour of 1932–33. He remains a character of great fun and zest.

[307]

CHAPTER 5

H. D. 'Hopper' READ (Born 1910)

'Hopper' Read's first-class career was really compounded into two seasons, but he was a very quick bowler, and he was looked upon as a possible successor, to Larwood. His country cricket was for Essex, and he took six wickets in the one Test match he played, against South Africa in 1935. An amateur, he was unable to give his time to cricket and followed a business career.

N. S. MITCHELL-INNES (Born 1914)

Norman Mitchell-Innes played for England in 1935 while still in his second year at Oxford. He was recognized as an outstanding talent, but his career was blighted by severe hay-fever. His appearances for Somerset were restricted by his professional career, for, on leaving university in 1937, he took up a post with the Sudan Civil Service. He was joint captain of Somerset in 1948. He was also a very fine golfer, and he remains actively interested in all sport.

W. H. V. 'Hopper' LEVETT (Born 1908)

An amateur wicket-keeper who played for both Kent and England in the same period as his friend Les Ames, 'Hopper' Levett remains a man of great enthusiasm and has done much to help young cricketers in Kent.

W. H. R. ANDREWS (1908–1989)

One of the game's great characters, Bill Andrews was an all-rounder with Somerset from 1930 to 1947, although he was sacked after 1932 but returned three years later. He later coached Somerset.

R. H. MOORE (Born 1913)

Dick Moore played for Hampshire from 1931 until the outbreak of the Second World War. He captained them for a period and hit 316 against Warwickshire in 1937. He played for the Gentlemen against the Players the following season, but his eagerness to attack probably cost him higher honours.

CHAPTER 6

Sir Donald BRADMAN (Born 1908)

The greatest of Australian cricketers and the most prolific run-scorer the game has known, Don Bradman has left a record in first-class cricket at which one can only gaze in awe and admiration. He averaged 95.14 in first-class cricket, and 99.94 in Test cricket. He had a mighty presence on the cricket field, and he was an outstanding captain of a great side.

T. N. PEARCE (Born 1905)

Tom Pearce captained Essex before and after the Second World War. He was a most capable batsman and a genial leader. He was a Test selector for a period, and he is now president of the Essex Club.

W. B. MORRIS (Born 1917)

An all-rounder who played for Essex from 1946 to 1950, Bill Morris became noted as a fine coach and did much to help the development of players like Gooch, John Lever, Ray East and others of the outstanding Essex side of the eighties.

Harry SHARP (Born 1917)

Harry Sharp could never hold a regular place in the Middlesex side for much of the nine years he spent with the county, but he was a good servant who hit nearly 6,500 runs and took over 50 wickets. He later became an excellent coach and was scorer to the county side for a time.

B. G. BROCKLEHURST (Born 1922)

Ben Brocklehurst played for Somerset between 1952 and 1954 and captained them in the last two of those three seasons. He did much to unite the club at a difficult time, and he has ever been both dynamic and visionary in the game. He saved and revitalized the *Cricketer*, the world's leading cricket magazine.

Stuart SURRIDGE (1917–1992)

The most successful county captain in the history of the game in that Surrey won the championship in all five seasons when he led them, 1952 to 1956. A medium-pace bowler, outstanding fielder and hard-hitting batsman, he was an exciting leader of men, and a great enthusiast.

CHAPTER 7

Frank TYSON (Born 1930)

Frank Tyson is one of the fastest bowlers to have appeared in first-class cricket. He played for Northamptonshire, 1952–60, but it was for England in Australia, 1954–55, that he had his greatest triumphs. He later settled in Australia and has become highly respected as a coach, a writer and a commentator.

ALIM-UD-DIN (Born 1930)

The youngest player ever to appear in first-class cricket, Alim-ud-din opened the batting for Pakistan between 1954 and 1962 and appeared in twenty-five Tests. He was a member of the Pakistan side which gained victory over England at the Oval in 1954.

Trevor GODDARD (Born 1931)

A left-handed all-rounder who captained South Africa in thirteen Tests, Goddard has a fine Test record. He was noted for his sound defence and his naggingly accurate bowling. A man of impeccable integrity.

Peter van der MERWE (Born 1935)

A steady middle-order batsman, Peter van der Merwe was perhaps short of Test class as a batsman, but he was an outstanding captain and led South Africa in eight of his fifteen Test matches. He was an excellent fielder.

CHAPTER 8

E. R. DEXTER (Born 1935)

Ted Dexter was a fine golfer and a brilliantly exciting cricketer. He captained both Sussex and England. He was a fine attacking batsman and a useful medium-pace bowler. He has become the 'supremo' of English cricket.

A. S. BROWN (Born 1936)

An all-rounder of no mean ability, Tony Brown played for Gloucestershire for twenty-three years and captained them in one of their most fruitful periods. A brilliant fielder, he held seven catches in one innings against

Nottinghamshire in 1966. He was later secretary/manager of both Gloucestershire and Somerset and a manager of England touring sides. He is now a highly respected administrator with the TCCB.

Richard HUTTON (Born 1942)

The son of one of England's greatest cricketers and captains, Richard Hutton established himself as a positive all-rounder of Test class for both Yorkshire and England. He bowled medium-pace and hit hard and was an entertaining cricketer. He is now executive editor of the *Cricketer.*

CHAPTER 9

Ashley MALLETT (Born 1945)

Ashley Mallett bowled his off-breaks for Australia between 1968 and 1980 and claimed 132 Test wickets in 38 matches. He was also a fine fielder in a very good Australian side. He is now a coach of spin bowlers at the highest level and a respected journalist.

Dilip DOSHI (Born 1947)

A slow left-arm bowler whose Test record stands equal to those of the other great Indian spinners of the period, Dilip Doshi played for both Nottinghamshire and Warwickshire with considerable success. He played in 32 Test matches. He is now a successful businessman in London.

Peter KIRSTEN (Born 1955)

One of the generation of South African cricketers whose best years were spent in isolation from Test cricket, Peter Kirsten led South Africa in one of the rebel series and ultimately made his Test debut in 1992. He was very successful with Derbyshire between 1978 and 1982, scoring heavily.

CHAPTER 10

Eddie HEMMINGS (Born 1949)

Eddie Hemmings is the oldest player still active in first-class cricket in England. An off-break bowler of Test quality, he played for his native

Warwickshire from 1966 to 1978 when he moved to Nottinghamshire. He gained international recognition with his new county, but Nottinghamshire released him at the end of the 1992 season. He joined Sussex for 1993.

John CHILDS (Born 1951)

A slow left-arm bowler whose career appeared to be over when he was released by Gloucestershire in 1984. Surprisingly, he was signed by Essex, the champion county. He made no immediate impact, but, in 1986, he took 91 wickets and Essex won the title. He was again a member of the championship-winning side in 1991 and 1992, and he has played twice for England since being with his new county.

INDEX

Adcock, Neil 221
Alcock, C. W. 52, 305
  quoted 52–3, 54
Alderman, Terry 287
Alim-ud-din 217, 219, 310
  quoted 217–19
All-England XI 8, 24, 28, 29, 30,
  31, 32–3
Allen, David 238, 247, 263–4
Allen, Sir G. O. B. ('Gubby') 85,
  109, 130, 140, 142, 167, 181,
  182, 210, 251
Alley, Bill 186–7
Allom, Maurice 103, 107, 109, 115,
  116, 307
  quoted 103–10, 111–14, 115
Ames, Leslie 113
Anderson, George 43–4, 304
Andrew, Keith 215
Andrews, Bill 150, 152, 158, 308
  quoted 158–9
apartheid politics and cricket
  115–16, 286, 287, 300
Armstrong, Warwick 179
Atherton, Michael 169

Bailey, Trevor 201, 231, 256
Barber, Wilf 131
Barlow, Eddie 222, 223, 224, 227,
  283, 284
Barnes, S. F. 98, 117

Barnett, Charlie 185, 248, 249
Barrington, Ken 194
Bartlett, Hugh 145–6
Barton, Michael 193
Bedi, Bishen 214, 277, 282
Bedser, Alec 176, 182, 193, 195,
  201, 202–3, 216, 245
Bedser, Eric 193, 195, 196, 245
Beldham, William 12–13
  quoted 13–15
Bell, Sandy 119, 120
Benaud, Richie 212, 217, 221, 222,
  225, 226, 234
Benson and Hedges Cup 242
Binks, Jimmy 260
Bissex, Mike 239
Blackham, J. M. 51, 61
Bland, Colin 223, 225
Blythe, Colin 98
'body-line' tour 108–9, 122
Bond, Jack 239, 240, 279
Booth, Brian 223, 224
Border, Allan 274
Botham, Ian 210, 211, 251, 254
boundaries 46–7
Bowes, Bill 88, 114, 136, 168, 182
bowling actions
  controversial 43, 107, 108–9,
    167, 224
  early 7, 15–17, 45
  googlies 92–3

bowling actions – *contd*
  measuring pace of 210–11
  spin-bowling 213–14
Box, Tom 22, 23, 24, 31
Boycott, Geoff 168, 191, 203, 237,
  255, 261, 265, 272, 287
Boyes, Stuart 162, 165
Bradman, Sir Donald 107, 124, 125,
  129, 138, 152, 166, 175–6,
  206–7, 212, 222–3, 251, 274,
  309
  quoted 176–9
Brain, Brian 299
Brearley, Mike 257, 285
Brett, Thomas 4–5, 9
Bridge, Basil 295–6
Broadbridge, James 16
Brocklehurst, Ben 186, 187, 189,
  190, 309
  quoted 186–92
Brown, Bill 178
Brown, David 246
Brown, Freddie 113, 122, 145, 215
Brown, George 169–70
Brown, Tony 235, 240, 241, 243,
  246, 251, 310–11
  quoted 235–8, 239–43, 244–54,
  255
Buller, Syd 268
Burnet, Ronnie 261–2
Buse, Bertie 150, 156

Caesar, Julius 36, 44
Caffyn, William 24, 33, 35, 36, 37,
  38, 303–4
  quoted 18–19, 20, 24–5, 26–7,
  28–9, 31–2
Cahn, Sir Julian 141
Calthorpe, Freddie 113
Cameron, Horace 106, 118, 119, 148

captaining a team 250
Cardus, Sir Neville 260
Carr, Arthur 114, 129, 139, 153,
  161
Catterall, Bob 121
Chapman, Percy 97, 167
Chappell, Greg 273–4
Chappell, Ian 278
Cheetham, Jack 179, 180, 181
Childs, John 249, 297, 298, 300,
  301–2, 312
  quoted 297–8, 299–300, 301
Christy, Jack 121
Clark, E. W. ('Nobby') 121, 142–3
Clark, Tom 194
Clarke, Charles Cowden 4
Clarke, William 25–6, 28–9, 31, 32
Close, Brian 260, 262, 263, 265
Compton, Denis 86, 99, 111–12,
  130, 151, 176, 182, 183, 184,
  201, 207–9, 210, 218, 220,
  240, 258
Constable, Bernard 193, 194–5
Cope, Geoff 260
Copson, Bill 125, 127, 137, 156
Cornford, ('Tich') 103, 113
Cotter, ('Tibby') 97
county cricket
  differs from Test cricket 232–3,
  296, 301
  origins 23–4
  qualification for 34–5
Cowdrey, Colin 99, 201, 209, 212,
  235, 240, 263
Cox, Dennis 194
Craig, Ian 226
Crapp, Jack 185, 235, 236, 241,
  250
Crawley, Leonard 136, 181
Cricketer 189, 190, 192

Crisp, Bob 119
Crowe, Martin 288

Daft, Richard 17, 25, 47, 303
    quoted 25–6, 29–30, 33, 41, 42
Dark, James 28, 34
Davidson, Alan 180–1, 221
de Saram, F. C. ('Derek') 146–7
Deane, H. G. 116
Dexter, Ted 99, 231, 310
    quoted 231–5
Diver, Alfred 35, 36
D'Oliveira, Basil 115, 240–1, 259
Dooland, Bruce 212, 213
Doshi, Dilip 278–9, 311
    quoted 279–83
Douglas, Johnny 82, 97–8, 114
Duckworth, George 95, 113,
    124–5, 129

Eckersley, Peter 111, 114, 182
Edrich, Bill 130, 166, 182, 183,
    184–5, 204, 209, 212, 240
Emburey, John 287, 293
Emmett, George 185, 204, 236,
    241, 244, 250
Engineer, Farokh 239, 279
Evans, Godfrey 179, 182, 201, 211,
    215, 216

Farnes, Ken 136, 138, 153–4, 182
Favell, Les 207, 278
Fender, Percy 95, 107, 108, 114,
    131, 167, 196, 236
Fingleton, Jack 129, 206
Fishlock, Laurie 195
Fletcher, Keith 237, 257, 298, 299
four-day cricket 242, 247
Freeman, ('Tich') 113, 120, 121–2,
    128, 157, 158, 170, 181

French, Bruce 280, 294
Fry, C. B. 58, 60, 66, 305–6
    quoted 59, 66–7, 68

Gatting, Mike 248, 287, 293
Gavaskar, Sunil 203, 281, 282
Gentlemen v. Players 16, 20, 41,
    233
Gibbs, Lance 214, 219, 276
Giffen, George 53, 62–3, 306
    quoted 53, 61, 62
Gifford, Norman 245, 253
Gilchrist, Roy 219
Gillette Cup 209, 233, 242
Gilligan, Harold 103, 104
Gimblett, Harold 150, 188–9
Goddard, Tom 184, 185, 244,
    247
Goddard, Trevor 219, 220,
    221, 222, 225, 226, 227,
    310
    quoted 220, 221, 222–3
Gooch, Graham 183, 237, 248, 287,
    292, 299, 300
Gower, David 252, 253
Grace, E. M. 34, 37–8, 41, 48
Grace, G. F. 54–5
Grace, W. G. 41–2, 45, 46, 54–7,
    65–7, 71, 76–7, 91, 94, 95,
    304–5
    quoted 46–9, 50–1, 57–8, 67
Graveney, David 238, 249, 298
Graveney, Tom 201, 236, 240, 241,
    255, 263
Gregory, J. M. 88, 97, 99
Greig, Tony 257, 279
Grimmett, Clarrie 177
Grinter, Trayton 141–2, 181
Grout, Wally 179, 225
Gupte, S. P. 212, 213, 219

Hadlee, Sir Richard 210, 211, 281, 294

Hall, Wes 219

Halliwell, E. A. 61

Hambledon Club 3–4, 7, 8, 10, 14

Hammond, Wally 106, 111, 124, 126, 132, 138, 147, 151, 159, 165–6, 166, 177, 181, 248, 249

Hardstaff, Joe jnr 140, 149, 182

Harris, David 11–12, 13, 15

Harris, Lord 51, 52, 53, 305
quoted 55

Harvey, Neil 179, 180, 207, 216

Hawke, Lord 60, 64, 78, 79, 80, 306
quoted 60–1, 64–5, 78, 79–80

Hayward, Tom 43, 60, 77, 89–91, 93, 96

Hearne, J. T. 80, 81

Hearne, J. W. ('Young Jack') 81–8, 106, 119, 307

Hemmings, Eddie 291, 292, 293, 294, 296, 297, 311–12
quoted 291–2, 293, 294–5, 296–7

Hendren, E. P. ('Patsy') 83, 84, 106–7, 120, 126, 130, 150, 151

Hill, A. J. L. 60

Hillyer, Billy 19, 24, 31

Hobbs, Robin 128

Hobbs, Sir Jack 88–9, 92, 93, 94, 95, 96, 103, 104–5, 126, 196, 307
quoted 89–93, 94–5, 96–9

Hogg, Rodney 287

Holmes, Errol 140, 147, 148, 149

Howarth, Hedley 277

Hutton, Sir Leonard 111, 131, 150, 152, 155, 168, 178, 182, 190–1, 201, 203–4, 207, 209, 212, 215, 234, 240, 257–8

Hutton, Richard 191, 255, 257, 259, 263, 311
quoted 255–68

Illingworth, Ray 231, 260, 276, 277, 278

Imran Khan 210, 211, 219

Insole, Doug 205–6, 251, 299

Jackson, Sir F. S. 68

Jackson, G. R. 127

Jackson, John 33, 36, 45, 304
quoted 33–5

James, Ken 104, 113

Jardine, Douglas 107, 108, 124, 125, 129, 130, 135, 166–7

Jenner, Sir Herbert 20–1, 304
quoted 21–3

John Player League 242

Johnson, Ian 179, 213, 214

Johnston, Bill 179

Jones, Alan 279

Kallicharran, Alvin 281, 287

Kapil Dev 210, 211

Kirsten, Peter 283, 284, 287, 288, 311
quoted 283–8

Knight, A. E. 55–6, 69, 305
quoted 56–7, 59, 68, 69–70, 75, 77–8

Knight, Barry 243

Knight, G. T. 16

Knight, Roger 238, 239, 244

Knott, Alan 179, 215, 257, 276, 277

Laker, Jim 195–6, 212, 218

Lamb, Allan 254, 283
Langridge, John 248
Larwood, Harold 88, 97, 107, 108, 109, 114, 124, 125, 128–9, 135, 153, 161–2, 167, 169
Lawry, Bill 224, 226, 227, 271, 272–3, 278
le Roux, Garth 283, 284–5
Lear, George 7, 9
Lee, Charles 187–8
Lee, Harry 80, 88, 131, 306
    quoted 80–2
Lee, Jack 131, 151
Legge, Geoffrey 111
Lever, John 282, 294
Levett, W. H. V. ('Hopper') 157, 308
    quoted 157–8
Leyland, Morris 120–1, 167
Lillee, Dennis 210, 273, 274–5, 284
Lillywhite, Fred 35, 304
    quoted 36–7
Lillywhite, James 49, 52
Lillywhite, John 35, 36, 43–4
Lillywhite, William 16, 22
Lindsay, Denis 223, 225, 226, 227
Lindwall, Ray 179, 180, 201, 210, 215, 217
Lloyd, Clive 239, 263, 276, 279
Loader, Peter 195, 245
Lock, Tony 194, 195, 212, 214, 215, 219, 232, 241, 262, 273
Lohmann, George 60, 77
Lord's 16, 44, 46
Lowry, Tom 104, 181–2
Luckes, Wally 150, 152, 156
Lyttleton, Hon. C. J. 140, 149
Lyttleton, Hon. R. H. 305
    quoted 55

Macaulay, George 88–9, 114, 170

McCabe, Stan 178
McDonald, Colin 205, 221–2
McDonald, E. A. 88, 97, 99
McEwan, Ken 279, 283–4
McGlew, Jackie 205, 206, 219, 220–1
McKenzie, Graham 273, 276
MacLaren, Archie 66, 67–8, 96
McLean, Roy 207, 220, 221
Mallett, Ashley 271, 274, 311
    quoted 271–8
Mann, Noah 10, 14
Marsh, Rodney 215–16, 277–8, 293
Marshall, Roy 240, 242
Martingell, W. 24–5, 31, 45
Marylebone Cricket Club (MCC) 16
May, Peter 99, 194, 196, 201, 209, 212, 232, 236, 240, 241, 251
Mead, Philip 161, 162–3, 164, 165, 170
Meckiff, Ian 221, 224
Miller, Keith 176, 179–80, 201, 211–12, 217
Milton, Arthur 231, 235, 237, 241, 245–6
Mitchell, Arthur ('Ticker') 151–2, 260, 261
Mitchell, Bruce 117–18, 121, 148
Mitchell, T. B. 122–3, 125, 128, 307
    quoted 122, 123–32
Mitchell-Innes, Norman 140, 144, 147, 154–5, 158–9, 308
    quoted 144–54, 155–6
Mitford, Revd John 303
    quoted 11–12
Moore, Richard 159–60, 161, 163, 168, 308
    quoted 160–71

Morkel, Denys 104–5, 119, 120
Morris, Arthur 176, 179, 180
Morris, Bill 182, 183, 309
  quoted 182–3
Mortimore, John 231, 232, 235,
    237, 238, 239, 244, 245, 263,
    264
Murdoch, W. L. 51, 53, 54
Murrell, Joe 84–5
Mynn, Alfred 17, 18–19, 20, 22,
    24, 31

Newland, Richard 5
Newman, George 119
Nichols, Morris 103, 136, 137, 153,
    154, 166, 181
North v. South 17–18, 25
Nyren, John 4, 303
  quoted 4–8, 9, 10, 12–13
Nyren, Richard 4, 5

O'Connor, Jack 123, 181
Oldfield, Bert 118, 179
one-day cricket 128, 163, 165,
    209–10, 247, 264–5
O'Reilly, Bill 98, 176–7, 206
origins of cricket 3
Oval 46, 140
Owen-Smith, H. G. ('Tuppy') 116,
    121, 145, 307
  quoted 116–19, 120–1,
    179–81

Packer, Kerry 253
Paris, Cecil 164, 165, 168–9
Parker, Charlie 247
Parks, Jim 99, 140
Parr, George 26–8, 29, 31, 33, 35,
    36, 37, 41
Pataudi, Nawab of 146, 147

Pearce, Tom 123, 141, 142, 181,
    309
  quoted 181–2
Peate, Edmund 78
Peebles, Ian 119, 122, 128, 141,
    142, 145
Peel, Bobby 78–9
Pepper, Cecil 212–13
Pickering, W. P. 35, 36
Pilch, Fuller 19, 20, 24, 31, 44
Pocock, Pat 272–3, 276–7
Pollock, Graeme 225, 263, 271–2,
    284, 285–6
Pollock, Peter 223, 225
Ponsford, Bill 105–6, 130, 177
Pooley, Edward 49, 50, 305
  quoted 49–50
Prasanna, E. A. S. 214, 277, 282
pre-match training 156, 157, 164
Prince's cricket ground 23
Procter, Mike 227, 235, 237–8, 239,
    240, 244, 245–6, 248–9, 252,
    253–4, 284, 286–7, 298
professional cricketers
  attitude towards the game 245,
    261, 267
  distinction between amateurs
    and professionals abolished
    233
  early status 75, 159
  pay and conditions 33–4, 76,
    77–8, 79, 126–7, 142, 154,
    170, 255
protective clothing 21, 50, 204
Pugh, Tom 236–7
Pullin, A. W. 33, 42, 49, 76
Pycroft, Revd James 13, 303
  quoted 20, 28

Quinn, Neville 118, 119, 120

Rackemann, Carl 287

Ramadhin, Sonny 201, 212, 213, 219

Ranjitsinhji, K. S. 58–9, 66, 306
quoted 75–6

Read, H. D. ('Hopper') 135, 308
quoted 135–44

'rebel' tours 287

Rhodes, Wilfred 79, 96, 98, 111

Rice, Clive 280, 281, 284, 285, 287, 291–2

Richards, Barry 240, 251, 273, 284, 286

Richards, Viv 251, 273, 274

Rixon, Steve 287, 288

Roberts, Andy 276

Robertson, Jack 85, 86, 184

Robins, Walter 85, 93, 118, 122, 141, 185

Robinson, Emmott, 152, 260

Rose, Brian 254

Sadiq Mohammad 235, 298

Sainsbury, Peter 245–6

Sandham, Andrew 96, 105, 112, 194

Scarborough Festival 51

Seamer, Jack 149, 154, 155

Sellers, Brian 107, 114, 131, 138, 151, 152, 156, 167, 193–4, 260–1

Shackleton, J. H. 244, 262, 263

Sharp, Harry 183, 184, 186, 309
quoted 184–6

Sheppard, David 234, 235

shining the ball 245

Shrewsbury, Arthur 57–8, 77

Simpson, Bobby 224, 226, 227, 241

Sims, Jim 87, 184, 185

Sinclair, J. H. 60–1, 64, 65

Sinfield, Reg 236, 255

Small, John 6, 8, 15

Snow, John 275–6, 277, 278

Sobers, Sir Gary 177–8, 207, 211, 240, 251; 279–80

Spofforth, F. R. 51, 54, 62, 63

Stackpole, Keith 227

Statham, Brian 201, 210–11, 256, 264

Steel, A. G. 51

Stephenson, H. H. 35, 36, 37

Stevens, Edward ('Lumpy') 8–9, 12

Stoddart, A. E. 71

Stott, Brian 262

Sueter, Tom 6, 9

Sunday League 209, 265

Surridge, Stuart 167, 193, 195, 309
quoted 193–7

Sutcliffe, Herbert 96–7, 106, 126, 138, 147, 150, 152–3, 158, 167, 267

talent money 170

Tallon, Don 179, 215

Tarrant, Frank 80–1, 82, 86

Tate, Maurice 94, 98, 112, 113, 117, 176

Tayfield, Hugh 209, 212, 214, 222

Taylor, Bob 179, 215, 277

Taylor, Herbie 106, 117

Taylor, Ken 260, 262

Tennyson, Lionel, Lord 160, 161, 168

Test cricket
differs from county cricket 232–3, 296, 301
first Test matches 49, 53, 54
playing at Test level 301

Thomson, Jeff 211

Thornton, C. I. 50–1, 305
three-day cricket 242
Tinley, R. C. 30
Titmus, Fred 248, 300
Todd, Les 267
Tribe, George 212, 215
Trott, Albert 63–4, 65
Trott, Harry 63
Trueman, Fred 192, 201, 218, 234,
 245, 260, 262–3
Trumper, Victor 69–71
Turnbull, Maurice 103, 109–10,
 182
Tyldesley, Johnny 64, 65
Tyldesley, Richard 122
Tyson, Frank 191–2, 193, 201–2,
 209, 215, 217, 218, 219, 310
 quoted 202–7, 208–9, 210–17

umpires 267–8
Underwood, Derek 257, 277
United England XI 32–3

van der Merwe, Peter 223, 225–6,
 310
 quoted 223, 224–5, 226–7
van Geloven, Jack 267
van Ryneveld, Clive 220, 221
Varsity matches 21
Verity, Hedley 111, 118, 119, 125,
 139, 147–8, 151, 153, 168,
 170, 171, 182
Vincent, Charlie 119, 120
Voce, W. 114, 129, 153, 161, 176,
 182

Waite, John 220, 225
Walker, Harry 11, 14, 15
Walker, Tom 11, 13, 14–15

Walker, Vyell 42, 44, 45, 304
 quoted 43, 44–6
Walsh, Jack 212, 213
Wanostrocht, Nicholas ('Felix')
 19–20, 31
Wardle, Johnny 212, 214–15, 219,
 258–9, 262
Warner, Sir Pelham ('Plum') 65,
 82, 85, 129, 148, 182
Washbrook, Cyril 183, 204, 234
Wellard, Arthur 150, 152, 156, 188
Wenman, Ned 19, 20, 22
Wessels, Kepler 283, 288
White, Jack 120, 139, 144, 145
wickets 46, 140, 213–14, 247,
 294–5
Wilcox, Denys 136, 138, 142
Willes, John 16
Willis, Bob 211, 248, 276, 281
Willsher, Edgar 43–4
Wisden, John 24, 25, 31–2, 35, 36,
 37
Wood, Arthur 118, 119, 267
Woof, William 76, 306
 quoted 76–7
Woolley, Frank 113, 120, 139, 157
World Series Cricket 253, 281, 284,
 286
Worthington, Stan 103, 125, 127,
 128, 131
Wright, Doug 128
Wyatt, Bob 113–14, 124, 132, 147,
 148, 164

Yardley, Norman 181, 182, 266
Young, Jack 184, 185, 192

Zaheer Abbas 235, 237, 248,
 253–4, 298